DATE DUE

JAN 7 1963	OCT 16 '69		
AP 9 '63			
NO 25 '63	APR 2 1970		
MY 27 '64	NOV 4 1971		
	NOV 1 1973		
JY 17 '64	NOV 15 1973		
DE 7 '64	OCT 18 1975		
APR 19 '65	NOV 10 1975		
MAY 3 '65	DEC 1 1975		
MAY 19 '65			
FEB 17 '66	DEC 18 1975		
	DEC 12 1975		
NOV 6			
DEC 15 1969	MAR 31 1986		
JAN 5 1970	DEC 13 1993		
DEC 2 1971			
GAYLORD			PRINTED IN U

Shakespeare
and the
Craft of Tragedy

Shakespeare and the Craft of Tragedy

WILLIAM ROSEN

HARVARD UNIVERSITY PRESS
CAMBRIDGE · MASSACHUSETTS
1 9 6 0

TO MY MOTHER AND FATHER

PREFACE

No one who writes about Shakespeare's tragedies can hope to convey their definitive meaning or re-create their precise emotions. Because criticism must, of necessity, abstract elements, it can never be a substitute for the complexity which is the play. However, in helping to reveal the craft of drama, it enables us to understand why works of art elicit their particular response.

Criticism is a co-operative enterprise. It brings together various methods: historical knowledge saves us from monstrous errors of fact and judgment; analysis illuminates the unique value of the literary work. But criticism, especially of the drama, can become too specialized. When it narrows to an intense examination of imagery alone, or intellectual background, or dramatic conventions, it can seriously wrench the meaning of a play by imposing a straitjacket on what is essentially dynamic. Performed before an audience, drama constantly moves to readjustments in the relationship between its characters and audience.

Familiarity with the customs and attitudes of Shakespeare's age is a prerequisite for intelligent discussion of the plays, but the critic must be wary of reconstructing a mythical Elizabethan mind to explain what every Elizabethan playgoer would have indisputably thought of pride, passion, old age, love, honor. The plays, not the concepts derived by historians from Elizabethan treatises and hack works, guide an audience into the emotions which the dramatist wishes to elicit. One can imagine how three hundred years from now an eager student of drama, insisting that his age can understand Arthur Miller's *Death of a Salesman* only by re-establishing our age's attitude towards salesmen, will draw material from novels, sociology texts, *Fortune* magazine, *The Saturday Evening Post,* to explain what every American would have felt while viewing the play. Historical criticism provides invaluable knowledge about the customs and vocabulary of an age; it is no substitute, however, for the dramatic experience which a playwright fashions.

We are greatly indebted to students of Shakespeare's imagery for their close, vigorous examination of his language. To those who have increased our knowledge of Elizabethan dramatic conventions we owe thanks for clearing away many of the fruitless problems that engaged 19th-century critics. Yet these specialized studies often seem unsatisfactory. Patterns of imagery, where they shape a deeper coherence beneath the surface of the work, enriching our understanding of a play's action and characters, can be of great importance, but we need to recognize the distortions which can result when a critic abstracts from imagery secret meanings which contradict the fundamental meaning of action and character. In the fascinating work of discerning the ironic tension that one word or image may exert against another, critics sometimes confound Shakespeare's plays with Chapman's poems and retrogress to something not unlike Delia Bacon's unfolding of Shakespeare's hidden philosophy. And though our knowledge of dramatic conventions has clarified much, we must resist the temptation to explain all in terms of conventions, for while they set certain limits to an artist's technique of representing experience, the artist still has the freedom to create an independent world to which, if his artistry be sufficiently compelling, the audience must assent.

This study of Shakespeare's last four major tragedies does not attempt to establish a revolutionary method that will set misguided thinking right. It is built on critical works of the past and of the present, for whoever writes on Shakespeare's plays is greatly indebted to those with whom he agrees and disagrees. This study concentrates on the play's dramatic techniques; more specifically, it investigates how the point of view of an audience is established towards the protagonist. Though such an approach has been extensively applied to the novel, it has not yet been used in the study of drama. This particular method is perhaps no more important than others; however, it is, I believe, a fundamental one, or as some might suggest, the most elementary. But an elementary reading, one that gets at meaning and response through dramatic structure and technique, can tell us much about the craft of drama.

I have chosen these four plays of Shakespeare because they represent two different methods of characterization. The so-called "Christian tragedies," *King Lear* and *Macbeth*, are so constructed that rapport is established between audience and protagonist; in the "Roman tragedies," *Antony and Cleopatra* and *Coriolanus*, that rapport is, to a great extent, missing. The contrast in Shakespeare's handling of point of view explains why these plays communicate different kinds of experience. However, in discussing these plays, I have not treated the problem of point of view in a single-minded fashion because drama is more than technique and more than form. In so public an art as the drama, techniques and conventions are available to all playwrights. But great tragedy, in the last analysis, issues from a unique vision that encompasses problems of value and personality, and these exert a powerful influence on the playwright's choice of techniques.

All Shakespeare quotations are taken from *The Complete Plays and Poems*, ed. William Allan Neilson and Charles Jarvis Hill, Boston, 1942.

Permission has been granted by St. Martin's Press to quote from A. C. Bradley's *Oxford Lectures on Poetry*, and by

Chatto and Windus to quote from C. F. Tucker Brooke's edition of *Shakespeare's Plutarch*.

While writing this work I have been helped by friends who gave unstintingly of their time, and I am most grateful for their kindness. To Miss Setsuko Shoda, who spent many hours transcribing material unavailable to me, I am indebted for aid as well as encouragement. Dr. Leonard Nathanson was particularly generous in discussing at length almost every point in this book; I profited greatly from his keen observations and judgments. To Miss Barbara Cooper I owe many thanks for her invaluable criticism; she suggested many changes in matters of style, argument, and organization, and took time from her own work to read proof. Miss Anne Brunhumer read the manuscript and offered helpful suggestions; the final manuscript was considerably improved because of the excellent editorial criticism of Miss M. Kathleen Ahern.

I am under a happy obligation to Professor Herschel Baker and the late F. O. Matthiessen for introducing me to an understanding and appreciation of drama and the theatre. I am grateful to Professor Alfred Harbage for reading the manuscript and dissuading me from errors of interpretation. My greatest debts are to Mrs. Wilma Kerby-Miller, who taught me how exciting the study of language could be, and to Professor Harry Levin, from whose lectures and conversation came the stimulus for this work. To Professor Levin I owe more than formal acknowledgment can express.

W. R.

Madison, Wisconsin

Contents

Shakespeare
and the
Craft of Tragedy

CHAPTER I

KING LEAR

APART from action, there are two major devices that delineate character on the stage: direct self-characterization — what the hero says of himself — and the characterization of the hero by others. Often Shakespeare anticipates and prefigures the entrance of the tragic hero by having characters talk about him before he actually comes onto the stage; and such a technique is used notably in *Romeo and Juliet, Julius Caesar, Othello, Antony and Cleopatra* and *Coriolanus*. By prefiguring the hero the dramatist imposes upon the audience a certain angle of vision: the playwright provides the audience with a dramatic attitude towards the central figure by having others preview his traits or impart value judgments on him. Thus we actively entertain certain emotions towards the hero before meeting him; and when he does appear, his words and actions are inevitably compared to the brief portrait already sketched for us.

In *King Lear*, though the king's character is not sketched before he appears on stage, he nevertheless comes immediately into a certain frame of reference, not through the technique of prefiguring, but through his own exalted status. For an Elizabethan audience particularly, his figure would expand in minds to encompass a whole context of values. The person of Lear is from the very beginning associated with great honor, for he can be viewed as the highest human embodiment of all the elements which give order and dignity to society: he is king of his nation, father of his family, and he is an old man. Hence the respect which he should command is triply compounded. Now it is not absolutely necessary to turn to Elizabethan concepts of kingship or order to understand the respect and honor due to one who is king, who is father, and who is old. Such ideas have not disappeared with the passing of some three hundred and fifty years. However, a brief reference to Elizabethan attitudes is appropriate here because the respect due to Lear is central to the play.

Certainly "kingship" had an evocative power for Elizabethans. There is divinity that hedges a king — we find this idea reiterated in much of the writing of the age.[1] Furthermore, the correspondence between the power of the king and that of the father was an Elizabethan commonplace illustrating the order of a universe in which, as God governed all, so kings ruled states, and fathers, families.[2] In *The French Academie*, whose popularity is attested by its many English editions from 1586 to 1614, La Primaudaye makes an observation that might serve as a commentary on *King Lear*:

Everie house must be ruled by the eldest, as by a king, who by nature commandeth over everie part of the house, and they obey him for the good preservation thereof. . . . This commandement over children, is called roiall, bicause he that begetteth, commandeth by love, and by the prerogative of age, which is a kind of kingly commanding. . . . The father is the true image of the great & soveraign God, the universal father of al things.[3]

Thus the ordered family, the private life of a nation, is a mirroring in miniature of the ordered hierarchy of public society; and analogies between the king and his subjects and the father and his children prevailed.

It is within such a context that we first see King Lear: his figure activates in the minds of an audience patterns of value of which he is the embodiment. His formal entrance highlights all the dignity and authority associated with kingship.

The set of notes sounded, the "sennet," ushers in the concrete symbol of royalty, "enter one bearing a coronet"; and the stage directions give the precise order of entrance which accords with the prerogatives of rank: "King Lear, Cornwall, Albany, Goneril, Regan, Cordelia, and Attendants." On the Elizabethan stage this would be a stately procession of splendor, Lear the central figure in a crowded scene. All are Lear's subjects, dependent on him.

Lear's stature is even further magnified in his first extended pronouncement in which he tells of his intentions to divest himself of "rule,/ Interest of territory, cares of state" (I.i.50), for we see him in the role of public and private figure at one and the same time. Because he is king, his actions in dividing the realm have public consequences affecting the destiny of the state; as benefactor to his children, in this division, his actions affect the private life of the family as well. And yet, though the figure of the king bodies forth the ideal, the highest good of family and nation, it is important to see that in this scene Shakespeare presents his central character as an ironist would; and in this way: that the audience does not fully engage its sympathies with Lear or those who oppose him since the dramatist supports the values which Lear represents while revealing the king's misguided position.

Lear's character is objectively dramatized at the beginning. And in situations that are dramatized rather than narrated, the task of projecting states of mind devolves upon the language itself. In Lear's first lengthy speech, which is balanced and regally formal, Shakespeare has the king dramatically reveal himself as proud, authoritative, at the height of his power, wishing to hear not truth, but flattery:

> Tell me, my daughters, —
> Since now we will divest us both of rule,
> Interest of territory, cares of state, —
> Which of you shall we say doth love us most,
> That we our largest bounty may extend

> Where nature doth with merit challenge? Goneril,
> Our eldest-born, speak first.

(I.i.49)

Lear's abdication is thus the occasion for a pageant of flattery: each daughter is to vie with the other in a public display of love. Goneril fulfills his expectations:

> Sir, I love you more than word can wield the matter;
> Dearer than eye-sight, space, and liberty;
> Beyond what can be valued, rich or rare;
> No less than life, with grace, health, beauty, honour;
> As much as child e'er lov'd, or father found;
> A love that makes breath poor, and speech unable:
> Beyond all manner of so much I love you.

(I.i.56)

Shakespeare makes it obvious that Lear already has in mind the kind of answer he expects from his daughters. It is significant that after Goneril's fulsome protestations of love Lear does not evaluate or praise her remarks. He makes no comment at all on her speech. He has heard what he has wanted to hear, and he immediately bestows upon her a share of the kingdom. It is interesting to note that in *The True Chronicle History of King Leir,* when Gonorill proclaims her love for him, Leir comments, "O, how thy words revive my dying soul" (I.iii.54).

Shakespeare reinforces this imperious characteristic of Lear. Again, after Regan's testimony of love, Lear makes no reference to her speech; in *The Chronicle History* he says, "Did never Philomel sing so sweet a note" (I.iii.74). He allots her portion and calls on Cordelia to "Speak." And it is important to observe that in the three instances where Lear asks the daughters to proclaim the extent of their love, he imperiously concludes with the curt, monosyllabic, "Speak." (The Folio omits the concluding "Speak" addressed to Regan.)

Thus, when Cordelia refuses to follow her sisters in answering with "glib and oily art," the stage has been dramatically set for Lear's wrathful indignation.

> *Lear.*   what can you say to draw
>   A third more opulent than your sisters? Speak.
> *Cordelia.* Nothing, my lord.
> *Lear.* Nothing!
> *Cordelia.* Nothing.
> *Lear.* Nothing will come of nothing. Speak again.
> *Cordelia.* Unhappy that I am, I cannot heave
>   My heart into my mouth. I love your Majesty
>   According to my bond; no more nor less.
>
>   (I.i.87)

Lear's real attitude comes out when in thwarted rage he revealingly says to Cordelia: "Better thou/ Hadst not been born than not t' have pleas'd me better" (I.i.237).

The situation presented here is the problem of any human relationship: shall we attempt to understand another, really understand another person, or will we accept him only on our own terms? Shakespeare presents Lear as a powerful king, wilful and unyielding, a man who has no desire to understand others or communicate with them. He has not here the humanity of thinking beyond himself. He hears only what he wants to hear, tinting everything with the color of his own mind. When Cordelia speaks these words:

>   Good my lord,
> You have begot me, bred me, lov'd me: I
> Return those duties back as are right fit;
> Obey you, love you, and most honour you.
> Why have my sisters husbands, if they say
> They love you all? Haply, when I shall wed,
> That lord whose hand must take my plight shall carry
> Half my love with him, half my care and duty.
> Sure, I shall never marry like my sisters,
> To love my father all.
>
>   (I.i.98)

Lear, expecting an entirely different answer, the kind of satisfying flattery given by the politic Goneril and Regan, makes no attempt to understand what Cordelia is really trying to say, and casts off the person dearest to him.

Though Lear acts in wrathful haste and blindness, his actions are analyzed, his motivation unfolded, that the audience may see and understand his character fully and unambiguously. Lear even explains himself, like an onlooker unfolding the psychology of action. When he shouts to Cordelia, "Better thou/ Hadst not been born than not t' have pleas'd me better" (I.i.237), he is, in a way, impartially describing himself as one who values love only as a means of adding to his own vanity. And in Kent's banishment there is the same self-revelation. In violent outburst Lears says that Kent must be banished because he sought to make the king break his vow and reverse his sentence which "nor our nature nor our place can bear" (I.i.174). Yet such statements cannot be taken as indications of a high degree of self-awareness on the part of the protagonist. They are best viewed as a mode of partial narrative which S. L. Bethell has described as "appropriate to poetic drama, since it renders the psychological situation clear without transferring attention from the verse to the process of naturalistic induction." [4]

One can say that in the beginning Lear equates "nature" with his own "conception" of himself; that for Lear the natural rights inherent in majesty, fatherhood, and age demand — or, rather, take for granted — the unquestioning and undivided love of children for parent, benefactor and king; the respect of youth for age; and the complete obedience of subject to ruler. Thus, when Cordelia refuses to conform to Lear's own conception of what is natural, the king arbitrarily casts her off as unnatural, disclaiming all "paternal care,/ Propinquity and property of blood" (I.i.115). He banishes Kent because his "nature" allows not the breaking of vows. For Lear, then, nature is not the external world, or reason, but his own image; and he looks out onto a world which must mirror back his own conceptions of loyalty, love, justice, perfection. Proudly independent in the omnipotence of self,

he is detached from all, and in his isolation feels no responsibility and kinship towards others. Lear's folly, like that of
Oedipus, is one of blindness, the overweening belief in the
infallibility of one's own being, the failure to recognize the
limitations of mortality.

To characterize Lear's folly as anything but the result of
misguided intellect is to reduce his stature and worth, and
turn him into a pathetic figure, as Lamb's version of a "painful and disgusting" spectacle, "an old man tottering about
the stage with a walking-stick, turned out of doors by his
daughters in a rainy night"; [5] or Lily B. Campbell's version
of Lear as "the slave of habitual wrath"; [6] or the very extreme view of G. W. Knight who pictured Lear as the supreme
pathetic figure of literature because of his "puerile intellect." [7]

That Lear has no true insight into himself, his actions, and
those about him can, on analysis, be seen as the leitmotif of
the opening scene. The loyal Kent draws attention to the
problem of appearance versus reality when he says to Lear:

> Thy youngest daughter does not love thee least;
> Nor are those empty-hearted whose low sounds
> Reverb no hollowness.

(I.i.154)

Certainly hollowness is Kent's judgment of Goneril and
Regan, a pointed reference to their earlier professions of
love. Notice the abstractions that Goneril used when she af-
firmed her love to be dearer than space, liberty, life, grace,
health, beauty, honor. In his blind pride Lear has been deceived by the world of appearances; he mistakes the outward
appearance of Goneril and Regan, their veneer of words
which cover the evil within them, for the real, sincere and
speechless love of Cordelia. As has often been noticed, a
similar situation exists in Sophocles' *Oedipus Rex* where
Oedipus is at first blind to the realities of the world in which
he lives. The prophet who was blind, Tiresias, saw; and the
king who saw was blind.

When the bluntly speaking Kent, who sees true relations and is not deceived by appearances, is banished with Lear's words echoing, "Out of my sight," he replies, "See better, Lear," — an exhortation which is given further significance at the end of the scene when Regan tells Goneril that the king "hath ever but slenderly known himself" (I.i.296). And when Lear's explosive, "now, by Apollo, — " is picked up by Kent, "Now, by Apollo, king,/ Thou swear'st thy gods in vain" (I.i.162), it is an ironic comment on the king's inability to distinguish true value, the faithful Cordelia and Kent, from mere appearance, the seemingly dutiful Goneril and Regan. It is to be remembered that Apollo was the god of light, and that inscribed on the temple of Apollo at Delphi was the famous "Know Thyself." Also inscribed there was the injunction "Nothing in Excess."

The first scene presents us with the basic facts of the play: the division of kingdom, the scorning of the faithful Cordelia and Kent. Shakespeare gives the audience a point of view towards the hero of the play: through Lear's own speech and actions we see him as proudly blind and regal; and this view is substantiated for us by Lear's friend, Kent, and by his future antagonists, Goneril and Regan. These three appraise him and reach the same conclusions. Kent slightingly calls him "old man," characterizes his actions as "folly" and "hideous rashness." At the end of the scene, when Goneril and Regan review the happenings in businesslike prose, their final judgment of the king, shrewd and incisive, has already been dramatized as truth:

> *Goneril.* You see how full of changes his age is; the observation we have made of it hath not been little. He always lov'd our sister most; and with what poor judgement he hath now cast her off appears too grossly.
> *Regan.* 'Tis the infirmity of his age; yet he hath ever but slenderly known himself.
> *Goneril.* The best and soundest of his time hath been but rash; then must we look from his age to receive not alone the imperfections of long-engraffed condition, but there-

withal the unruly waywardness that infirm and choleric
years bring with them.

(I.i.291)

The speeches of Goneril and Regan at the end of this exposition scene attune us to their later treatment of Lear by arous-
ing a state of expectation, of speculation as to how they will
curb their father and king, who has given up his power and
yet would, as Goneril fears, still "manage those authorities/
That he hath given away!" (I.iii.17)

In analyzing the way in which Shakespeare portrays Lear
at the beginning of the play it becomes evident that the audience sees and understands events not primarily through
Lear's eyes, thus becoming one with him, sympathizing with
his actions, but through the eyes of Kent and Goneril and
Regan who interpret him for us. Friend and foes, by agreeing
on the folly which impels Lear, formulate a dramatic attitude towards the character.

2

When next we encounter Lear there begins a shift in the
audience's point of view because there is an attendant change
of focus. Certainly the ideal of Lear is the world which precedes the division of kingdom: a world of his own order, of
undivided loyalty, of absolute respect for king and father and
age. These values were not attacked as values in the opening
scene of the play. Shakespeare portrayed Lear's great stature
and dignity while at the same time incisively criticizing his
misguided intellect. When Lear acted, he acted blindly, un-
wisely, and with morally shocking consequences. Now, Lear
suddenly moves precipitously from an old world of his own
conception into a tough new world which stretches him upon
its rack. In this new world Lear finds himself a stranger, rejected, and his is a continual battle to maintain self-respect,
to hold desperately to the vision of the man he once was. His
values — true values — are no longer recognized; and it is

this sudden shift into a new world that drastically changes the dramatic point of view towards Lear.

In Lear's act of dividing the kingdom we saw him at the height of his power. From this high point begins a fall which culminates in the stripping of Lear to the very bone in the storm scene on the heath, a stripping of the respect and honor due him as king, father, and old man. And it is this profound respect which he should command, which is his natural and inherent right, that comprises the informing context of values and determines the audience's point of view towards Lear.

There are several direct references to "stripping" in the play. France, questioning Lear's treatment of Cordelia, stresses the idea of dismantling:

> This is most strange,
> That she, whom even but now was your best object,
> The argument of your praise, balm of your age,
> The best, the dearest, should in this trice of time
> Commit a thing so monstrous, to dismantle
> So many folds of favour.   (I.i.216)

Goneril, commenting on Lear's treatment of Cordelia, tells "with what poor judgement he hath now cast her off" (I.i.294); Lear sees himself as a "discarded" father (III.iv.74); Kent, discussing Lear's remorse over his treatment of Cordelia, says that Lear is overwhelmed with the shame of "His own unkindness,/ That stripp'd her from his benediction" (IV.iii.44). Indeed, R. B. Heilman has gone to extremes in abstracting from the play what he has termed "The Clothes Pattern" to show that "the poor naked wretches of the play, the victims of the world, will survive in spirit. The gorgeous are doomed. In proud array, Lear failed; uncrowned, half-naked, he is saved. This is a central paradox of the play." [8]

That Lear's stripping is a preparation for his regeneration has been noted by all who discuss this play. What has not been noticed is the integral part that this concept of stripping has in the dramatic design of the play, reminiscent of *Everyman*, where the hero is stripped of all save Good Deeds.

An analysis of *Lear's* dramatic line of development shows
that up to the point of the actual tearing off of clothes on the
heath, in every scene in which Lear appears he undergoes
relentless stripping — of honor, of dignity.

The stripping process is the major movement of the first
part of *King Lear*. It begins when Lear disinherits himself.
With a pointing of a finger to the map before him he divests
himself of his lands and retains only the name and honor of
king without responsibility or power. Next Lear strips from
himself Cordelia, then Kent. We note the further fall of the
king and his further dismantling in the colloquy between
Goneril and Oswald. When Goneril learns that Lear struck
her gentleman for chiding his fool, she tells Oswald that
when the king returns from hunting she will not speak to
him; Oswald is to tell the king that she is sick. Furthermore,
she even instructs the servant to show disrespect to her father
and king:

> Put on what weary negligence you please,
> You and your fellows; I'd have it come to question.
> If he distaste it, let him to my sister,
> Whose mind and mine, I know, in that are one,
> Not to be over-rul'd. Idle old man,
> That still would manage those authorities
> That he hath given away!
>
> (I.iii.12)

Goneril, evincing this attitude to Oswald, triply compounds
her felony: she is disrespectful to kingship, fatherhood and
old age.

The relentless stripping of the king continues. When Lear
asks Oswald where Goneril is, Oswald does not answer; he
merely departs. And when Lear asks his knight why Oswald
did not return when called, the knight reports, "he would
not" (I.iv.59). Such an answer is given to the king, and we
must remember that he still commands the respect owing
to a king, and that here a servant has given him insult. The
knight feels impelled to speak out: "to my judgement, your

Highness is not entertain'd with that ceremonious affection as you were wont. There's a great abatement of kindness appears as well in the general dependants as in the Duke himself also and your daughter" (I.iv.61). Lear's reply, "Thou but rememb'rest me of mine own conception," is a poignant recognition of what is beginning to take place. And immediately after this, when Lear and Oswald meet, and Lear commandingly asks Oswald, "Who am I, sir?" (I.iv.85), Oswald replies with what can only be considered a deliberate insult: "My lady's father." Here the superiority of degrees so central to the Elizabethan conception of an ordered hierarchic society is completely overthrown and the position of king is subverted.

In this same scene the Fool, acting as chorus, focuses attention on these aspects of overturned degree. It is the Fool who gives the king a lesson in government, pointing out his folly in dividing the kingdom: "When thou clovest thy crown i' th' middle, and gav'st away both parts, thou bor'st thine ass on thy back o'er the dirt. Thou hadst little wit in thy bald crown when thou gav'st thy golden one away" (I.iv.175). "Thou art an O without a figure," the Fool tells Lear, "I am better than thou art now; I am a Fool, thou art nothing" (I.iv.212). It is natural that a king should rule a kingdom; it is unnatural for him to give it away. It is natural that a man should ride an ass; it is unnatural that he should carry the ass on his back. This is the complete overturning of what is natural. As in *Gorboduc,* an undivided kingdom symbolized order and due subordination in the realm; with the division of kingdom comes the breaking of all natural bonds, and chaos ensues.

The Fool holds up before Lear the mirror of his follies that he might clearly see his actions and their consequences. In the beginning of the play Kent, Goneril and Regan framed Lear's figure by objectively analyzing him. Now the Fool's utterances help frame the king, and the audience, seeing Lear in terms of the Fool's remarks, quickly perceives the relations between the two. While the Fool is certainly the disinterested truthteller, the "punctum indifferens" of the play, as Enid Welsford tells us in her social and literary history *The Fool*,[9] his truth narrows upon the folly of a king who would give away his titles; of a father who would allow the child to rule him; of a man who deserves to be beaten for being old before his time. The Fool is, as it were, a mirror for magistrates and fathers. But it is to be noticed that Lear does not seem to recognize his own figure in the Fool's mirror. It is we, the audience, who see it far more clearly than Lear. Thus, the audience is drawn into sympathetic participation with Lear because it can see, Lear cannot; it shares the Fool's superior knowledge, unintelligible to Lear for the most part, and recognizes in Lear the collision of opposites: a man who would still cling to the conception of proper place, the values taken for granted before; yet now, in a new world, put in his improper place. And once having entered into Lear's perspective we are forced to look on the world with his eyes.

Though Kent has said to Lear concerning the Fool, "This is not altogether fool, my lord" (I.iv.165), Lear will not recognize the significance of the Fool's wisdom until later, and it will be a self-recognition, not the result of another's explanation, but gained through his own suffering. In Act I, scene iv, Lear does not realize the significance of the Fool's statement: "thou mad'st thy daughters thy mothers; for when thou gav'st them the rod, and puttest down thine own breeches. . . ." No sooner does the Fool say this than his statement is demonstrated: Goneril, the daughter, comes in and reproves the king for what she considers to be his insolent retinue. Here we have an example of the daughter instructing the father. Again we see the stripping of Lear — in this instance, of the dignity and respect which a daughter owes him. Again, the Fool acts as chorus: "May not an ass know when the cart draws the horse?" (I.iv.244) — another reference to the inversion of order: the cart drawing the horse; the daughter applying the rod to the father.

And when the daughter, Goneril, wants to diminish the king further, when she suggests that he reduce the number of his retinue, he breaks forth in impassioned anguish, calling her degenerate bastard, and goes off to his other daughter, Regan, who he thinks will not, could not, be so unkind.

The whittling away of the king's stature continues unabated. When the disguised Kent becomes a messenger for the king and is put into the stocks by Cornwall for striking Oswald, it is a further insult to Lear, and this is pointed out by both Kent and Gloucester. To Cornwall, Kent exclaims:

> I serve the King,
> On whose employment I was sent to you.
> You shall do small respects, show too bold malice
> Against the grace and person of my master,
> Stocking his messenger.
>
> (II.ii.135)

while Gloucester protests to Cornwall, "The King must take it ill/ That he, so slightly valued in his messenger,/ Should have him thus restrain'd" (II.ii.152). And when Lear sees his messenger in the stocks, this insult against kingship is the first thing to come to mind: "What's he that hath so much thy place mistook/To set thee here?" "They durst not do't," he cries out. "They could not, would not do't. 'Tis worse than murder/ To do upon respect such violent outrage" (II.iv.12).

But the outrage proceeds. Lear now learns that Cornwall and Regan refuse to speak with him. He still has not attuned himself to the realities of his new world where the inversion of which the Fool speaks has become the norm; and he tries to rationalize and minimize the affront; and still he cannot do so:

> Deny to speak with me? They are sick? They are weary?
> They have travell'd all the night? Mere fetches;
> The images of revolt and flying off.
> Fetch me a better answer.
>
> (II.iv.89)

Gloucester, by speaking of "the fiery quality of the Duke," his "fix'd" nature (II.iv.93) only heightens the contrast between the respect due to Lear and the ignominious situation into which Lear is continually being pushed. Lear is torn between a conception of his elevated position and dignity, what should be, and an awareness, now growing more intense, of how that pattern of hierarchal values is being violated. These clashing views and Lear's struggle within himself are caught up and juxtaposed in a single speech:

> The King would speak with Cornwall; the dear father
> Would with his daughter speak, commands her service.
> Are they "inform'd" of this?   My breath and blood!
> "Fiery"? The fiery duke? Tell the hot duke that —
> No, but not yet; may be he is not well.
> Infirmity doth still neglect all office
> Whereto our health is bound; we are not ourselves
> When nature, being oppress'd, commands the mind
> To suffer with the body. I'll forbear;
> And am fall'n out with my more headier will,
> To take the indispos'd and sickly fit
> For the sound man.
>
> (II.iv.102)

Here the verse is flexibly mimetic, immediately conveying the curve of Lear's emotions. In the beginning, authority communicated in determined commands; the stressing of kingship, of fatherhood. With Lear's shift from the indicative mood in "would speak" to the imperative "commands her service" there is an indication of a rage that grows within him, as if Lear at that moment recognizes that he is losing his authority as king and father. And with his words, "Tell the hot duke that — " there is a sudden breaking off, reflecting a will to disbelieve the calculated affront to his person, a reluctance to accept the indignity as truth, and an attempt to reason himself into calmness. But when he looks upon Kent in the stocks there can be no doubt of the insult being done himself; and he passionately commands that his servant be released and that Cornwall and Regan be immediately summoned.

In this scene Lear is further degraded. After Regan finally comes, she says to Lear:

> I pray you
> That to our sister you do make return;
> Say you have wrong'd her, sir.
>
> (II.iv.152)

And Lear replies:

> Ask her forgiveness?
> Do you but mark how this becomes the house:
> "Dear daughter, I confess that I am old;
> Age is unnecessary. On my knees I beg
> That you'll vouchsafe me raiment, bed, and food."
>
> (II.iv.154)

The king actually kneels before Regan in enacting the shame that would be his were he to return to Goneril, forced to beg her forgiveness and favors. Here we have a picture of the grandeur that was king, now plundered of dignity, bent at the knees.

A further reminder of his ignominy comes when the trumpet heralds not a person of eminence, but, ironically, Oswald, who brought galling shame upon him. The indignities against Lear are compellingly, mordantly dramatized when, in a stylized manner, the king is forced to turn from one daughter to the other as they relentlessly reduce the number of his followers. What began as a retinue of one hundred for the king is halved to fifty by Goneril; halved to twenty-five by Regan (here Lear cries out, "I gave you all"). And when Lear turns to Goneril with the words:

> I'll go with thee.
> Thy fifty yet doth double five and twenty,
> And thou art twice her love.
>
> (II.iv.261)

the number is further reduced, until Regan divests him of all — "What need one?"

The daughters have finally stripped him of everything: honor, respect, filial devotion, retainers. The dismantling of the king is almost completed; its culmination is to come in the scene on the heath. When Regan says to Lear, "What need one?" he replies in words which show a turning point in his characterization:

> O, reason not the need! Our basest beggars
> Are in the poorest thing superfluous.
> Allow not nature more than nature needs,
> Man's life is cheap as beast's. Thou art a lady;
> If only to go warm were gorgeous,
> Why, nature needs not what thou gorgeous wear'st,
> Which scarcely keeps thee warm. But, for true need, —
>
> (II.iv.267)

If man is stripped of that which gives him dignity — his true need, if he is judged solely by his basic needs, is he no more than an animal? Is it only clothes which make a man, which separate him from the beast? Deprived of the last vestige of outward dignity, Lear asks questions about the status of human values. His speech is an address not only to Regan, but to the world,[10] an agonizing attempt to find universal meaning, universal justice. His particular fate therefore becomes the fate of mankind, and the audience can no longer take an objective view of Lear. To see a man fall from greatness and be reduced to nothingness is an awful spectacle. But when Lear universalizes his particular experience in his address to the world the dignity of all men is at stake: "not the dignity of kings and robes," as Melville was to write of the anguish at the undraped spectacle of Starbuck, his valor-ruined man, "but that abounding dignity which has no robed investiture." [11] Sympathizing with Lear's values and his precarious position, through his speech we move into his consciousness; we see the world with his eyes, we are committed to his point of view. Commenting on Yeats' poetry, C. M. Bowra explained an analogous experience in this way: "In the highest moments of all great poetical drama the personality of the character does not count so much as his situation, which is typical of a tragic human destiny, and . . . at such moments individuality is merged in poetry." [12]

The particular experience of Lear achieves its universality when in his speech to Regan he attempts to pierce through superficialities to the realities they disguise, to expose the real as it should be; for in this he presents the universal human desire to find in the world meaning and order. Waging a heroic battle to preserve his self-control and dignity in the face of the abuses which his daughters have heaped upon him, Lear, in his great agony, turns to address the heavens themselves:

> You heavens, give me that patience, patience I need!
> You see me here, you gods, a poor old man,
> As full of grief as age; wretched in both!
> If it be you that stirs these daughters' hearts
> Against their father, fool me not so much
> To bear it tamely; touch me with noble anger,
> And let not women's weapons, water-drops,
> Stain my man's cheeks!
>
> (II.iv.274)

Isolated, forsaken, despairing of men on earth, Lear can only call upon cosmic powers for help. This sense of isolation, of alienation from society, is characteristic of the tragic hero. Lear, like Job, has had his values and beliefs shaken, and finding no comfort or understanding in men of his own society, turns to the heavens. So Job, understood neither by his wife nor the comforters, had only one recourse: he carried on a monologue directed not so much to the comforters as to the heavens above, pleading to see and reason with God.

In this climactic speech Lear's thoughts focus upon the respect due to age and fatherhood. In a previous speech he poignantly summarized all the respect and honor which should have been his by right: " 'Tis not in thee," he told Regan,

> To grudge my pleasures, to cut off my train,

To bandy hasty words, to scant my sizes,
And in conclusion to oppose the bolt
Against my coming in. Thou better know'st
The offices of nature, bond of childhood,
Effects of courtesy, dues of gratitude.
Thy half o' th' kingdom hast thou not forgot,
Wherein I thee endow'd.
                                          (II.iv.176)

Lear therefore bodies forth the traditional values which give order and cohesion to society: the offices of nature, bond of childhood, effects of courtesy, dues of gratitude. No longer, as in the opening scene of the play, is a balanced point of view maintained towards Lear, where the audience is put in the position of his opponents, seeing the events primarily through their eyes. All the former tensions and conflicts are viewed in a new light because they are seen in a new intellectual and emotional perspective: the ideal of objective values, the order and civilized decency which Lear represents. When Goneril and Regan degrade their father, more than an individual is threatened; the civilized values of humanity are imperilled.

The gulf between the real and the ideal, between what Goneril and Regan actually do and what they should do, is so enormous that it tears Lear's reason to shreds, pitching him into insanity. Lear has come to recognize fully what his daughters are doing to him; and after appealing to the gods, he turns upon his daughters in bitterness. Stripped of his authority to command respect, his appeal to natural courtesies unheeded, the broken rhythms and thoughts of his speech reflect his impotency and aching bewilderment:

                    No, you unnatural hags,
I will have such revenges on you both
That all the world shall — I will do such things, —
What they are, yet I know not; but they shall be
The terrors of the earth. You think I'll weep:
No, I'll not weep.
I have full cause of weeping; but this heart
                    (*Storm and tempest.*)

Shall break into a hundred thousand flaws,
Or ere I'll weep. O, Fool! I shall go mad!

(II.iv.281)

The oncoming storm in the macrocosm, indicated by the
Folio stage direction, *"Storm and tempest,"* coincides with
the storm which is beginning in the microcosm, the seething
conflict within Lear's own mind. Driven to the edge of madness, Lear flees to an inhuman nature which is on the very
edge of the civilized world. This nature to which he flees is
a nature of chaos corresponding to the chaos in himself. Both
the macrocosm and the microcosm are rent and in discord, no
longer an expression of cosmic harmony and reason.

3

Serving as a skeletal framing device for *King Lear* is the
contrast between the values of an old and a new world, which
can also be viewed as the conflict between generations/ one
of the archetypal themes suggested by the Jungian psychol-
ogist Maud Bodkin.[13] Lear himself calls attention to this contrast early in the play when he announces his intent "To
shake all cares and business from our age,/ Conferring them
on younger strengths" (I.i.40) — a marked change from the
religious motivation of the older play of *Leir* where the king
says:

> The world of me, I of the world am weary,
> And I would fain resign these earthly cares,
> And think upon the welfare of my soul:
> Which by no better means may be effected,
> Than by resigning up the crown from me,
> In equal dowry to my daughters three.[14]

(I.i.24)

The young and the strong are to inherit the earth — "The
younger rises when the old doth fall" (III.iii.26) is how
Edmund pithily expresses the matter. The leading representatives of the new regime are Goneril and Regan in the
main plot of the play, and Edmund in the subplot.

With varying emphases, critics have repeatedly noted basic similarities in the characters of Goneril, Regan and Edmund.[15] While all three share certain traits, they are most closely related by a common philosophical outlook: representatives of a new world, they hold values radically different from Lear's. Their world is one in which nature is not fundamentally good, and evil is not a mere aberration, the result of misguided reason. Nor is the new moral and political order built upon the natural and divine law expounded by Hooker, in whose orthodox Elizabethan world view the will continually seeks the good: "evil as evil cannot be desired: if that be desired which is evil, the cause is the goodness which is or seemeth to be joined with it." [16] Rather, the desire for power and sexual pleasure — natural emotional drives — are the dominant urges of those who represent the new world. The bastard Edmund would top his legitimate brother and expropriate his land, disclaiming "the plague of custom" (I.ii.3); to gain all the property he betrays his father to Regan and Cornwall. The daughters, Goneril and Regan, strip their father of all; both lust after Edmund. Goneril would even have Edmund murder her husband, thus freeing her to marry him.

For Elizabethans this naturalistic aspect of human life was above all associated with the name Machiavelli — in Marston's description, "deepe, deepe observing, sound brain'd Macheveil." [17] Machiavelli provided in his writings, particularly in *The Prince*, a rational appraisal of the human condition, man as he is, rather than man as he ideally should be.[18] His emphasis was on the here and now, his concern was not with moral considerations but analytic observation and practical action whose end was the security and well-being of the ruler.[19]

To call the new world in *King Lear* Machiavellian is not to say categorically that Shakespeare patterned his characters exclusively on Machiavelli's writings. It is merely to affirm that Machiavellianism was part of a prevailing mode of thought which undermined established beliefs and hierarchic values. One might also cite many other figures who contributed to this movement, and point to philosophies which were as challenging to orthodoxy as Machiavelli's realism and materialism: epicureanism, naturalism, skepticism.[20] What is important is to see the fundamental differences which put the two conflicting societies of *King Lear* in sharp dramatic opposition.

The representatives of the new society look at the world in the same way. They advance their fortunes by scrutinizing men and events to gain mastery over them. They have a rational account of everything; they live in the realm of fact where only the things that are seen have worth because these can be pragmatically evaluated. That Goneril repeatedly refers to Lear's condition as "dotage" (I.iv.315; I.iv.349; II.iv.200) is revealing, an indication that hers is a reason that works from the visible world. She would not recognize that duty and honor befit old age, for these are of the unseen, known only to the spirit. The same can also be said of Regan and Edmund.[21]

Regarding as negligible such values as love, loyalty, respect, the things that are unseen and of the spirit, the leaders of this new society would hold in contempt the traditional humanistic concern for "right reason" and "virtue," for these would be considered but the shadows of reality, mere customs, having no foundation in the nature of things. Cicero can be taken as representative of the humanistic point of view when he writes that "Law is the highest reason, implanted in Nature, which commands what ought to be done and forbids the opposite. . . ."[22] Machiavelli would substitute the vision of the fox and the lion for a transcendent reason shared with gods and beyond transient occasions. He would maintain that for nations and individuals to survive successfully, force and policy are necessary to combat human savagery. But, warned the humanists insistently, without transcendent reason to guide and reprove man, the sacred

is profaned, man turns into a beast, all the bonds of nature
fly asunder, and chaos and bestiality reign. This upheaval of
everything traditional patterns the whole new order of *King
Lear*. We are projected into a world where everything turns
upside-down: the daughters become rulers of the father; the
father and the king becomes their subject. "Sons at perfect
age and fathers declin'd, the father should be as ward to the
son" (I.ii.77) is a conviction which Edmund himself holds,
but ascribes to Edgar. The cart draws the horse; the fool
who should be mad is wise; and the king who should be
wise is a fool and actually becomes mad. Those who are really
good, Cordelia, Kent and Edgar, are rejected. The good even
have to hide in this paradoxical world: both Kent and Edgar
are forced to go into disguise.

Everything is topsy-turvy. And this reversal of what is
natural comes out most overpoweringly in the imagery of
bestiality used to depict the leaders of the new society. Of all
the characters in the play, only Edmund, Goneril and Regan
are pointedly likened to beasts.[23] Though Gloucester calls
Edgar "Unnatural, detested, brutish villain! worse than
brutish!" (I.ii.81) when told that Edgar has often maintained
that "fathers declin'd, the father should be as ward to the
son" (I.ii.78), the sentiments are Edmund's, not Edgar's, and
Gloucester's imprecations rightly apply to his bastard son.
Lear recurringly sees his daughters as unnatural and loath-
some; he pictures them as animals and diseases. Goneril is
called "degenerate bastard" (I.iv.275), "detested kite" (I.iv.-
284); she is seen as "wolvish" (I.iv.330), as a "vulture"
(II.iv.137), a "serpent" (II.iv.163). Regan is called a "disease" (II.iv.225), a "boil" (II.iv.226), a "plague-sore" (II.iv.-
227). Both Goneril and Regan are referred to as "pelican
daughters" (III.iv.77) and "she foxes" (III.vi.24). Albany calls
both daughters "tigers" (IV.ii.40), "Most barbarous, most degenerate" (IV.ii.43), and likens them to "monsters of the
deep" (IV.ii.50).

These recurring references to the bestial in *Lear* call to

mind the brute tooth-and-claw nature of Machiavelli's world. The actions of Edmund, Goneril and Regan are patently Machiavellian. However, it is important to recognize that the bestial imagery also relates to an equally significant association: the unnaturalness of ingratitude. Certainly one source of Lear's great torment is the shock of discovering that those whom he loves most are his worst enemies and unworthy of his love. His mind is torn apart because he cannot believe that the apparent falseness of Goneril and Regan is reality, and that what is reality can be so hideously monstrous. At the same time thoughts of ingratitude and unkindness also combine to force Lear into madness. Goneril and Regan owe their kingdoms to Lear; he is their benefactor, as well as their father and king. But once they gain their lands and authority they so fail in their corresponding duty to remain grateful that thoughts of filial ingratitude continually sear Lear's mind. He calls Goneril "thankless child" (I.iv.311), designates her actions as "sharp-tooth'd unkindness" (II.iv.-137). He rails against "ingratitude, thou marble-hearted fiend" (I.iv.281). The corrosive thought of "monster ingratitude" (I.v.43) forces from him the first agonizing mention of madness as he exclaims:

> O, let me not be mad, not mad, sweet heaven!
> Keep me in temper; I would not be mad!
>
> (I.v.49)

"Unkindness" and "ingratitude" are often used synonymously in the sixteenth century, and are invariably called "unnatural." The basic meaning of "unkindness" being "unnatural conduct," [24] "ingratitude," a form of unnatural conduct, came to be linked with it. Together they form the most reprehensible qualities to be found in man, against which Elizabethan writers constantly inveigh.[25] Ingratitude in *Lear* becomes so monstrous that its intensity is expressed in language that conveys immense physical pain. Lear exclaims in anguish:

> Filial ingratitude!
> Is it not as this mouth should tear this hand
> For lifting food to 't?
>
> (III.iv.14)

The image of the intimate natural bond which should exist between father and child is here transformed into a vision of the unnatural and bestial tearing of one part of a human body by another. Lear can only believe that "nothing could have subdu'd nature/ To such a lowness but his unkind daughters" (III.iv.72). And his knotted, internal frustration is so urgent and pressing that at times he sadistically explodes into a fitful verbal attack on all nature —

> Crack nature's moulds, all germens spill at once
> That makes ingrateful man!
>
> (III.ii.8)

— while at other times he tortures himself:

> I tax not you, you elements, with unkindness;
> I never gave you kingdom, call'd you children;
> You owe me no subscription. Then let fall
> Your horrible pleasure.
>
> (III.ii.16)

Job and Lear face similar torments. Both are isolated because they can no longer understand their worlds; both impose upon life a kind of contract: Job, by being an eminently virtuous man, expects God to reward him; and Lear, by giving his daughters all, expects them, in a like manner, to fulfill their contractual obligation. Both Job and Lear confront a world which is indifferent to their demands.

Thoughts of ingratitude, of obligations unfulfilled, so tear at Lear's mind that he must either purge himself of them or else go mad:

> O Regan, Goneril!
> Your old kind father, whose frank heart gave all, —
> O, that way madness lies; let me shun that;
> No more of that.
>
> (III.iv.19)

But the idea of filial ingratitude, and the accompanying frustration of being in a world which refuses to conform to his conception of what it should be, continually overwhelms him. The first time he sees the begrimed Edgar who is reduced to animal existence, Lear can only think of one cause for such misery: "Did'st thou give all to thy daughters, and art thou come to this?" (III.iv.49) And again, when he hears Edgar's mad gibberish, he can only think of one explanation for such derangement: "Has his daughters brought him to this pass?/ Couldst thou save nothing? Wouldst thou give 'em all?" (III.iv.64) Shakespeare, in projecting Lear into a new order of things, a world which makes no provision for the old ways of life, concentrates keen attention on the dramatic clash of values and on a human being who is forced to undergo the ultimate of all tests: to see the world anew; to re-examine himself and his past.

4

Having described the conflicting values of the old and new world in *Lear*, we return to an analysis of Shakespeare's dramatic technique in establishing a certain point of view towards Lear. Much has been written of Lear's personality, of the flaw that leads to his downfall, of his regeneration, and even of his salvation. However, there is, in connection with Lear's personality, an important point to be considered: is it the king's character that accounts for his greatness? Can the greatness of any tragic hero be established solely in terms of a definite personality? Or does Melville's declaration, "To produce a mighty book, you must choose a mighty theme," [26] demand equal consideration? The matter can be answered best through an analysis of structure and dramatic technique, for these, after all, shape the work, and elicit particular emotions and attitudes from an audience.

Beginning with Act III, Shakespeare puts at the center of the stage not the personality of Lear, a particular king, but a moral problem which transcends a particular personality.

Not character, but values, become most important; not personality, but a situation typical of tragic human destiny. Several considerations of structural emphasis lead to this judgment. An investigation of the shifting of scenes in Act III, the calculated playing off of the subplot against the main plot for definite effects, will point to the main dramatic preoccupation of the act. An analysis of what *dramatis personae* say of the hero and what the hero says of himself will reveal the central concern of the action. And finally, by seeing the change that takes place in Lear's personality in connection with the dramatic context, we gain full perspective.

Before proceeding to an analysis of the interplay between the main plot and subplot in Act III, it would first be best to set forth the general pattern of interrelationships in the play. Many critics of Shakespeare have commented on the parallelism of characters and events in *Lear,* and we shall review these only briefly. Pervading the realms of the cosmos, society, and the individual is a breakdown of order, testimony to all the natural bonds which are broken in the play: the natural bonds of kingdom are broken with its division; the natural ties of family are broken when Lear casts off Cordelia, when Goneril and Regan degrade and persecute their father and even seek his death, when sister turns against sister, when Edmund turns against his brother Edgar, and against his father Gloucester. And on the individual level, Lear's madness is the wrenching of human order; and the storm in the macrocosm becomes a projection of the storm in the microcosm.[27]

In respect to plot, the story of Gloucester and his two sons Edgar and Edmund parallels the story of Lear and his daughters. Resembling many of the morality plays which bring forth their good and bad characters in two separate presentations, *King Lear* has a double opening, the subplot initiated by Edmund who, from the beginning, nakedly reveals his role as villain. The two plots of *Lear* finally merge in Act IV. There are also many other parallels in the play.

The plain-speaking of Cordelia is re-enforced by the bluntness of Kent and contrasted with the flattery of Goneril and Regan. Lear's mock court (III.vi.18–59 — omitted in the Folio) metes out justice in fantasy; Cornwall's kangaroo court (III.vii) imposes injustice in reality. Gloucester first learns to see the truth about Edmund and Edgar when he is physically blind; Lear fully penetrates the world of appearances and sees reality when he is mad.

Turning to Act III, we find that the subplot has very important functions. That it mirrors and reinforces the main plot has been duly noted by all. But the subplot provides more than intensification. We are made to see that the filial ingratitude and treachery which Lear endured is no isolated occurrence; it has happened in the past and it will happen again. In Act III, Gloucester experiences what Lear had previously undergone. We have a merging of past and present, and the force and depth of evil are brought upon us. Drama becomes the chronicle and brief abstract of the time, revealing how the reality of evil is not a mere passing phenomenon, but rooted in the spiritual structure of an era.

Let us briefly consider the interplay of plots in Act III. Scene iii, placed in Gloucester's castle, is the first shift from main to subplot; and it shows how history repeats itself. Here Gloucester reveals how Lear's daughters "took from me the use of mine own house" (III.iii.3). Though Edmund calls this "most savage and unnatural" (III.iii.7), he is hypocritical; he ends the scene with a bold sentiment which has already characterized the actions of Lear's daughters: "The younger rises when the old doth fall" (III.iii.26). The two plots become more intimately connected when Gloucester's efforts to mitigate Lear's suffering bring about his own misery. This is developed in the next change from main to subplot (scene v) where we also see history further repeat itself: the unnaturalness of Lear's daughters is paralleled when Edmund betrays his father to Cornwall. Finally, in the last scene of Act III we have Lear's situation paralleled in

detail. Gloucester, like Lear, has furnished Regan and Cornwall with all. They reside in his castle, yet they scant his
courtesies. "You are my guests" (III.vii.31) . . ., "I am your
host" (III.vii.39), Gloucester would vainly remind them, just
as Lear vainly repeated to his daughters, "I gave you all."
Moreover, Cornwall and Regan again show little regard for
the respect that is due old age; Regan even shamelessly plucks
Gloucester's white beard. At the end of the scene Gloucester
is thrust out at the gates to "smell/ His way to Dover" (III.-
vii.93), just as at the end of Act II the castle doors slammed
shut against Lear. And blind Gloucester groping his way to
Dover in the opening scenes of Act IV parallels Lear's mad
wanderings in Act III.

In its contrast with the main plot, the subplot intensifies
and enlarges the theme of filial ingratitude and the depravity
of man. This is to see the events objectively, from the outside. Something of equal — perhaps greater — significance
must be taken into account. And that is the cry of Gloucester,
"Give me some help! — O cruel! O you gods!" (III.vii.70) —
a cry for justice which corresponds to Lear's cry to the heavens
for understanding and justice at the end of Act II. Both Lear
and Gloucester are pushed into outer chaos and solitude,
forced to question the rightness of things. When these two
events occur we have a decided shift in the play's angle of
vision; we move from character which looks on the world
objectively, to character which suffers. Lear and Gloucester
can no longer act as though they still believed in the justice
of the world about them. And in their intense suffering, in
their appeal to the heavens, they actually address the conscience of the world. We, the audience, are that conscience.

We have therefore an important shift in vision: we move
from the plight of individual man to the terrors of everyman.
The personalities of Lear and Gloucester are also transformed. In their deepest loneliness they must blindly wander
in a wilderness to find truth. Action becomes a quest for
truth and certainty, and transcends mere personality. The

opening of Act III points to this shift in emphasis. At the
end of Act II the powerful members of the new order re-
treated "out o' th' storm" and the "wild night" and the doors
of the castle were shut behind Lear. At the beginning of Act
III, when the action moves to the heath, we feel that we have
reached the end of the human world. Nature's bounds are
broken. When Kent asks, "Where's the king?" a gentleman
paints in words the picture for the audience:

> Contending with the fretful elements;
> Bids the wind blow the earth into the sea,
> Or swell the curled waters 'bove the main,
> That things might change or cease; tears his white hair,
> Which the impetuous blasts with eyeless rage
> Catch in their fury, and make nothing of;
> Strives in his little world of man to out-scorn
> The to-and-fro-conflicting wind and rain.
> This night, wherein the cub-drawn bear would couch,
> The lion and the belly-pinched wolf
> Keep their fur dry, unbonneted he runs,
> And bids what will take all.   (III.i.4)

In the absence of scenery and lighting on the Elizabethan
stage, words alone establish atmosphere and description.
Through the eyes of the gentleman we see the king on the
wild heath, the rain pouring down upon his bare head, the
wind lashing him mercilessly. Shakespeare often sets up two
points of contrast, Egypt and Rome in *Antony and Cleopatra*,
for one example, or court and country, which is frequent in
the comedies, and by switching from one to the other,
heightens a situation or an emotion. Here we have a sudden
contrast between castle and moor. If one visualizes the play
as acted on the Elizabethan stage, where action is often un-
broken, unhampered by changing scenery and sets, the impact
of the contrast between castle and moor is heightened. We
get the impression that just outside the walls of a castle is the
world of animals and brute nature. Perhaps the only things
that divide men from the beasts are clothes and the comforts
of a hearth.

It is with the gentleman's speech that we begin our investigation of what the *dramatis personae* say about Lear. Such analysis, we suggest, will illuminate the central concern of the action. What does the gentleman's speech, which prefigures Lear, stress? We see all civilization a place of storm, with Lear at the center, raging thundering defiance. The king, once regally confident in his own conception of what constituted nature, now is a prey to the elements. Lear — the gentleman emphasizes — would impose upon nature his puny will; but nature is indifferent. Lear contends with the elements, "That things might change or cease." And the extremes of these two demands — change or complete destruction — give a most revealing insight into the king's condition. His present situation is so intolerable that it must either be temporary or give way to the end of the world.

We are concerned, then, with personality in conflict with the existing universe. Because of this monumental struggle, Lear's spiritual stature is greatly magnified; and because he represents civilized values which are threatened, all men are endangered. If we concentrate on the remarks made about Lear, we see that these form a significant pattern. Kent talks of the "hard rein" which Albany and Cornwall have "borne/ Against the old kind king" (III.i.27); of "how unnatural and bemadding sorrow/ The King hath cause to plain" (III.i.38). Gloucester predicts to Edmund that "These injuries the King now bears will be revenged home" (III.iii.12). To Regan's demand to know why Gloucester sent the king to Dover, he replies, "Because I would not see thy cruel nails/ Pluck out his poor old eyes; nor thy fierce sister/ In his anointed flesh stick boarish fangs" (III.vii.56). Going beyond Act III, we find Albany indicting Goneril:

> Tigers, not daughters, what have you perform'd?
> A father, and a gracious aged man,
> Whose reverence even the head-lugg'd bear would lick,
> Most barbarous, most degenerate! have you madded.
> Could my good brother suffer you to do it?

> A man, a prince, by him so benefited!
> If that the heavens do not their visible spirits
> Send quickly down to tame these vile offences,
> It will come,
> Humanity must perforce prey on itself,
> Like monsters of the deep.
>
> (IV.ii.40)

Cordelia explains her military expedition in this way:

> O dear father,
> It is thy business that I go about;
> Therefore great France
> My mourning and importun'd tears hath pitied.
> No blown ambition doth our arms incite,
> But love, dear love, and our ag'd father's right.
>
> (IV.iv.23)

And later, in the French camp, Cordelia speaks these impassioned words in reviewing Lear's experience on the heath:

> Had you not been their father, these white flakes
> Did challenge pity of them. Was this a face
> To be oppos'd against the warring winds?
> To stand against the deep dread-bolted thunder?
> In the most terrible and nimble stroke
> Of quick, cross lightning? to watch — poor perdu! —
> With this thin helm? Mine enemy's dog,
> Though he had bit me, should have stood that night
> Against my fire; and wast thou fain, poor father,
> To hovel thee with swine and rogues forlorn
> In short and musty straw? Alack, alack!
> 'Tis wonder that thy life and wits at once
> Had not concluded all.
>
> (IV.vii.30)

All the comments on Lear, except for Regan's reference to the "lunatic king" (III.vii.46), have a single focus: they serve as collective chorus and conscience, pointing to the dignity of fatherhood, age and kingship, the values that inhere in Lear's person. Even Edmund reveals this in his report to Albany:

> Sir, I thought it fit
> To send the old and miserable king
> To some retention and appointed guard;
> Whose age had charms in it, whose title more,
> To pluck the common bosom on his side,
> And turn our impress'd lances in our eyes
> Which do command them.
>
> (V.iii.45)

With Troilus it might be asked, "Weigh you the worth and honour of a king . . . in a scale/ Of common ounces?" [28]

We see that all references to Lear's misfortune direct our attention to the king's value, and this value remains constant; it does not shift according to the point of view of the onlooker. The accidents of personality recede, and we confront not particular man or ideal man, but the image of Lear embodying institutions and obligations necessary to the continuance of a moral society. The opposition between moral systems has brought about this plight of values. While the conscienceless fail to remember obligations, Lear and Gloucester vainly invoke that memory. Instead of holding to the bonds of gratitude, the leaders of the new amoral world greedily batten on others, their abuse finally turning into horrors. And this clash of opposing worlds brings into focus the overriding concern of players and audience alike: once man is free from memory and responsibility, can there be any limits to presumption? At stake is the most pertinent question of all: from this conflict what mode of life will finally prevail? Albany objectifies this concern when he appeals for retributive justice to set things right:

> If that the heavens do not their visible spirits
> Send quickly down to tame these vile offences,
> It will come,
> Humanity must perforce prey on itself,
> Like monsters of the deep.
>
> (IV.ii.46)

And in the situation paralleling the injustice done to Lear, the Second and Third Servants in Gloucester's castle also uni-

versalize the particular when, after the gouging out of
Gloucester's eyes, they too question the meaning of their
world:

> 2. *Servant.* I'll never care what wickedness I do,
> If this man come to good.
> 3. *Servant.*   If she live long,
> And in the end meet the old course of death,
> Women will all turn monsters.
>
> (III.vii.99)

Shakespeare, in every dramatic technique he employs, concentrates our vision on world order and the predicament of
everyman. This results in a rapport between Lear and audience, which is explained by Aristotle, who reminds us of the
intimate relationship between fear and pity when he defines
fear as pity lest the undeserving misfortune of another over-
take us.[29]

Lear's own speeches also point to the concern for values
and justice. Arthur Sewell has provided a very stimulating
comment on exposition of character: there are two kinds, he
says, one in which "the character is presented or presents himself in general relation to the world and to society, and the
other in which the character is presented or presents himself
merely in terms of the facts and feelings of the particular
situation." [30] Almost all of Lear's speeches on the heath are
directed to the world and society, only incidentally to the
particular situation. When he refers to his immediate predicament, invariably it is to relate it to a larger context, universal
justice. His first utterance on the heath is an apostrophe to
the heavens; it is a lament; it is a wish for annihilation:

> Blow, winds, and crack your cheeks! Rage! Blow!
> You cataracts and hurricanoes, spout
> Till you have drench'd our steeples, drown'd the cocks!
> You sulph'rous and thought-executing fires,
> Vaunt-couriers of oak-cleaving thunderbolts,
> Singe my white head! And thou, all-shaking thunder,
> Strike flat the thick rotundity o' th' world!

Crack nature's moulds, all germens spill at once
That makes ingrateful man!

(III.ii.1)

Wolfgang Clemen has traced the development in pre-Shake-spearian drama of this type of speech, the "Klagerede," as he terms it.[31] From rhetorical formulas, unintegrated in the structure of earlier dramas, this type of speech developed in Shakespeare's mature work into an integral part of the play's structure.

How much a part of the play's structure these rhetorical formulas are, we see when we consider the meaning of Lear's plight. From the start of Act III Lear is an exile on the wild heath; and though he is accompanied in his wanderings by the Fool, Kent, Edgar, Gloucester — spiritually he is utterly alone as he searches for a meaning to his existence. Before the division of kingdom, we are led to believe, Lear was able to extend his own conception of reality to the external world. He rewarded Goneril and Regan because they conformed to his idea of what was natural. He banished Cordelia and Kent because they would not match their actions to his expecta-tions. Now, on the heath, his individual will is of no avail. Cut away from his former world, he has lost his identity. If there is to be any order and meaning in life he must search for it, or create it anew, or perish in despair.

In his wanderings he searches and aches for recognition, needing almost to clutch in his hand the "why" of his misery. His soliloquies, addressed to the heavens, become addresses to the world, and since we, the audience, are that world, he speaks to our moral conscience. A world devoid of con-tractual obligations makes no sense to him; it is a world where nature's bonds are broken, just as they are on the heath. Hence he exclaims:

Rumble thy bellyful! Spit, fire! Spout, rain!
Nor rain, wind, thunder, fire are my daughters.
I tax not you, you elements, with unkindness;
I never gave you kingdom, call'd you children;

> You owe me no subscription. Then let fall
> Your horrible pleasure. Here I stand your slave,
> A poor, infirm, weak, and despis'd old man;
> But yet I call you servile ministers,
> That will with two pernicious daughters join
> Your high-engender'd battles 'gainst a head
> So old and white as this. Oh! Oh! 'tis foul!
>
> (III.ii.14)

Shakespeare, we can see, has woven the formulaic and rhetorical patterns of the lament, the complaint, the wish for annihilation into the texture of the play. Lear's speech here and elsewhere is detached neither from the physical setting nor the dramatic concern of the moment.

In his speeches Lear continually refers his own situation to the problem of universal justice. The particular repeatedly gives way to the universal. At one moment he would seek personal recognition from nature's forces, calling upon them to obliterate the world. In this he would find satisfying retributive justice. At another moment he would find the seat of justice, search out the meaning of the universe — but in this too he is thwarted: he can only envision corruption festering everywhere, for his degradation is testimony of a lawless universe:

> Let the great gods,
> That keep this dreadful pudder o'er our heads,
> Find out their enemies now. Tremble, thou wretch
> That hast within thee undivulged crimes,
> Unwhipp'd of justice! Hide thee, thou bloody hand;
> Thou perjur'd, and thou simular of virtue
> That are incestuous! Caitiff, to pieces shake,
> That under covert and convenient seeming
> Has practis'd on man's life! Close pent-up guilts,
> Rive your concealing continents, and cry
> These dreadful summoners grace. I am a man
> More sinn'd against than sinning.
>
> (III.ii.49)

Whenever Lear calls attention to the concern of the moment, it is only briefly; he is continually seeing in the particular a higher meaning. Even when he thinks of simple things, when he asks the Fool, "Where is this straw?" he proceeds to translate the immediate concern into a recognition of values: "The art of our necessities is strange/ And can make vile things precious" (III.ii.70). On the heath Lear continually pushes his thoughts beyond his present moment to universal questions. He is concerned with the reason, the justice of an event. His terror, for example, is for that which is out of time:

> Thou think'st 'tis much that this contentious storm
> Invades us to the skin —

he tells Kent;

>   so 'tis to thee;
> But where the greater malady is fix'd,
> The lesser is scarce felt.
> . . . .
>   the tempest in my mind
> Doth from my senses take all feeling else
> Save what beats there. Filial ingratitude!
> Is it not as this mouth should tear this hand
> For lifting food to 't?

>   (III.iv.6)

Serving as a perfect contrast to Lear is the Fool, for the Fool feels terror for that which is in time, for the immediate occasion:

> O nuncle, court holy-water in a dry house is better than this rain water out o' door. Good nuncle, in; ask thy daughters' blessing. Here's a night pities neither wise men nor fools.

>   (III.ii.10)

For Lear the storm and his own physical hardship are significant only because they reveal the spiritual chaos of the time. The Fool, ever practical, sees only the bare facts.

That Lear now sees more meaning in things than the Fool is a significant reversal of what had previously taken place. Before the heath scene the Fool served as *raisonneur*, continually pointing out the significance of happenings of which Lear was hopelessly unaware. Before, the Fool asked questions of Lear; now it is Lear who asks many questions. He wants to know whether Edgar's daughters have reduced him to the level of a beast. He would talk with the disguised Edgar, calling him "philosopher," "learned Theban," "good Athenian" (III.iv). He asks Edgar, "What is the cause of thunder?" (III.iv.160) and "What is your study?" (III.iv.163) And when the Fool sings out the moral of an occasion:

> "He that has and a little tiny wit, —
> With heigh-ho, the wind and the rain, —
> Must make content with his fortunes fit,
> For the rain it raineth every day."
>
> (III.ii.74)

Lear replies, "True, boy" — a remarkable change from his previous reactions to the Fool's utterances. Before the heath scene Lear never recognized the Fool's pointed moralizing. He either threatened to whip the Fool for his words or paid them no heed.

All this points to the significance, in dramatic terms, of Lear's wanderings on the heath. His is a quest for knowledge and certainty, a journey to find, somehow, a way back to order and civilization. While many critics have treated Lear as the study of the unstoical man,[32] Lear's unstoical conduct must be related to the dramatic movement of the play — his search for justice. Lear repeatedly tries to reconcile himself to the rending occasions. He strives for stoic endurance, for this would lead to freedom from pain and suffering. "You heavens, give me that patience, patience I need!" (II.iv.274) he cries out when his daughters would deprive him of all his retainers. "No, I'll not weep" (II.iv.286) he steadfastly maintains. On the heath, overwhelmed with grief and on the edge of self-pity, he steels himself with these sentiments: "No, I will be the pattern of all patience; I will say nothing" (III.ii. 37). "I will endure" (III.iv.18) is his continual resolve.

That Lear does not unalterably continue in these stoic

thoughts is to be explained in terms of the dramatic concern of the action: his main preoccupation is with justice, not his physical condition. To accept a stoic morality would involve a hardening to suffering, an attainment of peace through withdrawal and indifference. It would mean the acceptance of Marcus Aurelius' counsel: "When you are grieved about anything external it is not the thing itself which afflicts you, but your judgment about it. This judgment it is in your power to efface." [33] Lear can not do this, for Shakespeare has focused all attention on the problem of man who seeks justice in a world that has no justice. And this is the basis of the dramatic conflict. To argue that Lear is completely unstoical is to give the impression that Shakespeare is advocating in the play a support for stoic conduct: that Lear brings on his misfortunes because he has not the discernment of a stoic. Such analysis neglects dramatic structure and technique and turns drama into moral and philosophical formulas.

Lear's search for values and justice on the heath is also an attempt to regain his identity and once again recognize his former figure. "Who am I?" Lear insistently repeats this question in various ways, endeavoring to clutch at the shadow of his former being. Does this not explain his repeated references to himself as king even in his most desperate moments of madness? When, completely deranged, he makes his appearance late in Act IV, his first words are: "No, they cannot touch me for coining;/ I am the King himself" (IV.vi.83). The blind Gloucester recognizes him by his voice, "The trick of that voice I do well remember./ Is't not the King?" And Lear replies with great majesty in his madness:

> Ay, every inch a king!
> When I do stare, see how the subject quakes.
> I pardon that man's life. What was thy cause?
> Adultery?
> Thou shalt not die. Die for adultery! No:
> The wren goes to't, and the small gilded fly
> Does lecher in my sight.
>
> (IV.vi.109)

Completely isolated, alone with himself, speaking to himself, Lear creates his own world where none are guilty, for all are guilty. Yet he must have justice; and in Act III, scene vi, he sits as judge of all humanity. Before the Fool, Edgar, and Kent he arraigns Goneril and Regan in a mad judgment day where he can still demand justice and assert the prerogatives of kingship. Finally, his pathetic statement, "Come, come, I am a king,/ My masters, know you that?" (IV.vi.203) is a desperate attempt to hold on to his identity.

Since the audience looks at the world through Lear's eyes, it shares his agony and his view; the more intense his suffering, the more heightened the experience of the audience. Through Lear's address to the world our vision is directed to the quest for justice. In searching for his own identity in the midst of chaos, he does so for all mankind. A bewildered Lear, who has lost his proper place, must set himself against a hostile world, while the pragmatic Edmund invokes its aid. Is the tragic view, then, the depiction of a man of great stature and value who is helpless against an indifferent or malevolent nature? Is "the key to it all" what Herman Melville has termed the "ungraspable phantom of life" when he alluded to the story of Narcissus, "who because he could not grasp the tormenting, mild image he saw in the fountain, plunged into it and was drowned. But that same image, we ourselves see in all rivers and oceans. It is the image of the ungraspable phantom of life; and this is the key to it all." [34] The answer is to be found in the much discussed transformation that Lear undergoes on the heath.

At the beginning of the play Shakespeare portrays Lear as a proud man who lacks the humanity of thinking beyond himself; he even values love only as a means of adding to his own vanity. On the heath there comes to Lear an emotion which has not shown itself in him before: a concern for others. We first see this in Lear's words to the Fool:

> My wits begin to turn.
> Come on, my boy. How dost, my boy? Art cold?

I am cold myself. Where is this straw, my fellow?
The art of our necessities is strange
And can make vile things precious. Come, your hovel.
Poor Fool and knave, I have one part in my heart
That's sorry yet for thee.

(III.ii.67)

For the first time Lear reaches out to touch another human being. Seeing the Fool's suffering, he makes a sympathetic connection, "I am cold myself." He notices the Fool's adversity first; and through sympathetic identification he comes to recognize his own condition. In spite of innumerable outward differences, in one respect Lear and the Fool are equals: they share a common fate; and in their humanity they are kin. No longer do we see Lear as proud and vain. He recognizes other human beings and shows compassion for them. When Kent bids him seek refuge in the hovel, Lear would torture himself further by remaining out in the storm; but he shows concern for Kent, counselling him, "Prithee, go in thyself; seek thine own ease" (III.iv.23). And when he does decide to go into the hovel, he bids the Fool enter first, "In, boy; go first." There follow significant statements which show his concern for the sufferings of "poor naked wretches" everywhere:

Poor naked wretches, wheresoe'er you are,
That bide the pelting of this pitiless storm,
How shall your houseless heads and unfed sides,
Your loop'd and window'd raggedness, defend you
From seasons such as these? O, I have ta'en
Too little care of this! Take physic, pomp;
Expose thyself to feel what wretches feel,
That thou mayst shake the superflux to them,
And show the heavens more just.

(III.iv.28)

Lear's whole personality undergoes a complete transformation. From a desire to find personal vindication and personal recognition, his thoughts turn to sympathy for each individual being. He approaches the view that a moral society depends on the recognition of each man's value. This stress on the responsibility of one man for all makes Lear one with all humanity and binds all humanity into oneness. In his speech he strips away all thoughts of comforts and superficialities to lay bare basic truth, the human condition which underlies the world of fleeting appearances. In an unforgettable moment on the heath Lear translates his verbalization of this necessity for bare truth into a physical act as he asks the tormenting question:

> Is man no more than this? Consider him well. Thou ow'st the worm no silk, the beast no hide, the sheep no wool, the cat no perfume. Ha! here's three on's are sophisticated! Thou art the thing itself; unaccommodated man is no more but such a poor, bare, forked animal as thou art. Off, off, you lendings! come, unbutton here.
>
> (III.iv.107)

And he tears off his clothes.

Two interpretations may be offered for Lear's action. First, consider Lear's statement to Regan when she argued that he had no need of any retainers:

> O, reason not the need! Our basest beggars
> Are in the poorest thing superfluous.
> Allow not nature more than nature needs,
> Man's life is cheap as beast's. Thou art a lady;
> If only to go warm were gorgeous,
> Why, nature needs not what thou gorgeous wear'st,
> Which scarcely keeps thee warm. But, for true need, —
>
> (II.iv.267)

If man's life is as cheap as beast's, if it is only clothes which make a man, which separate him from the beast, then it is unnecessary for man to borrow from animals the clothes which cover his nakedness. Thus, one can say that in stripping off his clothes Lear dramatically acts out his words to Regan. Casting off his lendings, he makes a radical return to nature, becoming one with the beasts. And we can only ask: is this the bare truth about man? Is this reality, naked man, man as beast?

One can also view Lear's tearing off his clothes as the stripping away of all the superfluous values by which he has lived. One can say that he is acting out his words,

> O, I have ta'en
> Too little care of this! Take physic, pomp;
> Expose thyself to feel what wretches feel,
> That thou mayst shake the superflux to them,
> And show the heavens more just.

If one views this act of the stripping of clothes as an act of purgation, a return to essential man, then a new Lear will emerge from such torments.

These two interpretations have equal validity, for one is part of the other. What we are concerned with now, it is quite obvious, is more than the personality of a particular king; it is a confronting of the universe, and in that crisis, a questioning and a recasting of one's vision of reality. Previous to the division of kingdom, reality for Lear consisted of the values in his mind, and these he imposed upon the external world. As long as he had power to control nature, he could project his expectations and, with a high degree of success, have them realized. But the will to believe does not constitute reality. Power is accidental and temporary; things can appear to be what they are not; man can seek more justice in the world than there is. Consequently, the most urgent problem — the concern of the greatest works of art — is to learn to see reality as it is. In tearing off his clothes Lear divests himself of the husks of appearance, the accidents of power and rank. The reduction to unaccommodated man puts him on an equal basis with all men; he is, therefore, akin to all men. This act looks forward to a theme which preoccupied Dostoevski: the idea that each man is responsible for all men. As Markel says in *The Brothers Karamazov,* "Every one is really responsible to all men for all men and for everything." [35] When man sees that he is like all men, neither better nor worse, he begins to feel a bond with all humanity.

The opposite — isolation — results from proud independence and selfish aloofness.

Lear's recognition of his kinship with all men makes him see more sympathy and understanding in the world than before. Through sympathy he discovers himself. We have a moral reorientation, a shift from individual power to the principle of universal justice. We have a different vision of society, which is now seen as organic. Each individual is so intimately united to another that the misery of all is the misery of one. And we approach a recognition that the most important bonds of society are inner and spiritual, not merely the external and the formal.

The stripping of Lear suggests even more levels of significance. It is the culmination of his daughters' stripping him of honor and dignity, the final dismantling of the king. It suggests that man by himself, against nature's forces, is insignificant; that he is not, as Protagoras maintained, the measure of all things; that he derives his strength from his dependence on his fellow men. It is a suggestion that all men, at one time or another, are outcasts and wanderers. It is a recognition that man's worth is independent of rank and power. It is a test of man's true strength, for, as William Segar wrote in his Elizabethan treatise *The Booke of Honor and Armes,* "Seneca saith, that who so will trulie judge what worthines is in man, must consider of him naked, laying aside his livings and titles of honor . . . and then weigh of what value or excellencie he is in minde, because nobilitie is placed in the minde." [36]

In *Lear* the mind confronts the universe to discover if there is any relationship between the world and man. Such action partakes of the religious experience, for as Alfred North Whitehead has observed, "Religion is what the individual does with his own solitariness." [37] Lear is not the only one who undergoes an experience which forces him to face his world alone, see himself anew, and make what settlement he can with the world. The numerous other addresses to the world — by Gloucester (IV.vi.34), Edgar (IV.i.10), Albany

(IV.ii.46), Cordelia (IV.vii.14) — show the play's recurring preoccupation with man's quest for values. From personal suffering each learns something; and whatever we call the individual's experience in confronting the universe or invoking its aid — whether *anagnorisis,* self-recognition, or epiphany — the very number of addresses to the world reveals the concern with the question, "What is man?" or in individual terms, "Who am I?" For many of the characters it is necessary that they first lose their way before they can find themselves; and this action also partakes of the religious experience, for it deals with the problem, "What must man do to be saved?"

Our concern is with Lear and what he learns from his experience on the heath. When the rain came to wet him and the wind made him chatter, when nature would not conform to his wishes, when, as Lear says in his madness, "the thunder would not peace at my bidding" (IV.vi.103), he learns that he is not everything, that he can not control nature, and in his madness he clearly sees the true character of Goneril and Regan:

> They flatter'd me like a dog, and told me I had the white hairs in my beard ere the black ones were there. To say "ay" and "no" to everything that I said! "Ay" and "no" too was no good divinity . . . . they told me I was everything; 'tis a lie, I am not ague-proof.
>
> (IV.vi.97)

Lear discovers that there are no special laws in the universe for man. Dostoevski's treatment of an analogous episode illuminates Lear's situation at this point. When, in *The Brothers Karamazov,* the saintly monk Zossima dies, Alyosha expects that nature would show signs of glorifying that death. That the monk's body prematurely stank, that the saint should be so dishonored, agonizes Alyosha and momentarily destroys his faith in the universe. It was not miracles he looked for in this instance, "it was justice, justice, he thirsted for." [38] Just as Lear sought, in time of great crisis, personal recognition from nature and the gods, so Alyosha looked for nature's special laws: "Where is the finger of Providence? Why did Providence hide its face 'at the most critical moment' (so Alyosha thought it), as though voluntarily submitting to the blind, dumb, pitiless laws of nature?" [39] While Alyosha had been taught to love everyone and everything, he had concentrated his love on one man, one ideal, and Dostoevski stresses the significant consequences. On the day that Zossima dies and there occurs the scandal of the stinking body, Alyosha forgets everyone and everything: he forgets about Dimitri's vexing problems; he forgets to take two hundred roubles to Ilusha's father, though he had firmly resolved to do so the previous evening. When nature will not fulfill Alyosha's expectations of justice, he sets himself apart from creation in judgment, refuses to accept the world and objectifies his rebellion by spitefully doing things he would never have done before. He asks for sausage, vodka; and finally, to complete his degradation and fall from saints to sinners, would go to Grushenka. In this spiritual crisis there comes to Alyosha the recognition that the self can be fulfilled only through communication with others. Where Alyosha goes to Grushenka to find a companion in degradation, he finds, instead, sympathy and loving pity, and because of her he is saved from despair. In turn, because Alyosha does not judge or condemn Grushenka, she is saved. Only when we see that all are equally guilty and equally worthwhile, Dostoevski stresses, can we live a meaningful life, for then we do not withdraw from sinful creation in horror and self-righteous judgment, but participate fully in the world, acknowledging individual responsibility for all and for everything. In this greatest of all recognitions for Dostoevski, man goes through a psychological and moral reorganization of personality; but even more: man makes a meaningful discovery about the world.

Lear's transformation on the heath is strikingly similar to the experience of Alyosha and other characters of Dostoevski. Lear also seeks personal recognition from nature and gods, and would have special laws recognize the justice of his

cause. Frustrated, he too finally finds that the abnegation of
self is prerequisite to communion with all men; and further
— that a person achieves true identity when his humanity is
recognized by others. While these ideas control the development of Dostoevski's characters and give structure to his
work, they operate less rigidly in *Lear*. Edgar's development,
to take but one example as contrast to Lear, is towards stoic
withdrawal. Finding nature a blank wall, he does not seek
for a justice immanent in nature, nor does he strive to impose
his will on nature. He is, nevertheless, a man of action; he
rights personal wrongs in combat. He acts where he has
power to act, not against the universe, but against evil embodied in men. His lament and address to the world in Act
IV serves as contrast to Lear's situation:

> Yet better thus, and known to be contemn'd,
> Than, still contemn'd and flatter'd, to be worst.
> The lowest and most dejected thing of fortune
> Stands still in esperance, lives not in fear.
> The lamentable change is from the best;
> The worst returns to laughter. Welcome, then,
> Thou unsubstantial air that I embrace!
> The wretch that thou hast blown unto the worst
> Owes nothing to thy blasts.   (IV.i.1)

Lear, like Edgar, comes to know that it is better to be contemned than still contemned and flattered. But their final
visions of the world differ. Lear, like many of Dostoevski's
characters, loses himself to find himself part of all humanity.
In terms of dramatic action, Lear is first stripped of all; then
he strips himself of all; and finally, his madness is the complete loss of self. In terms of personality, Lear intermittently
progresses to a denial and surrender of the individual will
which finally enables him to kneel before Cordelia and beg
for forgiveness.

5

Is there an explanation for the greatness of Lear? Is Lear's
stature to be wholly explained by pointing to the fact that

he is a king, a father, an old man? If such were the case the Lear of the opening scene, garbed in splendor and authority, would fulfill the essentials of true greatness. Is Lear's topmost grief his topmost greatness? A Hieronimo may rant and rave and still be a small figure; Gloucester and Edgar undergo equally painful torments, yet never achieve Lear's greatness. There is no simple answer, of course; we can only offer observations which provide, at best, partial explanations.

First, we can say that contributing to make Lear's stature greater than that of any other character in the play is the fact that we, as audience, know more about him than about any of the others. In a letter of Keats we find this statement: "There may be intelligences or sparks of the divinity in millions — but they are not Souls till they acquire identities, till each one is personally itself." [40] In drama the character shapes his identity in speech far more than in deeds. Though Lear, for most of the play, is acted upon, "more sinned against than sinning," he is the most vigorously eloquent of all. To be convinced of this we need only compare the moment when the main and subplot merge, when the mad Lear and the blind Gloucester meet on the heath. Gloucester speaks prosaically, though at times his trenchant conciseness is most effective, as when Lear tells him, "You see how this world goes" (IV.vi. 151), and the blind Gloucester replies, "I see it feelingly." Lear, on the other hand, continually speaks imaginatively and expansively. Throughout the play he reveals himself fully in his speeches.

"You should know, Sancho," said Don Quixote, "that one man is no more than another unless he does more than another." Lear does more than any other person in the play. Too often critics overemphasize the point that Lear is mainly acted upon; Mark Van Doren goes so far as to say that "the deeds of the tragedy are suffered rather than done; the relation of events is lyrical instead of logical, musical instead of moral." [41] Though most of Lear's struggle is inward, that conflict is externalized imaginatively in words, and we come to know that Lear wages the most heroic battles of all: against the cosmos, and the new society, and finally, against his own hardened self. He is glorified in his suffering because, for one thing, he represents a striving for justice and civilized values. There is another point. His situation is much like that of King Richard the Second; both are humbled to nothingness because of their own actions. But Richard does not grow spiritually, as Lear does. That is the most important distinction. Lear reaches the very lowest state of existence, unaccommodated man, he loses that which distinguishes man from animal, his reason, but from nothingness he progresses to Truth, about himself and others. He sees beyond the world of pomp, state, contractual obligations. His vision is of truth or perfection or blessedness, not the center of a flower or blinding light, but a secular vision of love and the community of mankind. Hell, Dostoevski continually reminds us, is "the suffering of being unable to love." [42]

In essential agreement with many of these points is Arthur Miller, himself a playwright trying to mold tragedy out of contemporary life, but faced with a difficulty which did not exist for Shakespeare, the "split between the private life of man and his social life." [43] Miller has written that all plays we call great are ultimately concerned with some aspect of a single problem: "How may a man make of the outside world a home? How and in what ways must he struggle, what must he strive to change and overcome within himself and outside himself if he is to find the safety, the surroundings of love, the ease of soul, the sense of identity and honor which evidently, all men have connected in their memories with the idea of family?" [44] In this statement Miller succinctly reviews considerations we have found to be so central to *King Lear*. Our analysis of the point of view established towards Lear has revealed how Shakespeare, through the dramatic clash of two worlds, has concentrated attention on the survival of civilized values; how, in the structure of the play, the individual's quest for truth and certainty and identity is so im-

portant; how, finally, Lear's plight is more than one of individual personality, but is typical of tragic human destiny.
While Miller maintains that the memory of family is man's
most abiding value, his ultimate truth, such a context is to
be associated more with drama since Ibsen; it is not so valid
for Greek or Shakespearian tragedy where the vision is more
cosmic. Lear finds his greatest happiness in Cordelia's unselfish love; but in preparation for this his view of the world has
extended beyond, to a recognition of the community of men.

Nevertheless, Lear's insight into truth and happiness is
not negotiable in this tough world. He cannot convert his
experience into saving advantages. To give the play a Christian interpretation and make of it a divine comedy is to distort the work. By the end of the play Lear's world has narrowed to Cordelia, but she is dead in his arms. "Is this the
promis'd end?" (V.iii.263) Kent cries out in anguish; and
Edgar joins in, "Or image of that horror?" "Fall, and cease!"
is Albany's tortured utterance. Evil is in the world and there
is no escape. It is much better, says Kent, that Lear die:

> Vex not his ghost; O, let him pass! He hates him
> That would upon the rack of this tough world
> Stretch him out longer.
>
> (V.iii.313)

In *King Lear* Shakespeare takes us to the edge of the human
world to front the terrors of life and the viciousness of man's
brutality. He offers no solution to the ungraspable phantom
of life. However, in the midst of terror we see the nobility and
greatness of man's spirit. Keats gives us one of the most illuminating insights into the nature of tragedy: "The excellence
of every art is its intensity, capable of making all disagree-
ables evaporate, from their being in close relationship with
Beauty and Truth. Examine 'King Lear,' and you will find
this exemplified throughout. . . ." [45] From the time of
Aristotle, men have maintained that great art has a civilizing
function: it tells us, like history or science, what is; but even
more, it can tell us what ought to be. Lear's suffering, his

search for justice and identity, is a facing of the fearful elements of the world. His vision of truth and his complete change of character give us a sense of the nobility of spirit which can transcend the confinements of man's condition. "There lies within the dramatic form," Arthur Miller tells us with great conviction, "the ultimate possibility of raising the truth-consciousness of mankind to a level of such intensity as to transform those who observe it." [46]

CHAPTER II

MACBETH

IN *Macbeth,* as in *King Lear,* the health and stability of society depend on a monarch whose office is divinely sanctioned and whose anointed person is tantamount to an agent of deity. When Macbeth kills the legitimate king and usurps the throne, he brings disorder into society, his own life, and even the cosmos. King Lear, in dividing his kingdom, also disrupts the harmonious workings of nature. However, what happens to Lear is to a great extent the reverse of what happens to Macbeth. While Lear is a legitimate king, Macbeth is a tyrannical usurper. At first irascible and imperious, showing little concern for others, Lear proceeds in the course of the play towards humility and enlightenment; he grows into perfection, standing forth as the representative of civilization's embattled values; he becomes a projection of all that is good and meaningful in life, hence a hero with whom an audience feels sympathetic rapport. Macbeth, on the other hand, begins as a valiant hero who fights for his king, but instead of growing into perfection, becomes progressively hardened in evil. Lear is sinned against; and he battles the representatives of a new society who would violate nature and scant the civilities owing to a sovereign, father, and benefactor. In *Macbeth* the central character is not sinned against; he himself perpetrates the most unnatural crimes. When he kills his king it is more than murder; it is, for Shakespeare's audience, sacrilege, for he "broke ope/ The Lord's anointed temple" (II.iii.72). King James I, before whom *Macbeth* was staged, reminds us of the widely held Elizabethan and Jacobean belief in the divinity of kingship in his *Basilicon Doron: Or His Maiesties Instrvctions to His Dearest Sonne, Henry the Prince*: "learne to knowe and loue that God, whome-to ye haue a double obligation; first, for that he made you a man; and next, for that he made you a little God to sitte on his throne, and rule ouer other men." [1] In murdering the legitimate King Duncan, acknowledged by Macbeth to be virtuous and meek, a king "clear in his great office" (I.vii.18), Macbeth kills God's vice-regent, a little God. And the crime, Macbeth observes in horror before committing the deed, is triply heinous, for he is Duncan's kinsman, subject, and host (I.vii.12–16). While Lear cries out in anguish against the unnatural acts committed against him, desperately searching for justice in the universe, Macbeth does not suffer such indignities; he commits them. It is Macbeth who endangers all civilization.

And yet Macbeth is the protagonist of the play; his personality, says A. C. Bradley, excites "horror, sympathy, and admiration." [2] The play has always posed a very important problem for actors studying the role of the main character, for those who would direct the drama, and for critics of literature: how can a villain be a truly tragic hero? [3] An investigation of this question is a major concern of this study.

2

That the tragic hero must elicit from an audience some degree of sympathy is almost a truism. It is therefore surprising that Shakespeare drastically changes his source, Holinshed's *Chronicles,* to heighten Macbeth's guilt and deliberately take away, it would seem, characteristics which might attract an audience's sympathy. Shakespeare gives an idealized picture of Duncan: he has not a single fault; he is, indeed, a saint — "Thy royal father," Macduff tells Malcolm, "Was a most sainted king" (IV.iii.108). Holinshed's Duncan, on the other hand, is a man of many faults. He is soft and gentle by nature, but so negligent in punishing offenders that his laxity actually encouraged the seditious to disrupt the peace of the land.[4] Makdowald, foremost rebel against Duncan, exploits the king's weakness to gather a mighty power against him, calling Duncan "a faint-hearted milkesop, more meet to gouerne a sort of idle moonks in some cloister, than to haue the rule of such valiant and hardie men of warre as the Scots were."[5] There is, in Shakespeare's play, not the slightest hint of this aspect of Duncan's character. Shakespeare makes no allusion to a cowardly side of Duncan; in the *Chronicles,* however, news of the military expedition against Duncan "did put him in woonderful feare, by reason of his small skill in warlike affaires."[6] Holinshed further relates that Macbeth harshly berates the king in council, "speaking much against the kings softnes, and ouermuch slacknesse in punishing offendors."[7]

Shakespeare takes away from Macbeth all justification for his crime. Macbeth recognizes that save for vaulting ambition he has not the slightest provocation to murder an old, sleeping, defenseless man who is his lord and trusting guest. Again, this is a radical departure from Holinshed, who provides Macbeth with greater grievances against the king. Duncan, in designating his elder son Malcolm to succeed him, crushed all hope in Macbeth that the kingdom would in time be legally his: "Mackbeth sore troubled herewith, for that he saw by this means his hope sore hindered (where, by the old lawes of the realme, the ordinance was, that if he that should succeed were not of able age to take the charge vpon himselfe, he that was next of blood vnto him should be admitted) he began to take counsell how he might vsurpe the kingdome by force, hauing a iust quarell so to doo (as he tooke the matter) for that Duncane did what in him lay to defraud him of all maner of title and claime, which he might in time to come, pretend vnto the crowne." [8] In Holinshed, further-more, Macbeth does not slay Duncan treacherously (for Duncan's murder Shakespeare turned to the murder of King Duff by Donwald); he does not violate the proprieties of hospitality; and compared to "the feeble and slouthfull ad-ministration of Duncane" [9] Macbeth, for ten years, ruled virtuously, with justice and magnanimity.

Various theories have been offered to explain Shakespeare's departures from Holinshed, and these often involve specula-tions about the dramatist's reason for writing this particular play. It has been suggested that Shakespeare composed his drama as a morality play.[10] It has also been held that since *Macbeth* was one of the first plays written during the reign of James I, Shakespeare intended to honor the king by glorify-ing Banquo, the legendary founder of the Stuart line; and hence the play also serves as a mirror for magistrates, a drama-tization of the theme of kingship.[11] Such explanations have large elements of truth; they establish a necessary historical context, but they tend to focus exclusive attention on the play's background. As L. C. Knights has observed, *Macbeth* is "a statement of evil; but it is a statement not of a philosophy but of ordered emotion." [12]

Critics, however, disagree about the elements of the play which determine the "ordered emotion." Those who direct all attention to character study invariably glorify Macbeth. Those who concentrate on pattern analysis find Macbeth either ignoble or, at best, unsympathetic. In character studies the term "sympathy" continually recurs: how can an audience sympathize with a bloody, usurping tyrant? — this is the ques-tion that is always posed and answered. In spite of Macbeth's vicious deeds, goes the argument, we are meant to sympa-thize with him. And the most popular explanation is given in terms of the romantic predilection to sympathize with the rebel, the man who dares greatly. Because A. C. Bradley has had such widespread influence upon Shakespeare criticism, I quote his eloquent argument at length:

What is the conflict here? It will be agreed that it does not lie between two ethical powers or universal ends, and that, as Hegel says, the main interest is in personalities. Let us take it first, then, to lie between Macbeth and the persons opposing him, and let us ask whether there is not spiritual value or good on both sides — not an equal amount of good (that is not necessary), but enough good on each to give the impression of spiritual waste. Is there not such good in Macbeth? It is not a question merely of moral goodness, but of good. It is not a question of the use made of good, but of its presence. And such bravery and skill in war as win the enthusiasm of everyone about him; such an imagination as few but poets possess; a conscience so vivid that his deed is to him beforehand a thing of terror, and, once done, condemns him to that torture of the mind on which he lies in restless ecstasy; a determination so tremendous and a courage so appalling that, for all this torment, he never dreams of turning back, but, even when he has found that life is a tale full of sound and fury, signifying nothing, will tell it out to the end though earth and heaven and hell are leagued against him; are not these things, in themselves, good, and gloriously good? Do they not make you, for all your horror, admire Macbeth, sympathise with his agony, pity him, and see in him the waste of forces on which you place a spiritual value? It is simply on this account that he is for you . . . a tragic hero, and that his war with other forces of indubitable spiritual worth is a tragic war.[13]

Other critics — particularly those who are concerned with pattern analysis — steadfastly maintain that Shakespeare does not intend his audience to sympathize with Macbeth. We cannot sympathize with evil, these critics contend; moreover, this is one of Shakespeare's most moral plays, it abounds in Christian imagery. Slighting action and character to the point where *dramatis personae* virtually disappear from the stage, pattern analysts focus attention on imagery of light and darkness, clothing, the elements of order and disorder, claiming that these direct an audience's response to the play. L. C. Knights — to take but one example — has argued that it is not Macbeth or Lady Macbeth who gives emotional coherence to the play, but opposing systems of values, the pattern of order played off against disorder.[14]

Our concern with the point of view which Shakespeare establishes towards Macbeth is based on the assumption that the force of the play is conveyed mainly through Macbeth's experience, which is the result of the artistic ordering of thought and emotion, mood, imagery, the interplay of characters. In this play Shakespeare presents clearly defined values. Duncan is completely virtuous; Macbeth is villainous. However, values serve as background in this play; they do not by themselves control our response to character and event, otherwise we would be greatly moved by Duncan's fate, which affects us less than the fate of Macbeth.[15] By establishing a certain point of view towards Macbeth, Shakespeare molds an audience's emotional response, and this response is the significant experience of the play.

In studying the perspective in which Shakespeare places Macbeth, we shall make use of the concepts "involvement" and "detachment" to describe an audience's reaction to character. Because the more popular term "audience sympathy" connotes both involvement and approval, it can lead us far astray in treating Macbeth, who exhibits commendable traits, yet commits heinous crimes. Oftentimes we are involved with Macbeth; we see events through his eyes, share his thoughts and emotions, and yet Shakespeare, at the same time, calls upon us to judge his actions. We can be involved with a character with whom we are not meant to be sympathetic.

3

The first scene of *Macbeth* has certain similarities with the opening of *Hamlet*. In both plays the action is initiated by supernatural figures; in both, the atmosphere is sullied and "the frame of things disjoint." In his other tragedies Shakespeare either prefigures the protagonist in the first scene, or, as in *Lear*, subjects his actions and characters to lengthy analysis. In *Hamlet* and *Macbeth* we hear the protagonist's name mentioned in the first scene, but we learn nothing significant about him. There is a reason for this. In *Hamlet* and *Macbeth*

Shakespeare is intent on creating an atmosphere of bewilderment. Indeed, both plays begin in darkness; the first words are questions. Bernardo's anxious shout, "Who's there?" introduces *Hamlet*. The first utterance of *Macbeth* is the witch's query: "When shall we three meet again/ In thunder, lightning, or in rain?" Immediately conveyed to an audience is the sense of restlessness, doubt, confusion. This deliberate evocation of perplexity helps explain the delayed appearance of the protagonists of both plays. We are first projected into a state of uncertainty; things are not as they seem; everything has to be examined. We have to feel our way through these hazy surroundings, just as Hamlet and Macbeth must feel their way, Hamlet to discover very gradually the nature of evil and the demands of duty, and Macbeth to waver in confusion, uncertain how he should act to fulfill the witches' prophecy. In both instances the atmosphere of uncertainty helps reinforce the protagonists' own uncertainty in acting.

An overwhelming sense that everything hangs in suspense, that nothing is a foregone conclusion, pervades the opening scenes of *Macbeth*. Each of the first four scenes begins with a question:

> When shall we three meet again. . . ?
>
> (I.i.1)
>
> What bloody man is that?
>
> (I.ii.1)
>
> Where hast thou been, sister?
>
> (I.iii.1)
>
> Is execution done on Cawdor?
>
> (I.iv.1)

In these first four scenes over twenty-five questions are asked, contributing to the atmosphere of urgent doubt and confusion. These elements of doubt and confusion are stressed in the bleeding sergeant's initial lines describing the battle against the rebellious Macdonwald:

> Doubtful it stood,
> As two spent swimmers that do cling together

And choke their art.

(I.ii.7)

Over and over in these opening scenes what is unnatural merges confusingly with what is natural. Customary associations are jumbled, as in the sergeant's battle report:

So from that spring whence comfort seem'd to come
Discomfort swells.

(I.ii.27)

Our imagination is directed towards a gloomy world where values and events are precariously unstable; opposites are yoked together in amazing paradox. The witches announce they will meet again, "When the battle's lost and won" (I.i.4); in an echoing of this phrase, Duncan, at the end of scene ii says of the rebel Cawdor, "What he hath lost, noble Macbeth hath won" (I.ii.67). Nature itself is unstable and bewilderingly enigmatic. "Fair is foul, and foul is fair" (I.i.11) chant the witches; and Macbeth later echoes them, "So foul and fair a day I have not seen" (I.iii.38). As in the fantastic turnings of a nightmare, everything seems to be topsy-turvy, unreal, yet strangely real. Appearances cannot be trusted. "There's no art," Duncan says of the rebel Cawdor, "To find the mind's construction in the face./ He was a gentleman on whom I built/ An absolute trust" (I.iv.11).

Nowhere is this unsettling confusion more pronounced than in the encounter by Banquo and Macbeth with the witches. Here reality is indeed an enigma; the witches themselves speak in riddling ambiguities:

1. Witch. Lesser than Macbeth, and greater.
2. Witch. Not so happy, yet much happier.
3. Witch. Thou shalt get kings, though thou be none;
So all hail, Macbeth and Banquo!

(I.iii.65)

Previous to this meeting we were made to feel that perhaps there was no clear-cut division between reason and unreason, order and disorder. Now that feeling becomes more of a conviction as Banquo and Macbeth repeatedly doubt their senses:

> *Banquo.*   What are these
> So wither'd and so wild in their attire,
> That look not like th' inhabitants o' th' earth,
> And yet are on't?
>
> (I.iii.39)

> *Banquo.*   You should be women,
> And yet your beards forbid me to interpret
> That you are so.
>
> (I.iii.45)

> *Macbeth.* Are ye fantastical, or that indeed
> Which outwardly ye show?
>
> (I.iii.53)

And finally, to the amazement of Macbeth and Banquo, the witches, who seemed corporeal, melt as breath into the wind.

As in the preceding scenes, conflicting emotions are made to exist together, intensifying the atmosphere of confusion. After the witch's prophecy that Macbeth will be king, Banquo's reaction to the startled Macbeth is expressed in terms of conflicting opposites:

> Good sir, why do you start, and seem to fear
> Things that do sound so fair?
>
> (I.iii.51)

Macbeth, too, balances opposites when he conjectures about the possible consequences of the witches' visitation:

>   This supernatural soliciting
> Cannot be ill, cannot be good.
>
> (I.iii.130)

And this same suspension of opposites, which can result only in a moral dilemma where the impulses to good and evil meet in paralyzing equipoise, occurs when Macbeth, thinking of murder, relates how it

> Shakes so my single state of man that function

Is smother'd in surmise, and nothing is
But what is not.

(I.iii.140)

It is apparent that at the beginning of *Macbeth* Shakespeare, in numerous ways, deliberately creates a background of doubt, confusion, irresolution. We, as audience, confront a world in which it is difficult to distinguish between sense and nonsense, sanity and insanity, right and wrong, because they are continually made to blur, one into another. Banquo aptly describes the experience:

Were such things here as we do speak about,
Or have we eaten on the insane root
That takes the reason prisoner?

(I.iii.83)

In this atmosphere of confusion we first see Macbeth. The first words he utters on stage, the paradoxical "So foul and fair a day I have not seen" (I.iii.38), would seem to be Shakespeare's brilliant stylistic device of linking him with the weird sisters, for it is an echo of the witch's paradox which ended the first scene, "Fair is foul, and foul is fair;/ Hover through the fog and filthy air." Such a view has generally led to the assumption that Macbeth, from the moment of his first entrance, is inexorably inclined towards evil. Edward Dowden, commenting on the parallel between the witch's utterance and Macbeth's, presents such a position, which has had widespread acceptance, arguing that "although Macbeth has not yet set eyes upon these hags, the connection is already established between his soul and them. Their spells have already wrought upon his blood." [16] However, is it not a serious error in interpretation to say that by this linkage Shakespeare portrays Macbeth from the outset as already fallen into evil? The weird sisters have the gift of foreseeing the end of events, but they are not depicted as having the power to compel man to act in a predetermined way. They can only tempt; man still has free will. Of them

Holinshed wrote that they were "reputed at the first but some vaine fantasticall illusion. . . . But afterwards the common opinion was, that these women were either the weird sisters, that is (as ye would say) the goddesses of destinie, or else some nymphs or feiries, indued with knowledge of prophesie by their necromanticall science, bicause euerie thing came to passe as they had spoken." [17] In the *Chronicles*, as in *Macbeth*, the scope of the witches' power is left to the imagination; the only certainty is that they foretell the outcome of specific occasions, that they tempt Macbeth, but not Banquo. Consequently, it is idle speculation to read more into events than what is actually presented on the stage, to propound, as does one writer on Shakespeare, the view that "Macbeth killed Duncan not because they [the weird sisters] had come into his life; they came because he wanted to kill Duncan." [18]

Macbeth's first statement, "So foul and fair a day I have not seen," is deliberately cryptic, part of the design already outlined, whose purpose is to establish an atmosphere of doubt and confusion as a setting for Macbeth's own moral confusion. There are several reasons for questioning the view that his words establish his immediate connection with evil. First, consider the matter from the standpoint of acting. If an actor believes that Shakespeare intended Macbeth to be inclined towards evil from the beginning, and that the clue to this conception is in his first words, he would, from the moment he appears on stage, try to convey a sense of evil and guilt through his tone of speaking and his body gestures. But such an interpretation would have to play down the intense moral struggle which Macbeth undergoes.

Secondly, there arises the question whether Shakespeare, an astute dramatist, would expect an audience, hearing Macbeth's paradoxical statement, to associate it immediately with the witch's statement which occurred a full scene before. Such an association can be made in reading and studying the play, but drama works an immediate effect.[19] We should take into consideration the dramatic context of Macbeth's first utterance. His words, combined with the numerous other utterances that build up a sense of uncertainty, can be seen as contributing to a cumulative effect, the evocation of confusion and doubt. In this scene, in which Macbeth makes his first appearance, turmoil reaches a high point as Banquo and Macbeth repeatedly voice their uncertainty about the weird sisters' existence and their nature; in this scene they also hear of the witches' prophecy, which further provokes mystification and suspense.

If we accept the view that Macbeth's words immediately link him with the forces of evil, we reduce his stature and minimize the crucial moral struggle that sets him apart from the stock figure of the villain. Furthermore, we would completely undercut Shakespeare's deliberate heightening of Macbeth's stature in the opening scenes of the drama. We should neither overlook nor undervalue the fact that at the beginning of the play Shakespeare brings about the involvement of an audience with Macbeth by portraying him as the greatest of men. When Macbeth first appears on stage, an audience has already been prepared to view him as the mighty warrior and heroic savior of the realm. The bleeding sergeant prepares his entrance. He tells of a brave Macbeth who, disdaining fortune, "like Valour's minion carv'd out his passage" (I.ii.19) until he faced the merciless rebel Macdonwald and slew him. Macbeth alone turned doubtful battle into victory. And Shakespeare magnifies Macbeth's figure even more by having the sergeant faint because of his wounds, breaking off at the crucial moment his report of Banquo and Macbeth's fate when powerful Norwegian forces attacked after Macdonwald's death. Because of this unexpected interruption, an audience's curiosity and attention are greatly aroused and its interest is focused upon Macbeth, for in his prowess lies the safety of the state. Suddenly Ross enters; he completes the account, and once again Macbeth is glorified as the greatest of men:

>   Norway himself,
> With terrible numbers,
> Assisted by that most disloyal traitor,
> The thane of Cawdor, began a dismal conflict;
> Till that Bellona's bridegroom, lapp'd in proof,
> Confronted him with self-comparisons,
> Point against point, rebellious arm 'gainst arm,
> Curbing his lavish spirit; and, to conclude,
> The victory fell on us; —
>
>   (I.ii.50)

Even before his entrance Macbeth looms as a figure of enormous stature. And this exaltation of his person continues after his entrance. Following the disappearance of the weird sisters, Ross and Angus come on stage. Ross tells of the king's wonder at Macbeth's marvelous exploits, and of the numerous men who streamed to the king bearing news of Macbeth and praise of his deeds:

>   As thick as hail
> Came post with post; and every one did bear
> Thy praises in his kingdom's great defence,
> And pour'd them down before him.
>
>   (I.iii.97)

A man of great courage and military ability, Macbeth, single-handed, defeated his country's powerful enemies. To him the nation owes its survival.

Shakespeare purposely elevates Macbeth's stature above that of Duncan and Banquo. Too often this is not stressed in discussions of the play, particularly in studies which set off patterns of order against those of disorder, or in analyses of imagery only. We have before us the image of a Macbeth who is the noble deliverer of his nation. He has the potentialities of ideal man. The third witch, in prophesying that he will "be King hereafter" (I.iii.50) suggests the consummation of greatness.

But there is the intimation that something terribly unnatural threatens to destroy the potentially perfect image. "Good sir, why do you start, and seem to fear/Things that do sound so fair?" says Banquo to Macbeth, who "seems rapt withal" at the witch's news that he will be king. It is hardly necessary, or appropriate, to take Banquo's words as proof that guilty thoughts lurk within Macbeth at this moment. An audience is not involved in speculations about Macbeth's innocent or guilty thoughts here. Banquo's words build up indeterminate expectations and the tensions of uncertainty. When Ross calls Macbeth by his newly acquired title, "thane of Cawdor," he bears out the truth of one part of the witches' prophecy. And tension increases as Banquo voices his suspicion that the witches are evil forces: "What! can the devil speak true?" (I.iii.107)

The events of this scene do not point to a guilty Macbeth, but to a Macbeth overcome with uncertainty, tempted to an act whose horrid image, he says, unfixes his hair and makes his seated heart knock at his ribs. By contrasting the reactions of Banquo and Macbeth to the same event, the visitation and prophecy of the witches, Shakespeare quickly and incisively delineates each man's character. Banquo's reactions are the exact opposite of Macbeth's. Though he is told that he is lesser than Macbeth and greater, not so happy, yet much happier, that he will get kings though he be none, he remains unimpressed. He refuses to express any personal emotion, even when Macbeth asks whether he hopes his children will be kings. Instead, he presents a reasoning, detached evaluation of the strange visitation:

> But 'tis strange;
> And oftentimes, to win us to our harm,
> The instruments of darkness tell us truths,
> Win us with honest trifles, to betray's
> In deepest consequence.

> (I.iii.122)

Macbeth is so excitedly involved in the prophecy that he does not seem to hear Banquo's observations. Immediately following Banquo's speech is Macbeth's reaction to the event, his unquestioning belief, spoken in an aside:

> Two truths are told,
> As happy prologues to the swelling act
> Of the imperial theme.
>
> (I.iii.127)

Where Banquo takes an objective and impersonal view of the situation, making no reference to personal advantage, Macbeth reacts in a completely subjective manner:

> This supernatural soliciting
> Cannot be ill, cannot be good. If ill,
> Why hath it given me earnest of success,
> Commencing in a truth? I'm thane of Cawdor.
> If good, why do I yield to that suggestion
> Whose horrid image doth unfix my hair
> And make my seated heart knock at my ribs,
> Against the use of nature? Present fears
> Are less than horrible imaginings.
> My thought, whose murder yet is but fantastical,
> Shakes so my single state of man that function
> Is smother'd in surmise, and nothing is
> But what is not.
>
> (I.iii.130)

In this speech Macbeth's point of reference is himself: he repeatedly uses "I" and "my." Banquo, it should be noticed, uses only the collective "we": "to win us to our harm . . . tell us truths,/ Win us with honest trifles, to betray's." Banquo's references point outward to the community of men; Macbeth's point inward to the isolated self.

Banquo is steadfast in his virtue; Macbeth shows an inclination to evil. Yet our involvement is with Macbeth, not Banquo. Rapport between character and audience does not depend, in a simple way, on our being in favor of the good and against those who contemplate evil. Several elements combine to establish audience rapport with Macbeth. Because he has been portrayed as the greatest of men, he commands our primary interest. Furthermore, we are more intimately caught up in his situation because the action of the play points towards a possible murder and subsequent ascension to the throne, and these depend on the kind of decision Macbeth will make. Until the actual murder of Duncan, attention focuses upon Macbeth's moral choice. Another point: we know Macbeth more fully than we know Banquo; his soliloquy externalizes his inner being and pulls us into the midst of his conflict. Finally, moral judgment towards Macbeth is as yet unformulated. Setting the mood for Macbeth's own uncertainty is a confused and unnatural atmosphere which helps shape our response to him. His sudden thought of an unnatural deed is made understandable to a certain degree when Shakespeare, with great care, makes us feel that Macbeth is in a world where confusion is the norm. Doubt prevails. Opposing attitudes remain unresolved. Macbeth, too, is torn by opposing attitudes. Verbalizing the good and evil existing within him, he effects a contrast between the two, unsure which will prevail, but acknowledging the malignancy of evil. Because he condemns his own horrible imaginings, we are not alienated from him; there is no need to detach our emotions in order to entertain or pass moral judgment.

Our response is to character, but character cannot be separated from society and its ethical and political order. The prefiguring of Macbeth's greatness, for example, had a social and political frame of reference. Macbeth achieved his noble reputation because he fought heroically against powerful rebels and preserved society from chaos. And when in Act I the scene shifts from the heath to Duncan's palace Shakespeare firmly establishes Macbeth's position in the social and political order. We move from confusion to the stately, ordered proceedings of the court. After the defeat of the rebel forces unity replaces chaos. The central figure of the scene is Duncan. The king is seen as the embodiment of society's health and fertility; he assures the stability and continuance of the natural order. Duncan even speaks in terms of growth, fertility, emphasizing the gracious life-giving quality of his person. He tells Macbeth:

> I have begun to plant thee, and will labour
> To make thee full of growing.

(I.iv.28)

And when Duncan tells Banquo that he has deserved no less than Macbeth, and that he holds him to his heart, Banquo also brings forth associations of fertility:

> There if I grow,
> The harvest is your own.

(I.iv.32)

Through their loyalty to the king all the members of society are harmoniously joined together. This homage is not enforced, but freely given; and while it promotes the glory of the king, it redounds to the glory of each individual, for this unifying homage promotes the order and prosperity of a nation. From Macbeth comes a formal enunciation of the relationship that exists between subject and king:

> The service and the loyalty I owe,
> In doing it, pays itself. Your Highness' part
> Is to receive our duties; and our duties
> Are to your throne and state children and servants,
> Which do but what they should, by doing everything
> Safe toward your love and honour.

(I.iv.22)

It does us little good to speculate whether Macbeth actually believes what he says. We have no basis for believing otherwise. In the context of the situation his speech is not subtly ironic, masking Machiavellian guile, but a general's natural pronouncement of the proper devotion owed to his king. Only in retrospect does it gain irony.

While the person of Macbeth excites admiration and praise, Shakespeare places him in perspective: though Macbeth is the greatest of all men, he acknowledges and reaffirms his proper and subordinate place in a system of political and social relationships which order life. In a state dependent on the king, the well-being of man is involved in the fate of the monarch. But now Macbeth would threaten that pattern of civilization. When Duncan proclaims his eldest son Malcolm successor, naming him Prince of Cumberland, he topples Macbeth's previous expectation that chance would bring him the crown:

> If chance will have me King, why, chance may crown me
> Without my stir.
>
> (I.iii.143)

No longer able to gain a crown without stirring, Macbeth is forced to confront the contingency of immediate and direct action:

> The Prince of Cumberland! That is a step
> On which I must fall down, or else o'erleap,
> For in my way it lies. Stars, hide your fires;
> Let not light see my black and deep desires;
> The eye wink at the hand; yet let that be
> Which the eye fears, when it is done, to see.
>
> (I.iv.48)

Macbeth no longer evenly balances good and evil intentions; he does not recoil in horror from unnatural thoughts; he appeals to black and deep desires. And yet, though he reveals guilty thoughts of regicide, they are general and vague. He is still uncommitted to a specific act, and this needs to be stressed, for he is not to be viewed as the villain at this point in the play, as so many commentators have insisted. He speaks of black and deep desires — but his thoughts are as yet desires, not convictions. The focus of interest in this scene is not on a villainous Macbeth, but on his future mode of action, on the way he will fulfill the promise of the witches' prophecy. An audience, therefore, is not called upon to condemn the protagonist. Moral judgment is held in abeyance. Shakespeare guides an audience into feelings of apprehension as the question of Macbeth's future decisions is purposely left unresolved.

If, instead of emphasizing the point of view established

towards the hero, we were to employ a thematic approach to this scene, stressing the interplay of good and evil, appearance and reality, imagery of light and darkness, we would come to an entirely different conclusion: that Shakespeare *expects* an audience to pass moral judgment on Macbeth. Duncan, perfectly virtuous, would be associated with radiant light. Indeed, in proclaiming his eldest son Malcolm successor to the crown, he invokes symbolic light, saying that the honor of title should not

> unaccompanied invest him only,
> But signs of nobleness, like stars, shall shine
> On all deservers.
>
> (I.iv.40)

Macbeth, on the other hand, is associated with the dark, and in words which contrast with Duncan's, calls upon darkness to engulf him:

> Stars, hide your fires;
> Let not light see my black and deep desires.
>
> (I.iv.50)

Duncan is gracious and honest, Macbeth is not what he seems to be. Certainly these contrasts establish a clear division between good and evil; as Caroline Spurgeon has noted, "light stands for life, virtue, goodness; and darkness for evil and death." [20] But such contrasts do not determine the audience's response to character; they do not lead to involvement with Duncan or detachment from Macbeth. The imagery of light and darkness and the contrast between appearance and reality are of peripheral importance to the main action, which points to a decision of Macbeth as yet unformulated. We lose focus completely if we ignore dramatic context and emphasize secondary suggestion at the expense of primary action.

The contrasts of this scene enhance the effect of the unfolding action; they help establish the tension of uncertainty and the foreboding of future conflict. We see this most clearly when we consider the function of irony in this scene. Provid-

ing the basis for the effective dramatic irony at the scene's beginning and end is the difference between appearance and
reality. Towards the beginning of the scene Duncan says of
the rebel Cawdor,

> There's no art
> To find the mind's construction in the face.
> He was a gentleman on whom I built
> An absolute trust.
>
> (I.iv.12)

At precisely the moment Duncan finishes this statement, Macbeth, who has just revealed his secret thoughts of regicide,
comes on stage. Duncan's statement is therefore highly ironi-
cal: it has literal application to the dead Cawdor, but an audience knows, as Duncan does not, that it might also have application to the living Cawdor. And at the end of the scene we
have a repetition of this same kind of dramatic irony as Duncan extols Macbeth for being a "valiant" man in whose com-
mendations he is fed. Again, the irony derives from the juxtaposition of the good in appearance with the bad in reality.
Duncan's trusting words are spoken immediately after Macbeth, confronted with the news of the king's successor, has
revealed in an aside to the audience just before his exit the
evil he contemplates against his king. Duncan thinks that
Macbeth is honest and completely trustworthy; an audience
knows otherwise. Hence the fearful and ominous note of
irony which concludes the scene as Duncan joyfully hastens
into imminent danger:

> Let's after him,
> Whose care is gone before to bid us welcome.
> It is a peerless kinsman.
>
> (I.iv.56)

The dramatic irony of this scene — as well as the irony of Act
I, scene vi — heightens the expectation of unknown things to
come; it creates suspense and foreboding. Excited by the tension that irony produces, we are not primarily involved with

the virtue of Duncan or the evil of Macbeth, but with the uncertainty of future action. To say, with A. C. Bradley, that Shakespeare uses irony here "to excite the vague fear of hidden forces operating on minds unconscious of their influence" [21] is to neglect the unfolding action of the moment.

In presenting a contrast between a heroic Macbeth, the pride of his country, and a Macbeth who is tempted to violate the natural order, thus betraying the ideal he represents, Shakespeare establishes an ambiguous point of view towards the protagonist; for while we remember his greatness, we anticipate his evil — yet we are still in doubt as to what he will finally do.

4

In the early part of the play we view Macbeth in the context of society's order and the individual's duty. When his character is prefigured and glorified it is in terms of his public role: the most valiant of men, he rescues his nation from rebels who would overturn the natural order. In moving to Inverness Castle we have another prefiguring of Macbeth, this time by his wife, but now there is a significant shift from the prefiguring of a public figure to that of a private personality. After reading Macbeth's letter recounting the witches' prophecy that he will be king, Lady Macbeth gives to an audience an account of her husband's moral nature. She dwells on what to her are Macbeth's vulnerable qualities which would keep him from murder and greatness. His nature is "too full o' th' milk of human kindness"; he would be great, he is not without ambition, but he does not want "the illness should attend it." Between desire and fulfillment are the curbing restrictions of moral sensitivity and fear:

> What thou wouldst highly,
> That wouldst thou holily; wouldst not play false,
> And yet wouldst wrongly win. Thou'dst have, great Glamis,
> That which cries, "Thus thou must do, if thou have it";
> And that which rather thou dost fear to do
> Than wishest should be undone.   (I.v.21)

Emphasizing Macbeth's weaknesses, Lady Macbeth establishes his connection with society and morality, a bond that did not exist for Iago or Edmund, Goneril or Regan. What she holds to be his vices are to society virtues. Because Shakespeare delineates the moral personality of Macbeth, we do not confront a conscienceless villain, an Iago or an Edmund, but a good man, a great man, who is tempted to do what he would rather not do. In anticipating her husband's moral scruples, Lady Macbeth also prepares an audience for the impending conflict he will wage with himself; she anticipates the reasons for his torment in facing the act of murder.

Constructed on the compositional principle of contrast, scene v of Act I distinctly establishes the differences in character between Macbeth and his wife. In her soliloquy Lady Macbeth indirectly contrasts herself with her husband by associating herself with all that is evil, inhuman, unnatural. What Macbeth is, she is not. In her there is no "milk of human kindness." Callously repudiating all moral responsibilities, she calls upon the spirits to "unsex" her, to turn the milk of her breasts to gall. She earnestly craves to be filled "from the crown to the toe top-full/ Of direst cruelty!" Renouncing what Macbeth still retains, remorse and the "compunctious visitings of nature," she visualizes with precision what Macbeth has as yet never pictured, the actual deed of murder:

> Come, thick night,
> And pall thee in the dunnest smoke of hell,
> That my keen knife see not the wound it makes,
> Nor heaven peep through the blanket of the dark
> To cry, "Hold, hold!"
>
> (I.v.51)

Freed from the restraints of morality, Lady Macbeth can override all qualms to reach her goal of murder. However, morality inhibits Macbeth. He allows his imagination to approach the thought of murder, but he cannot go beyond, to visualize the act itself. These different moral views shape the dramatic interplay between the two. With her lengthy

speeches and bold thoughts of action, Lady Macbeth is reso-
lute in her purpose: "Glamis thou art, and Cawdor; and shalt
be/ What thou art promis'd" (I.v.16). Macbeth, uncommitted to action, is by comparison reticent when he is with her,
for he really has nothing to say; he speaks no more than a
brief sentence at a time. He seems innocent of any scheme
that might bring him the crown, and Shakespeare brings this
out most effectively in the exchange between a naïve Macbeth
and his fierce wife:

> *Macbeth.*   My dearest love,
>   Duncan comes here to-night.
> *Lady Macbeth.*   And when goes hence?
> *Macbeth.* To-morrow, as he purposes.
> *Lady Macbeth.*   O, never
>   Shall sun that morrow see!
>
>   (I.v.59)

Caught in his wife's determination, Macbeth is still un-
decided. "We will speak further" is his answer to her design
that would give to all their nights and days to come "solely
sovereign sway and masterdom" (I.v.71). And the scene closes
with Macbeth's indecision set against his wife's commanding
firmness as she has the final say: "Leave all the rest to me."

The strategy of the scene is machination, and Lady Macbeth, its author, employs Machiavellian terminology in its
exposition; "look like the innocent flower,/ But be the serpent under't" (I.v.66), she counsels her husband. Opposed
to a completely amoral and Machiavellian individual, Macbeth's morality, however tenuous, stands out. Shakespeare's
careful contrast of the two personalities, and its subsequent
effect upon our view of Macbeth, subverts any suggestion that
in this scene Lady Macbeth is admirable in her passionate
courage and that Macbeth, by contrast, is weak and cowardly.

The audience at this point is involved with Macbeth for a
moral reason: unlike the stock villain, he recognizes the sancti-
ties of life, the horror of murder, the duty of one kinsman to
another, of subject to king, of host to guest. Unable to reason

with his wife, who is obsessed with a single unquenchable
purpose, Macbeth reasons and debates with himself; he becomes his own antagonist. His long soliloquy in Act I, scene
vii, exposes to an audience a mind arguing with itself. Emphasizing not the attractions of murder, but the deterrents, Macbeth would talk himself into steadfast virtue. From the practical argument that bloody deeds will only return to plague the
inventor, he proceeds to the ethical, acknowledging his obligations as kinsman, subject, host; and finally, testifying to the
unimpeachable virtues of Duncan, Macbeth sees all humanity pierced by a most unnatural and indefensible murder:

> his virtues
> Will plead like angels, trumpet-tongu'd, against
> The deep damnation of his taking-off;
> And pity, like a naked new-born babe
> Striding the blast, or heaven's cherubin hors'd
> Upon the sightless couriers of the air,
> Shall blow the horrid deed in every eye,
> That tears shall drown the wind.
>
> (I.vii.18)

After describing the cosmic reverberations that would attend
the murder of Duncan, Macbeth offers the only justification
he has for prompting such a catastrophe, vaulting ambition,
which seems by contrast, petty and ignominious.

In his lengthy soliloquy Macbeth rises from his initial concern with practicalities and the narrow concentration on the
self, reaching out to all people of good will who would mourn
the taking-off of innocent virtue. It is this shift from self-
sight to insight that produces in him compassion for another.
By getting outside himself into a state of sympathy — which
is, after all, the projection of the self — he sees his intended
act of murder from an objective vantage-point, and he indicts
that action. And so, when he tells Lady Macbeth, "We will
proceed no further in this business" (I.vii.31), his disavowal
does not result primarily from cowardice, the fear of personal
consequences; it proceeds from his moral sensitivity. His

thought of murder is, by itself, no great crime — many men
have had such thoughts at one time or another. Holding him
back from the actuality of crime is his responsiveness to moral
considerations. This is not to say that Macbeth completely
frees himself— as does Lear — from a narrow preoccupation
with his own being. When he tells his wife that he will not
carry on in her design, he argues from personal, not ethical,
motives:

> He hath honour'd me of late; and I have bought
> Golden opinions from all sorts of people,
> Which would be worn now in their newest gloss,
> Not cast aside so soon.
>
> (I.vii.32)

Having gained personal honor and national esteem, Macbeth refuses to jeopardize these, but his wife, lacking the restraints that moral consciousness imposes, would push him
into perpetrating a deed he would rather not execute.

We have already heard Lady Macbeth's indictment of her
husband's moral scruples — this, upon her first appearance in
the play. What she foretold, Macbeth enacts, drawing back
from murder for the very reasons she anticipated. Now Lady
Macbeth will play out the role she previously envisioned as
necessary to enlist her husband: she will pour her spirits into
his ear; the valor of her tongue will win him over. Relentlessly
harping on what is, to a military man, of the utmost repug-
nance — cowardice — she lets him think of nothing else:

> Art thou afeard
> To be the same in thine own act and valour
> As thou art in desire? Wouldst thou have that
> Which thou esteem'st the ornament of life,
> And live a coward in thine own esteem,
> Letting "I dare not" wait upon "I would,"
> Like the poor cat i' th' adage?
>
> (I.vii.39)

When Macbeth objects that he dares do all that may become
a man, she evades the ethical implications of his words, hur-

riedly subjecting him to a stream of recriminations: that he revealed the enterprise to her when neither time nor place was ripe for the deed, yet then he was truly a man; but now, though the proper occasion be present, he is unmanned. Offering herself as the prototype of hardened courage, she swears that had she been resolved to the deed as he, no tenderness would have hindered her purpose. Her words are fierce and frightful,

> I have given suck, and know
> How tender 'tis to love the babe that milks me;
> I would, while it was smiling in my face,
> Have pluck'd my nipple from his boneless gums
> And dash'd the brains out, had I so sworn as you
> Have done to this.

> (I.vii.54)

The reference to Macbeth's being sworn to murder has caused considerable speculation and has important bearing on our view of the protagonist's character. Those who believe that when Macbeth first enters the play he is already committed to evil because "he would not have been chosen by the witches had his soul not been prepared for them," [22] can point to Lady Macbeth's words as an indication that plans to murder Duncan might have been formulated even before the play began. And there are those who would take Lady Macbeth's words as evidence that a scene depicting Macbeth's acceptance of the murder plot has been lost. [23] But there is no need to go outside the text into the realms of speculation. Our concern is with the effect of Lady Macbeth's words on her husband, the relation of speech to the action of the moment. We can say, with equal justification, that Macbeth never swore to murder the king, that Lady Macbeth, intent on forcing her husband to join her, takes his wish for fact, and by means of this catches him firmly in her plot. In this scene, it is to be noted, Shakespeare forcefully dramatizes Lady Macbeth's strength of will, which so overwhelms Macbeth that he no longer thinks of moral considerations. Forced into

accepting his wife's premise, Macbeth considers only the practical aspects of murder, questions of failure and discovery,
but to these his wife has immediate, bold answers and strate-
gies, and Macbeth is trapped into full acceptance of "this
terrible feat." His final words in this scene, the Machiavellian
pronouncement,

> Away, and mock the time with fairest show;
> False face must hide what the false heart doth know,
>
> (I.vii.81)

affirm his union with Lady Macbeth; he adopts, as his own,
her Machiavellian strategy, uttered in a previous scene:

> To beguile the time,
> Look like the time; bear welcome in your eye,
> Your hand, your tongue; look like the innocent flower,
> But be the serpent under 't.
>
> (I.v.64)

Succumbing to a will stronger than his own, rather than
to the temptation of murder's gain, Macbeth still retains
moral qualms. And we see this when he calls the murder "this
terrible feat" (I.vii.80), when he pauses before the act, imagin-
ing not a glittering crown, but, instead, tortured by a guilt
which takes on the palpable shape of a bloody dagger (II.i.33–
47).[24] Committed to action, despairing of its evil, Macbeth
is in conflict with himself. It is this conflict within Macbeth
which commands an audience's attention. And this explains
why the murder of Duncan will not affect us greatly: we are
more involved with Macbeth's torment in facing murder
and its consequences than with the act itself. Duncan has all
the outward majesty; his virtues are reported aright; but we
do not know his soul.

5

Before the murder of Duncan, Shakespeare concentrated
attention on Macbeth's doubt and on his decision. After the
murder, focus is upon the consequences: what Macbeth does

to society, and, what is of far greater dramatic import, what he does to himself. To kill a king is to violate nature, to tear apart the harmonious order of all the interrelated hierarchies of the macrocosm and the microcosm, the great world outside man, and its counterpart and reflection, the little world within. Macbeth's lawless act destroys all law; it occasions confusion and disorder in the world of men and animals as well as in the heavens above. Everywhere there is upheaval: on the night when the murder is done, chimneys are blown down, lamentings and strange screams of death are heard in the air, and some say the earth was "feverous and did shake" (II.iii.66). Such portents are reported before the discovery of murder; Lennox calls that night a "woeful time" (II.iii.64) and his memory cannot parallel a fellow to it. All this confirms the interdependency of man and nature, and Ross, after the discovery of the murder, voices that conviction: "Thou seest the heavens, as troubled with man's act,/ Threatens his bloody stage" (II.iv.5). The natural elements, following the death of Duncan, are in strange disorder: though by the clock it is day, darkness entombs the face of earth (II.iv.6–9). " 'Tis unnatural," says the Old Man, in a chorus-like statement, "Even like the deed that's done" (II.iv.10). And there is the further recounting of other amazing violations of nature, the unnatural behavior of animals no longer acting according to their wont, of the falcon hawked at and killed by a mousing owl (II.iv.13), of Duncan's horses, "turn'd wild in nature," eating one another (II.iv.16).

We are, however, more intimately involved with Macbeth and what he does to himself. Shakespeare does not present the murder of Duncan directly, thus alienating rapport with the protagonist; instead, we see the murder through the eyes of Macbeth. Projected into his consciousness, we neither judge the murder objectively, nor do we observe Macbeth detachedly, from a distance. We are committed to Macbeth's point of view and to the intensity of his sensations when he contemplates the horror of murdering a benefactor and king, when

he assesses his intent and experiences the terrors of degradation. In having Macbeth reveal the torments of his mind,
Shakespeare shifts our view from the fact of murder and its
public consequences, from the social and political situation
rooted in a particular time and place, to the spiritual, a time-
less realm, giving to Macbeth's personal life universal significance. Macbeth, Arthur Sewell has said, is like a soul in hell,
"and we know a little more about hell because Macbeth has
had a glimpse of it. These tragedies, then, all imply a metaphysical world in which what matters is not what men do to
society but what they do to themselves. This is the major
vision which seeks to fulfil itself in the tragic heroes." [25]

In *King Lear,* as in *Macbeth,* there is a stripping process
which forms an integral part of the play's dramatic design.
The stripping of Lear produces a spiritual change, a re-form-
ing of personality, and a vision of love and sympathy which
leads him to a communion with men. In *King Lear* truth's
vision is associated with virtue, and Hooker's words might
serve as commentary on the knowledge which Lear gains:
"Goodness is seen with the eye of the understanding. . . .
For the Laws of well-doing are the dictates of right Reason." [26]
While the stripping of Lear results in his humanization and
fellowship with others, the stripping of Macbeth leads to de-
humanization and the complete isolation from all men. After
the murder of Duncan, Macbeth puts on the clothes of a king,
but he is gradually divested of those atttributes which set man
apart as exalted creation — judgment, the healing solace of
prayer, sleep, trust, human companionship — until, finally,
completely reduced to the bestial, he serves as unwitting re-
porter of his degeneration, likening his condition to that of
a baited animal:

> They have tied me to a stake; I cannot fly
> But, bear-like, I must fight the course.
>
> (V.vii.1)

A study of the play's dramatic line of development will confirm that in every scene in which Macbeth appears after the

murder of Duncan, he loses, or deliberately casts off, his humanity. Evil corrupts the mind, the imagination, the soul. The first humane trait to drop from Macbeth is his capacity to join in prayer: "I could not say 'Amen'/ When they did say 'God bless us!' " (II.ii.29) he reports to his wife, whose counsel is to forget the deeds lest they bring on madness. Macbeth's worldly rise is the consequence of Duncan's fall, but at the moment of greatest triumph there is no rejoicing, only horror,

> But wherefore could not I pronounce "Amen"?
> I had most need of blessing, and "Amen"
> Stuck in my throat.
>
> (II.ii.31)

Crime gags Macbeth, stifles his humanity, cuts him off from communication with the world. We witness his first step into the darkness of isolation.

Next, Macbeth reveals his fear that he has lost the capacity for sleep, which is most often associated in Shakespeare's plays with what is sweet, gentle, medicinal, for it "sometimes shuts up sorrow's eye" (*Midsummer-Night's Dream*, III.ii.435), it is "Nature's soft nurse" which steeps the "senses in forgetfulness" (*2 Henry IV*, III.i.6,8). Macbeth enumerates its precious, restorative functions:

> Sleep that knits up the ravell'd sleave of care,
> The death of each day's life, sore labour's bath,
> Balm of hurt minds, great nature's second course,
> Chief nourisher in life's feast.
>
> (II.ii.37)

The thought that he will sleep no more haunts him. In violating nature he placed himself outside its regulating rhythms.

The torments of Macbeth are of the spirit; his struggle is with himself and with the world of values. Our vision is directed, as in *King Lear*, to the predicament of all men who are forced to confront themselves and the universe and to make what settlement they can. While Lear searched for meaning in his world, Macbeth, because of his wilful crime, finds that he has destroyed that meaning, which is inseparable from life's order; he discovers that there is no longer any connection between himself and his world. Because he has moral sensibilities, his thought moves from the particularity of his crime to a consideration of universal consequence: in killing Duncan he has murdered not one sleeping person, but sleep itself,

> "Glamis hath murder'd sleep, and therefore Cawdor
> Shall sleep no more; Macbeth shall sleep no more."
>
> (II.ii.42)

In this recognition of the spiritual consequences of crime there is the suggestion that what Macbeth suffers is what all men would suffer, for in affirming that a deed is right or wrong the appeal is to mankind's judgment; every man is involved, and this accounts for audience rapport with Macbeth.

Murder has not yet changed Lady Macbeth's view of life. Practical, conscious only of the physical fact of murder, she responds accordingly, as she advises her husband,

> Go get some water,
> And wash this filthy witness from your hand.
>
> (II.ii.46)

But water can only efface a guilt that has not stained the mind. Murder does alter her husband's vision. He is not conscious of the exigencies of the particular occasion; he is preoccupied with its spiritual effects — "I am afraid to think what I have done" (II.ii.51) is his cry. Shattering his world is an awareness of guilt which so overtakes the mind that it sees only blood and death and fear. All the waters of Neptune's ocean can not wash the blood clean from his hands. After such knowledge there can be no self-exculpation. "To know my deed, 'twere best not know myself" (II.ii.73) is Macbeth's recognition when, at the porter's knocking at the gate, he thinks, in remorse and near-repentance, of a deed he would wish undone, "Wake Duncan with thy knocking! I would thou couldst!"

But there is no way Macbeth can unmake what he has done, recovering, thereby, his lost innocence. Henceforth Shakespeare charts Macbeth's descent into a self-created world of darkness. Having broken the bonds of nature, Macbeth finds that one law alone governs him now — personal power — antithetical to that law of the interdependency between the king and all men, which previously held the community together in harmony. Substituting the will of one for the willing and natural consent of all, Macbeth is thrown back upon himself. Alone, cut off from the community of men, he cannot live again in the world of reciprocal obligations and compromise. Lear progressed beyond the narrow concern with his own being, and in doing so, grew in sympathy and imagination. The act of sympathy and love involves one or more human beings, but guilt isolates; there is no giving of the self, only a retreat into one's own being. The consequence, for Macbeth, is an atrophy of the sympathetic imagination and a servitude to personal fears and uncertainties.

With inexorable rapidity Macbeth strips from himself all vestiges of humanity. Because he founded his reign upon the principle of individual power, and destroyed, in the process, traditions of custom and respect, he does not feel that the law of mutual obligations will sustain his rule, and he adopts, in its stead, the law of the jungle. He will murder again, for now he would be the practical realist, untouched by moral considerations, his imagination narrowed to the immediate situation which he subjects to a shrewd assessment: "To be thus is nothing,/ But to be safely thus" (III.i.48) — this is his first judgment. Having moved beyond the range of all men, Macbeth can no longer communicate with any human being, and one consequence is the loss of all feelings of mercy. Thus, it is politic to murder Banquo, who has such royalty of nature, wisdom, and valor, that Macbeth fears him as rival.

Macbeth is gradually converted to his wife's initial attitude; he becomes the pragmatist who considers only the physical facts of the immediate moment. But Lady Macbeth no longer adheres to that disposition. She displays, as Macbeth did earlier, a concern with things that are unseen, which cannot be pragmatically evaluated. Her speech of Act III, scene ii, addressed to herself — for no one else is on stage at that moment — reflects her change of vision:

> Nought's had, all's spent,
> Where our desire is got without content.
> 'Tis safer to be that which we destroy
> Than by destruction dwell in doubtful joy.

(III.ii.4)

The speech has several important functions. It is our first indication of how Lady Macbeth's spirits have been affected by murder. Composed of epigrammatic couplets, its rhythms conveying with fidelity the torments of an uneasy soul, the speech is a precise résumé of the despair which has ironically followed an act whose execution was to have brought great joy. It also serves to set the mood for Macbeth's entrance in this scene. When her husband appears, her address to him — "why do you keep alone"? (III.ii.8) — is an observation of the outward figure, the isolated man. We see Macbeth from the outside. But we come to know that this physical state is a reflection and consequence of his inner torment when Macbeth speaks of "terrible dreams/ That shake us nightly" (III.ii.18); when he longs to possess the peace of the dead rather than "on the torture of the mind to lie/ In restless ecstasy" (III.ii.21); when he begrudges Duncan his escape from "life's fitful fever" (III.ii.23). To talk himself into virtue and peace is no longer possible. He is forever exiled from the regenerating balm of sleep. He loses all touch with the community of men, even withdrawing from his wife, refusing to share with her the plot he has formed against Banquo and Fleance. To the question, "What's to be done?" comes his reply: "Be innocent of the knowledge, dearest chuck,/ Till thou applaud the deed" (III.ii.45).

Of all Shakespeare's tragic figures, Macbeth is the most isolated. The tragic lovers have one another. Hamlet can reveal himself to Horatio; Othello, to the villainous Iago. Lear has the company of the faithful Kent, the Fool, Edgar, Gloucester. Timon has Flavius. Coriolanus has a friend in Menenius, and though he rejects him, he does not reject his mother, for it is her pleading which makes him give up his attack on Rome. But Macbeth turns completely inward upon himself. His wife's question, "Why do you keep alone?" sounds the thematic note of isolation which Shakespeare renders in a carefully developed pattern of dramatic action.

Macbeth cannot find kinship even with his wife, the one person who shares his guilt. And after refusing to divulge to her the details of future plans, he willfully cuts himself off from his own humanity:

> Come, seeling night,
> Scarf up the tender eye of pitiful day,
> And with thy bloody and invisible hand
> Cancel and tear to pieces that great bond
> Which keeps me pale!
>
> (III.ii.46)

Invoking the powers of darkness, he would shut himself off from light, and suppress all feelings of pity, lest it interfere with the carrying out of his unnatural acts. The bond he would cancel and tear to pieces is Fleance and Banquo's lease on life, but there is the suggestion that it is also the bond of human fellowship which Macbeth must cast off before he can destroy, with deliberate calculation, another human being.

Free of the outer sanctions of social and moral doctrines, Macbeth derives authority from himself alone. His own pragmatic standards determine what is good and what is evil; consequently, good is that which affords him freedom from fear of the living. As Macbeth retreats from the light of day and the natural feelings that join people together in bonds of sympathy and trust, there is nobody he can depend upon completely. When he sends the two malcontent murderers to attack Banquo and Fleance, his mistrust of others is highlighted — he sends a third man to spy upon the two.

It is impossible, however, to murder all the living; and this is the import of Fleance's escape from death. That Banquo's son still lives is sufficient testimony that crime will be opposed, that it cannot succeed in making good of bad and friends of foes. Once again our view is not of man in conflict with society, the external world; our vision is of Macbeth confronting himself:

> But now I am cabin'd, cribb'd, confin'd, bound in
> To saucy doubts and fears.
>
> (III.iv.24)

Macbeth might advise his wife to assume the Machiavellian pose, to make the "faces vizards to our hearts,/ Disguising what they are" (III.ii.34), but he uncovers to an audience the reality behind the mask. Of *King Lear* Melville wrote that, "Tormented into desperation, Lear the frantic king tears off the mask, and speaks the sane madness of vital truth." [27] In unmasking himself to his audience, Macbeth also articulates vital truth, of a different kind, the reverse of Lear's truth, but no less of a discovery of what is beneath the seeming. Macbeth uncovers dark truths unchangeable: that if a man strikes out at law and nature, law and nature recede, leaving him to his aloneness; and though he possess crown and sceptre, there is no joy.

The banquet scene provides us with the play's most dramatic rendering of Macbeth's isolation, and, further, of the anguish that is continually his. Pointedly emphasized at the beginning of the scene are the ceremony and order traditionally surrounding the king. The first words of the scene are Macbeth's, his address to the assembled guests, "You know your own degrees; sit down" (III.iv.1). Contrasted with these words which inaugurate the banquet are Lady Macbeth's, which bring the feasting to an abrupt and disorderly conclusion:

> At once, good night.
> Stand not upon the order of your going,
> But go at once.
>
> (III.iv.118)

Contaminating and destroying the harmony which should prevail at such an occasion is the reminder of Macbeth's lawlessness which rises before him in the form of Banquo's ghost.

There has been much dispute concerning the nature and significance of the ghost. We have, for example, the rather extreme view of W. C. Curry: "Banquo's ghost is an infernal illusion, created out of air by demonic forces and presented to Macbeth's sight at the banquet in order that the murderer may be confused and utterly confounded." [28] The argument that external demonic forces control Macbeth has disturbing consequences, for Macbeth becomes a mere puppet, a helpless victim unable to will his own actions. Willard Farnham, taking another position, refers to an imposing array of Elizabethan moral treatises and plays in supporting his contention that fear was one of the passions stirred by conscience, and that tyrants were notable sufferers from guilty conscience.[29] However, that such a view had currency in Shakespeare's time is no guarantee that Shakespeare dramatized it in this particular scene. Actually, there is not within the play itself strong support for the supposition that the ghost's appearance is brought on by Macbeth's conscience; only by going outside the drama to Elizabethan writings and other plays can such a view be sustained. Indeed, after Macbeth's pragmatic assessment of his status — the turning point in his characterization — that speech of Act III, scene i, which begins, "To be thus is nothing,/ But to be safely thus," there is nowhere an indication that Macbeth is affected by conscience, save for a passing reference in his warning to Macduff, towards the end of the play,

> get thee back; my soul is too much charg'd
> With blood of thine already.

(V.viii.5)

Instead, Shakespeare portrays a Macbeth who deliberately casts off his conscience in the endeavor to consolidate his rule by eliminating all outward threats. Nevertheless, he cannot escape his own fears. Not conscience but fear and isolation arise from his guilt.

Too great a preoccupation with the nature of the ghost leads us away from the most important point of the scene, the dramatic impact which the ghost has upon Macbeth. In undergoing this most unexpected of experiences, Macbeth reveals his character, and his response determines our attitude towards him. Shakespeare uses Banquo's ghost to establish a certain point of view towards the protagonist. To determine this we need to examine first the dramatic context, for we do not react to character detached from the conditions which the dramatist builds about him; our emotions are very much affected by the interplay — particularly in the banquet scene — between character and occasion.

The banquet is a ritual: the king sits at the head of a community of guests, each in his proper place. In its way, then, the banquet is a kind of microcosm, its order a reflection of society's order. But Macbeth cannot join the festive circle; he must remain outside, for when he would take his seat at the head of the gathering, he finds it occupied by the ghost. Banquo was invited not to fail the feast; his spirit keeps the pledge. The grim irony of the returning spirit dominating the scene, while often commented upon, needs to be analyzed more fully in terms of the play's developing action, Macbeth's isolation from the community, and his retreat into the self.

On the two occasions when the ghost appears, Shakespeare surrounds the moment with irony. The first instance is when Macbeth feigns resentment at Banquo's absence:

> Here had we now our country's honour roof'd,
> Were the grac'd person of our Banquo present,
> Who may I rather challenge for unkindness
> Than pity for mischance.
>
> (III.iv.40)

Irony here operates on two levels. There is, first, the incongruity between what Macbeth says and what he knows: unlike his guests, Macbeth knows that Banquo lies dead in a ditch. There is, at the same time, a further use of dramatic irony. An audience is aware of what Macbeth and his guests do not perceive: that while Macbeth speaks his dissembling words, Banquo's spirit has menacingly appeared and now sits in Macbeth's place. And when the ghost makes its second appearance we have a repetition of the same two levels of irony as Macbeth offers a toast to his guests and to Banquo:

> Give me some wine; fill full.
> I drink to th' general joy o' th' whole table,
> And to our dear friend Banquo, whom we miss;
> Would he were here! to all and him we thirst,
> And all to all.

(III.iv.88)

That Shakespeare should present both occasions in a deliberately identical manner suggests unifying purpose and significance. In both instances irony works in two ways. First, it serves to characterize Macbeth. Sharing his knowledge that Banquo is dead, an audience catches him in the Machiavellian pose of saying what he does not mean, of seeming to be what he is not. If this irony existed alone it would only elicit moral judgment from an audience, and Macbeth would stand forth a traditional villain. But in both situations another kind of irony is also at work; it is brought on by the visitation of the ghost, and it effects a rapport between audience and protagonist which elevates Macbeth above the stock villain, making of him a tragic figure. Here the irony is what might be called Sophoclean, deriving from the contrast between the protagonist's ignorance and the spectator's knowledge, as well as from the principle of reversal, the terrible discrepancy between Macbeth's expectation and the occasion's actuality.

When Macbeth chafes at Banquo's absence, when he would drink to Banquo's health, knowing well the man is dead, he confidently expresses the unuttered belief that he is capable of controlling his destiny, that in dispatching Banquo he has rid himself of mortal danger, and reigns supreme. His words are testimony to a belief that he is the most important of beings, that he can, through individual power, impose order on the uncertainties of existence. But an audience, aware that Banquo's spirit has arisen, knows this belief to be an illusion. It is this moment of ironic reversal which creates a close bond between actor and spectator and accounts for pity and terror, for Macbeth's situation becomes typical of tragic human destiny. At the very moment of his supreme confidence we see the precariousness of the human condition.

Macbeth's fear is not the fear of conscience, it is the terror that springs from his inability to control his fate. He finds that his acts do not have purposeful finality: kill a man, and he is not dead. Macbeth cannot control nature, it seems to rise against him. "The time has been," he apprehensively recalls,

> That, when the brains were out, the man would die,
> And there an end; but now they rise again.
> With twenty mortal murders on their crowns,
> And push us from our stools. This is more strange
> Than such a murder is.
>
> (III.iv.78)

Murder brings to Macbeth terror instead of safety, it exiles him from the company of men. In numerous ways Shakespeare accentuates Macbeth's isolation in the banquet scene. Unable to trust others, he cannot even depend upon his own senses. Nor can he rely upon the orderly processes of nature, for when he wipes out his adversary, that adversary returns to confront him. And, it is significant to note, the visitations of the ghost occur at precisely those moments when Macbeth would join the community of men; first, when he would take his place at the head of the banquet; afterwards, when he would join his guests in drinking a toast. Separated from others and from the world of ordered nature, Macbeth has no proper place in this new world he has fashioned for himself.

Viewing the ghost's appearances in dramatic context, we see how they mark Macbeth's final estrangement from others.

Where Lear corrects his error, repenting the transgression against society's harmony, re-establishing his connection with others, Macbeth is blocked from rejoining the community and is driven deeper into himself. The ghost's appearances breed in him terror and also defiance, the kind of desperate self-will which so often characterizes the child who has not yet learned that he cannot always have his own way, and who, when frustrated in asserting his will, strikes out against natural order rather than giving in to it.

The ghost brings to Macbeth an omen that crime will not remain hidden, that his license to destroy also implies that he can be destroyed: "It will have blood, they say; blood will have blood" (III.iv.122). To stave off revenge he must blindly strike out at all who might jeopardize his person; he cannot dominate his world until his law of crime is fully accepted; therefore, he must destroy others before they have a chance to destroy him. The momentum of crime is so strong it pushes him forward:

> I am in blood
> Stepp'd in so far that, should I wade no more,
> Returning were as tedious as go o'er.
> Strange things I have in head, that will to hand,
> Which must be acted ere they may be scann'd.
>   (III.iv.136)

Macbeth alone will judge men and impose sentence upon them. In this way he places himself at the center of creation; the community falls away. Rejecting all laws and customs outside his own being, Macbeth is no longer cognizant of conscience. The sin of pride may be said to characterize him, and Saint Augustine provides a precise description of this greatest of sins — the attempt by man, essentially a dependent being, to exist for himself alone, "liking himself as if he were his own light." [30] In treating this subject of pride, some would stress man's duty to God, others, man's duty to society. There is common agreement, however, that to live completely isolated in the self is to live trapped in hell — this is what theo-

logians and humanists and psychologists warn against, and
what many artists have dramatized.

Oblivious to feelings of guilt, Macbeth, unlike Lear, does
not entertain thoughts of repentance. His journey is away
from society and morality, away from the humanity that
would make him akin to all men. Before the murder of Duncan, Macbeth lived within the confines of ordered nature,
acknowledging his responsibilities to king and nation; and
the thought of wrenching that ordered pattern brought him
terror because, as Joseph Conrad has phrased the matter, "The
real significance of crime is in its being a breach of faith with
the community of mankind." [31] After violating the natural
order, Macbeth finds that he is cut off from it; for him it has
neither sanctity nor dependable, unalterable stability. His
loss of faith in nature, his denial of its worth, becomes explicit when he demands from the weird sisters knowledge of
future events, for he conjures them to answer his request
even though they unloose every natural bond which assures
the world's harmony: though they untie the winds and let
them fight against the churches; though they cause the waves
to overwhelm navigation and man's cultivation of the land;
though castles topple and palaces and pyramids tumble. No
longer aghast at nature's chaos, he would, for private gain,
countenance it; for he seems to consider himself not only
outside but above nature's domain. He would gain personal
knowledge, even at the expense of all creation:

> though the treasure
> Of nature's germens tumble all together,
> Even till destruction sicken; answer me
> To what I ask you.
>
> (IV.i.58)

And while the weird sisters transform his uncertainty and fear
into a temporary illusion of safety by telling him that "none
of woman born/ Shall harm Macbeth" (IV.i.80), that he
"shall never vanquish'd be until/ Great Birnam wood to high
Dunsinane hill/ Shall come against him" (IV.i.92), he goes

beyond such assurances and would assert his own power over nature by obliterating mortal threat, by wiping out Macduff, his wife, and all who are of his lineage.

Still there is no joy. At Dunsinane castle, informed that military forces are marshalled against him, Macbeth finds comfort in the reassuring pronouncements of the weird sisters, spirits who know all mortal consequences. But, alone, he speaks of the corroding misery of isolation:

> I have liv'd long enough. My way of life
> Is fallen into the sear, the yellow leaf;
> And that which should accompany old age,
> As honour, love, obedience, troops of friends,
> I must not look to have; but, in their stead,
> Curses, not loud but deep, mouth-honour, breath
> Which the poor heart would fain deny, and dare not.
>
> (V.iii.22)

In this speech Macbeth reveals a humane quality we rarely see in him. Alone on the stage, he faces himself as well as the audience of mankind. He seems momentarily to stand back from the flow of life to assess its meaning. He does not, as before, rage against nature, question its purpose, or try to control his own destiny. He sees himself separated from the world because of his own deeds. Because he passes judgment upon himself, spectators are at one with him, for his judgment is our judgment. He speaks not just for himself, but for all men who might do as he has done. It is a moment of lucid self-recognition when man, in the person of Macbeth, faces the consequences of his actions and gives voice to the aching loneliness that inevitably results once he has stripped from himself honor, love, obedience, friends.

Nevertheless, there can be no turning back. Macbeth undergoes no transformation of character or vision. Shakespeare shows how hardened man becomes when he disowns others and when society disowns him: he must rely completely upon himself; he has no choice. "Give me my armour" (V.iii.33), Macbeth, after his soliloquy, commands Seyton. Although

advised it is not needed yet, twice again he repeats the bidding (V.iii.36, 48). This insistence that he be given his armor
stresses the imminence of battle; it enables the actor to ready
himself in full view of the audience; but, that the commands
are repeated three times also suggests a possible trait of character: Macbeth's impatient reliance upon no one but himself.

The stripping from Macbeth of social and humane qualities continues in the next scene in which he appears. His estrangement from others and his loss of natural human re-
sponses pervade his thoughts. When he hears the cry of women
within the besieged castle, he does not recognize its character;
he must ask of Seyton, "What is that noise?" (V.v.7) And this
brings on reflections of how insensate he has become since
steeping himself in murders:

> I have almost forgot the taste of fears.
> The time has been, my senses would have cool'd
> To hear a night-shriek, and my fell of hair
> Would at a dismal treatise rouse and stir
> As life were in 't. I have supp'd full with horrors;
> Direness, familiar to my slaughterous thoughts,
> Cannot once start me.
>
> (V.v.9)

Following upon this insensibility to the distress of the crying
women, comes his callousness to the plight of one particular
woman. "Wherefore was that cry?" he asks the returning Seyton; and learning that his wife is dead, he shows neither be-
reavement nor compassionate concern:

> She should have died hereafter;
> There would have been a time for such a word.
>
> (V.v.17)

The words are ambiguous; we are not sure whether he means
that Lady Macbeth had to die sometime, after all, or that too
many mishaps come at once, or whether he suggests that her
death should have taken place in a more peaceful time. But
the important thing to note is his wearied unconcern. He does
not even ask the cause of her death; and his thoughts hurry on

to a hopeless vision of life emptied of vital purpose, where
the future is petty, holding no meaning, and the past lights
fools the way to dusty death.

> It is a tale
> Told by an idiot, full of sound and fury,
> Signifying nothing.
>
> (V.v.26)

The manner in which Macbeth faces death gives a good indication of how he views himself and the world about him.
Informed that Birnam wood actually moves towards Dunsinane, he alludes to meeting death, but his is not a stoical
hardening, learning how to die; it is, rather, the evocation of
sheer futility, the necessity of facing an occasion which has no
great import; it must be met head-on and with determination, not from conviction, but because there is nothing else
to do:

> I gin to be aweary of the sun,
> And wish th' estate o' th' world were now undone.
> Ring the alarum-bell! Blow, wind! come, wrack!
> At least we'll die with harness on our back.
>
> (V.v.49)

Comparing this approach to death with analogous moments
in other Shakespearian tragedies, we see the quality of Macbeth's life in greater perspective. "Report me and my cause
aright," Hamlet asks of Horatio, for his actions have been
purposeful and of benefit to society; and in the moment of
death he thinks of honor and reputation, most sacred to man.
So also Othello, who asks only that his story be told honestly,
"Speak of me as I am; nothing extenuate,/ Nor set down
aught in malice." And he wishes, above all, that his service to
the state be remembered. In *King Lear*, too, the protagonist
comes to acknowledge his involvement with others. In these
moments of ultimate crisis the individual and society come together so that there is the sense not only of man's inner
strength but of the ties that bind him to others. Macbeth be-

longs, finally, to no one but himself; and his strength derives
not from wisdom but impotence as he finds himself reduced
to animal existence, cornered and alone. Macbeth discovers
how thoroughly the juggling fiends have paltered with him
in a double sense: Birnam wood does come to Dunsinane;
and Macduff, born of no woman, for he was from his mother's
womb untimely ripp'd, faces him in personal combat. At first
Macbeth will not fight; then, with the fortitude of desperation, he determines to do battle as again he thinks himself a
cornered animal:

> I will not yield,
> To kiss the ground before young Malcolm's feet
> And to be baited with the rabble's curse.
>
> (V.viii.28)

His final words in the play,

> Lay on, Macduff,
> And damn'd be him that first cries, "Hold, enough!"
>
> (V.viii.33)

are not without the nobility of an unbridled vigor that refuses to submit to inevitable defeat.

6

When we see Macbeth from his own perspective, we participate in his changing nature, go with him into isolation
and despair, know and share the terrors of spiritual descent.
Here the relationship is individual and personal; it is between audience and protagonist. However, we would distort
Shakespeare's presentation of Macbeth if we considered only
the protagonist's private life, his alienation from others and
the evil he does to himself. In the unfolding action on the
stage we also see the disrupting evil Macbeth brings into society and natural order. After the murder of Duncan, Shakespeare alternates his scenes. In one scene we are with Macbeth,
seeing him from within; the emotions are personal, the judgments are private. In another scene Shakespeare shifts the

focus so that we see Macbeth from the outside; the judgments are social and the emotions public.

In those scenes in which we leave the private life of Macbeth to view him with the perspective of other people in the play, there is a distancing of the protagonist; we become detached from his spiritual torments and are made to see the cosmic and social consequences of his actions. When we are with Macbeth we see the world with his eyes; we understand his private misery; and understanding involves, to a great degree, compassion. When an audience views Macbeth through the eyes of others, it is repelled by the destructiveness of his public acts. This deliberate, almost choric, framing of Macbeth and his actions begins immediately after the murder of Duncan when Ross and an Old Man are the sole participants of a scene (II.iv). Their speeches stress the effects of Duncan's unnatural death upon the world. They describe a universe which has suddenly changed; and the strangeness of that transformation is magnified as the Old Man, recalling his past seventy years, cannot remember a time which might equal the present dread. The heavens, says Ross, are troubled with man's act: though it is day, there is no light. Both men describe the horrors of a nature in turmoil, of animals gone mad, behaving in unbelievably unnatural ways.

In the colloquy between Lennox and an unnamed Lord after the banquet scene (III.vi) there is another framing of Macbeth's character and deeds. If, as is generally thought, III.v, IV.i. 39–43, 125–132, are interpolations and not Shakespeare's work, the exchange between Lennox and the Lord would immediately follow the banquet scene, reinforcing the contrast between the private and the public views of Macbeth. In this scene the Lord calls Macbeth, "tyrant"; he tells of Fleance's flight to England, of Macduff's voyage there to gather forces so that

we may again

Give to our tables meat, sleep to our nights,

Free from our feasts and banquets bloody knives,
Do faithful homage and receive free honours;
All which we pine for now.

(III.vi.33)

While the speeches of this scene convey necessary information concerning the preparations being undertaken against
Macbeth, they also place him in a social context. From the
close-up view of the protagonist established in the banquet
scene, where personal emotions of pity and fear are evoked,
we move away, seeing him from the vantage point of his
subjects. Since Macbeth's reign jeopardizes the health of society, since all men's lives are affected, an audience judges
and condemns the protagonist. And the scene ends on this
note of public concern as Lennox prays

that a swift blessing
May soon return to this our suffering country
Under a hand accurs'd!

(III.vi.47)

After the murder of Duncan, in almost every scene in
which Macbeth is absent, Shakespeare concentrates upon the
disastrous public consequences of his reign. This is true of
the scene presenting the murder of Lady Macduff and her
child, which has frequently been called "mere pathos." [32]
One of the scene's functions, as A. C. Bradley pointed out, is
to set up the conflict between Macbeth and Macduff. Above
all else, however, the dramatization of the slaughter of the
innocents brings out the unnatural changes in social and
domestic values occasioned by Macbeth's rule. In time of
greatest peril Lady Macduff finds herself deserted by her husband. She calls him "traitor"; "he wants the natural touch"
(IV.ii.9). Though Ross pleads that Macduff is "noble, wise,
judicious," that he knew what he was doing in fleeing without wife and children, this is of little solace to one left to
fend for herself. Love of country was Macduff's one motive
for his flight, A. C. Bradley offers as exoneration,[33] but this

cannot soften the stark brutality of the scene's happenings. Here Shakespeare gives visible proof that Macbeth has destroyed all that is customary and right in life. As Lady Macduff says of the new world in which she suddenly finds herself, "All is the fear and nothing is the love" (IV.ii.12). Recurring in the speeches of the scene, almost in the manner of a leitmotif, is the unnaturalness which pervades society, building up the feeling that what is happening and about to happen result from Macbeth's malignancy which makes unnatural all that is natural. Ross says,

> cruel are the times when we are traitors
> And do not know ourselves; when we hold rumour
> From what we fear, yet know not what we fear,
> But float upon a wild and violent sea
> Each way and move.
>
> (IV.ii.18)

And Macduff's son utters, in his innocent prattling, the new truth of contemporary life. Told by his mother that his father is a traitor, that a traitor is one who swears and lies, that all traitors should be hanged by honest men, the boy's reply serves as commentary on the bankruptcy of the time: "Then the liars and swearers are fools; for there are liars and swearers enow to beat the honest men and hang up them" (IV.ii.56). This sense of the time's uncertainty and lawlessness reaches a high point after the sudden arrival and hasty departure of the messenger who urges Lady Macduff to flee. "I have done no harm," she protests to herself; and then she draws the moral of this topsy-turvy world:

> But I remember now
> I am in this earthly world, where to do harm
> Is often laudable, to do good sometime
> Accounted dangerous folly.
>
> (IV.ii.74)

The slaughter of the innocent wife and child is final testimony to the public horrors of Macbeth's lawless reign. The world has become a fearful place as humanity falls prey to the law of the jungle. But evil is not a mysterious, universal condition of unfathomable origin. It is localized in Macbeth and his tyrannical regal powers.

In the next scene, often omitted from stage productions because it is an essentially nondramatic discourse on the requisites of the ideal king and the duties of loyal subject, Shakespeare offers a relatively simple answer to the existence of evil, and this has great bearing on the point of view established towards Macbeth. Each participant of the scene vividly describes the spreading consequences of evil. Macduff mourns the fate of Scotland, for each day, "New widows howl, new orphans cry, new sorrows/ Strike heaven on the face" (IV.-iii.5). Malcolm pictures the country sinking beneath the yoke, weeping, bleeding, and "each new day a gash/ Is added to her wounds" (IV.iii.40). Ross likens the nation to a grave, then to a wasteland filled with unheeded sighs and groans and shrieks, "and good men's lives/ Expire before the flowers in their caps,/Dying or ere they sicken" (IV.iii.171). At the scene's opening Malcolm would seek some desolate shade and there weep out his sadness at his country's travail. Macduff, however, counsels action, for evil is not cosmic, the result of indifferent or malevolent nature. Nor is the reality of evil rooted in the spiritual structure of an era, as in *King Lear*. It has its beginnings in one man, and it can be ended by extirpating that individual. The numerous references to Macbeth, more in this scene than in any other, are all alike. Repeatedly called "tyrant," "black," "devilish," "fiend of Scotland," Macbeth is stripped of all human characteristics.

> Not in the legions
> Of horrid hell can come a devil more damn'd
> In evils to top Macbeth.
>
> (IV.iii.55)

Such concerted condemnation alienates all compassion for Macbeth. The dramatist transforms the audience from participant in his doubts and torments to indignant judge of his destructive fury. When we are alone with Macbeth we become involved with action which is primarily inner and spiritual rather than outward and physical; our involvement is with Macbeth as man, not as king. When we move away, viewing him with the perspective of society, the dramatist shifts the center of interest from the problem "what is man?" to a consideration of the individual's responsibilities to his fellow men. This shift of focus is brought out in the colloquy between Macduff and Malcolm, and while Theodore Spencer has shown the relationship of the episode to the play's preoccupation with appearance and reality, suggesting that the reality of good which shines under the false appearance of Malcolm offsets and contradicts the reality of evil which is Macbeth,[34] we should also view the situation as affording dramatic occasion for explaining the ideal relationship which should exist between sovereign and subject, and determine the effect this has upon our attitude towards Macbeth.

When Malcolm, legitimate heir to the throne, catalogues Macbeth's sins only to announce that he himself would be a far worse ruler, that had he power he would

> Pour the sweet milk of concord into hell,
> Uproar the universal peace, confound
> All unity on earth,

> (IV.iii.98)

Macduff draws away from Scotland's rightful sovereign, refuses to assist him in acquiring the throne, and says, bitterly, that Malcolm not only is unfit to govern, he is unfit to live. Having tested Macduff's integrity and fidelity to country, Malcolm at this moment abjures the blames he put upon himself. By setting forth the dramatic contrast between virtue and overreaching pride, Shakespeare offers a coherent pattern of life: society is more important than any individual, even its lawful king. While Macbeth refuses to acknowledge the interdependency between the individual and his society, acting as if man were powerful enough to tear the universe apart and refashion it according to his will, Malcolm affirms his responsibilities to society. In his person he has all the king-becoming graces, for he is a man of virtue:

> I am yet
> Unknown to woman, never was forsworn,
> Scarcely have coveted what was mine own,
> At no time broke my faith, would not betray
> The devil to his fellow, and delight
> No less in truth than life.
> (IV.iii.125)

Unlike Macbeth, he does not believe that everything is possible for a king, and instead of glorifying personal power and prerogative, he would give of himself to all men:

> What I am truly,
> Is thine and my poor country's to command,
> (IV.iii.131)

he tells Macduff.

The play's final vision is highly optimistic: evil has no abiding mystery, no vestigial force which will linger on no matter how men act to overcome it. If only reciprocal obligations are acknowledged and maintained, society will grow and prosper. Though the death of Macbeth brings the play to a close, that death, we are made to feel, is no loss. "The time is free" (V.viii.55) cries Macduff, displaying the "usurper's cursed head." And Malcolm speaks of "this dead butcher and his fiend-like queen" (V.viii.69). The fall of the protagonist brings no tragic release, no feeling of woe or wonder, for Shakespeare mutes such feelings by transferring interest from Macbeth's personal plight to society's salvation, dispelling the terrors of man's conflict with destiny. We move from the despair of evil to the exaltation of righteousness, from spiritual and moral blindness to illumination. *King Lear* ends with an intense, agonized questioning of cosmic justice. *Macbeth* ends with a tentative resolution of universal problems, departing from the tragic world to enter the realm of chronicle and history. The play of character is subordinated at the end and becomes the story of Macbeth, whose example of tyranny is to be shunned. If, as some critics maintain, *Macbeth* is a great work, but not the greatest of tragedies, might its ending not afford partial explanation? Great tragedy does not offer the whole truth about life's meaning, affording, thereby, an easy release from life's uncertainties.

CHAPTER III

ANTONY AND CLEOPATRA

IF all texts of Shakespeare's *Antony and Cleo-patra* disappeared and only the criticism remained, we would confront such contradictory opinions about the play and its protagonists that we would wonder whether the critics had discussed the same work, or whether Shakespeare had written at least two different versions. Two opposing views predominate in the criticism of the play. Some regard the work as an exposure of corruption and human weakness; others view the play as a kind of lyrical poem which exalts love as life's greatest value, finally triumphant over death and the petty restrictions of the world. Some view Cleopatra and Antony as a strumpet and a fool; others give to them the role of Phoenix and Turtle. "A tragedy of disillusion, we might call it," [1] said Harley Granville-Barker and judged the work to be "a play of action . . . not of spiritual insight." [2] Completely opposed to Granville-Barker's interpretation is the verdict of E. E. Stoll, an equally eminent Shakespearian critic, who found the play's emphasis to be on greatness of character rather than action: Antony and Cleopatra are nobler than their action, "their love is greater than their natures." [3]

In addition to these opposing views, there are interpreters

of Shakespeare who hold the two extreme positions in tenuous balance. Willard Farnham characterized Antony and Cleopatra as "finished studies in paradoxical nobility." [4] S. L. Bethell, noting the many contradictory views of the play, attacked the attempt to isolate character and action as "precarious and inadequate" and maintained that only by beginning and ending with the poetry itself could the critic do justice to Shakespeare's true meaning.[5] His final judgment was that Shakespeare was investigating the problem: what are the positive bases of the good life? These positive values, said Bethell, are to be found in the affections rooted in the sensual nature; Egyptian values survive death. Thus we have a paradoxical combination of extreme positions when Bethell applies theological categories to the play: "In *Antony and Cleopatra* the strong sinners meet their purgatory here. They do not desire or seek it; it is forced upon them from without — grace which visits them in the guise of defeat." [6]

Critics disagree about the most important features of the play. Some condemn its construction as panoramic and loosely connected; others insist that it is superbly integrated. Critics disagree about the play's meaning, its morality, and the inherent worth of Antony and Cleopatra.[7] The most important reason why *Antony and Cleopatra* has been interpreted in so many ways is that we, as audience, are constantly forced to change our point of view. At one moment we are in Egypt; suddenly we are transported to Rome. We see the actions of Antony and Cleopatra through Roman eyes and Roman judgments; we see these same actions from the Egyptian point of view; we hear the lovers' own judgments of their actions. Antony is called "not more manlike/ Than Cleopatra" (I.iv.5); "the abstract of all faults" (I.iv.9); "libertine" (II.i.23); "amorous surfeiter" (II.i.33); "old ruffian" (IV.i.4). These are Roman views. Opposing them are Egyptian descriptions of Antony as "the demi-Atlas of this earth" (I.v.23); "the crown o' th' earth" (IV.xv.63); a being so wondrously magnificent that he was "past the size of dreaming" (V.ii.97). Nor do all Roman views denigrate Antony. Lepidus, a Roman, defends him against Caesar's denunciations:

> I must not think there are
> Evils enow to darken all his goodness.
> His faults, in him, seem as the spots of heaven,
> More fiery by night's blackness.
>
> (I.iv.10)

And a Roman soldier, who tells the renegade Enobarbus that Antony has sent Enobarbus' treasures to Caesar's camp, says:

> Your emperor
> Continues still a Jove.
>
> (IV.vi.28)

Whose point of view are we to accept finally? — this becomes a crucial problem in the analysis of the play. To render judgment is to choose from among conflicting opinions, and the critic must be alert against improper abstraction and generalization. In *Antony and Cleopatra* it is difficult to arrive at unconfuted judgment, for while we have, as in other Shakespearian plays, a clash of two worlds, the two worlds are so corrupt — as in *Troilus and Cressida* — that one is not morally superior to the other. Evil, therefore, is not clearly localized as in *Hamlet* or *King Lear* where we see the world primarily through the eyes of Hamlet or Lear, not through the eyes of Claudius or Goneril.

Even in the play's first scene the point of view can be a bewildering matter as an audience confronts the questions: through whose eyes are we to look upon Antony and Cleopatra and whose judgments are we to accept as truth? Antony's soldiers condemn his love; to them it is dotage and debauchery. Antony and Cleopatra exalt their love above all power and dominion; they call it divine. Commentators who choose the judgment of the observing soldiers over the lovers' own assessment generally regard Antony and Cleopatra as reprobate and strumpet in much the same way as George

Bernard Shaw, who wrote in his preface to *Three Plays for Puritans* that Shakespeare gave "a faithful picture of the soldier broken down by debauchery, and the typical wanton in whose arms such men perish." [8] G. Wilson Knight, on the other hand, accepted Antony's words in the first scene at face value and idealized his love: "man is transfigured by love's orient fire. Without it he is, as the beasts, mere product of 'dungy earth.' Love here translineates man to divine likeness — it is the only 'nobleness of life.' " [9]

It is possible to resolve such conflicting judgments on character and morality by defining the major concern of the play, the opposing forces that give to the drama its structure. The opening scenes of Shakespeare's mature plays often serve as a kind of overture to the entire work, setting forth the mood and themes that shape its central action. In *King Lear* and *Antony and Cleopatra* the first scenes have significant similarities: both end with recapitulating analyses of the hero. In *Lear*, Goneril and Regan review what has happened and incisively analyze the king. Their concluding speeches point to the dominant action of the play — their future treatment of their father. Through the speeches of Goneril and Regan at the end of the first scene of *Lear*, Shakespeare foreshadows the themes which order the entire drama: an old world of certain values embodied by Lear; the sudden transition to a new world of new values; and the mordant clash between the two.

One might well ask whether the concluding speeches of Demetrius and Philo in the first scene of *Antony and Cleopatra* also point to the major concern of the play:

> *Demetrius.*   Is Caesar with Antonius priz'd so slight?
> *Philo.* Sir, sometimes, when he is not Antony,
>   He comes too short of that great property
>   Which still should go with Antony.
> *Demetrius.*   I am full sorry
>   That he approves the common liar, who
>   Thus speaks of him at Rome; but I will hope
>   Of better deeds to-morrow. Rest you happy!   (I.i.56)

Their brief speeches emphasize Antony's heroic past as well as his ignominious present. Antony's life in Egypt is seen as a terrible fall from his heroic life. He is not what he should be. Yet the scene ends with the hopeful expectancy that Antony will belie his present disgrace, that he will soon regain the nobility he once had. While Caroline Spurgeon has noted that the word "world" occurs forty-two times in this play, far more often than in any other Shakespearian drama,[10] I suggest that the play is not concerned primarily with the clash between the values of Egypt and Rome but with Antony, his divided allegiance, and most important, his fulfilment as man, which demands that he recapture his heroic past.

In the first scene the introductory speech by Philo and the concluding remarks between Demetrius and Philo point to the forthcoming dramatic conflict as they sound the same questions: will the debauched private life of Antony prevail, or will he again assume his glorious public role? The opening speech prefigures the protagonists unfavorably as Philo invites us to remember the great Antony of the past and compare that memory with the Antony of the present:

> Nay, but this dotage of our general's
> O'erflows the measure. Those his goodly eyes,
> That o'er the files and musters of the war
> Have glow'd like plated Mars, now bend, now turn
> The office and devotion of their view
> Upon a tawny front; his captain's heart,
> Which in the scuffles of great fights hath burst
> The buckles on his breast, reneges all temper,
> And is become the bellows and the fan
> To cool a gipsy's lust.
>
> (I.i.1)

Philo defines for us the soldier's ideal of magnificent action in wars which made Antony the greatest of men. He now sees Antony as ridiculous and corrupt, for Antony has fallen away from that standard which shaped his noble reputation in the public world. Antony's descent from public virtue to private indulgence is abhorrent because it is the abnegation of moral discipline, an escape from duty and honor to a private world whose private values the soldier can neither sympathize with nor understand. "Look, where they come!" Philo points, as to an exhibition or a play to be enacted:

> Take but good note, and you shall see in him
> The triple pillar of the world transform'd
> Into a strumpet's fool. Behold and see.

(I.i.10)

Philo's words constitute a kind of prologue to the forthcoming action. And since his speech is addressed to soldiers and audience alike, we, the audience, are asked to view the ensuing performance in a very particular way: to determine whether Antony and Cleopatra, in their words and actions, either confirm or deny Philo's judgment.

There can be little doubt that Antony proceeds to act out the role Philo has attributed to him. The first words spoken by Cleopatra after Philo's introduction, "If it be love indeed, tell me how much" (I.i.14), are answered by Antony, "There's beggary in the love that can be reckon'd." The immediate preoccupation with love calls attention to Philo's preview of the two lovers. And upon entering into their private world we find that for Antony it is an escape from the world of honor and duty and public action. "I'll set a bourn how far to be belov'd" (I.i.16), says Cleopatra, and Antony replies, "Then must thou needs find out new heaven, new earth." His love would transcend mundane reality. He would escape into a world beyond the confines of the here and now, a world he must fashion in language of hyperbole. Freud would have characterized his desire as indulgence in the pleasure principle to escape from reality.

When the public world, in the form of messengers from Rome, harshly intrudes, Antony would flee. "Nay, hear them," Cleopatra objects, taunting him with the possible demands of public duty and public action: perhaps Fulvia has sent scolding reprimands, reminders of his conjugal duties; or perhaps Caesar has sent a powerful mandate,

> "Do this, or this;
> Take in that kingdom, and enfranchise that;
> Perform't, or else we damn thee."
>
> (I.i.22)

These social and political concerns would pull Antony back into the orbit of society. But he separates himself completely from society, refusing to face his obligations as triple pillar of the world. "Let Rome in Tiber melt, and the wide arch/ Of the rang'd empire fall!" is his cry of renunciation. Egypt is his refuge, and he turns from the gloomy thought of Roman duty to the glamor of sensual exaltation:

> Here is my space.
> Kingdoms are clay; our dungy earth alike
> Feeds beast as man; the nobleness of life
> Is to do thus, when such a mutual pair
> And such a twain can do't, in which I bind,
> On pain of punishment, the world to weet
> We stand up peerless.
>
> (I.i.34)

As the ideal of the lovers' private morality Antony invokes the "love of Love and her soft hours" (I.i.44); he would live in a world free from the entanglements of time, public duty, thought, a world in which not a minute of their lives "should stretch/ Without some pleasure now" (I.i.46).

We must view the words of Philo and Antony as part of the dramatic context of the scene. The meaning of the play cannot be said to derive wholly from what the hero says of himself. No matter how grandiose the imagery of Antony's speeches in this scene, to extract an imagery pattern stressing the overwhelming nature of love, to say that Shakespeare here magnifies Antony's figure and presents his love as life's highest value, is to neglect dramatic situation and indulge in romantic delusion. The actions of Antony and Cleopatra are unmistakenly framed in this scene. At the beginning, Philo judges them by the standard of public duty; an audience is prepared to accept this standard. When Antony and

Cleopatra come on stage, their words do not alter or contradict this point of view. Finally, the scene ends as it began,
with a soldier's condemnation; Demetrius joins Philo in dis-
approving Antony's present conduct. The deliberate framing
of the lovers cannot be dismissed. No matter how noble
Antony and Cleopatra wish to appear, the derogatory judgment of their actions by Philo and Demetrius reduces their
stature.

When Philo and Demetrius depict Antony's two opposing
personalities, they point to the conflict that will go on
throughout the play. Which of Antony's personalities will
ultimately prevail? This question arises even in the interplay between Antony and Cleopatra at the middle of the
scene. When Antony extols the sensual values of Egypt, calling on Rome to melt in Tiber, asserting that kingdoms are
but clay and that he and his beloved stand peerless, Cleopatra
dismisses his hyperboles and harshly challenges his honesty:

> Excellent falsehood!
> Why did he marry Fulvia, and not love her?
> I'll seem the fool I am not. — Antony
> Will be himself.

>   (I.i.40)

There are two Antonys: the illustrious public figure of the
past and the decadent private figure of the present, the
Antony of Rome and the Antony of Egypt. "Antony will be
himself," says Cleopatra, and almost immediately afterwards
Philo echoes a similar idea to Demetrius:

> When he is not Antony,
> He comes too short of that great property
> Which still should go with Antony.

>   (I.i.57)

Part of Antony endorses the soldier's ideal and urges him to
return to public life, recapture his reputation as peerless
warrior and become the magnificent man he used to be. The
other part of Antony yields to private emotion, the all-con-

suming passion for Cleopatra, and urges him to love in the grand manner, to deny and exclude the outside world and create a romantic paradise. However, to be at once Roman and Egyptian is impossible. If Antony is to return to his public role and regain his manhood, he must throw off Cleopatra and her influence. He can regain his manhood only through self-mastery; if he yields to passion, he is unmanned.

2

Antony's heroic past is significantly the only unquestioned ideal in the play. When his past is evoked, it serves as contrast to an ignominious present; but, equally important, it presents an image of perfection. By fulfilling the role of peerless soldier, Antony, on this basis alone, became a man of many splendid qualities, held the world's wonder, and earned his place in history. It is, indeed, most striking that not a hint of criticism is ever directed at Antony's past exploits, for this is a prominent departure from Shakespeare's primary source, North's *Life of Marcus Antonius*, where Antony's faults before his union with Cleopatra are amply illustrated. Shakespeare presents Antony's past as flawlessly heroic; he makes no use of Plutarch's references to Antony's dishonesty in money matters, his repeated riot and excess, his cruelty, his occasional lapses in generalship which lead to inefficiency and the botching of military expeditions.

In Shakespeare's play Antony is castigated for present actions, never for past performances. In the opening speech of the play Philo looks back to a time when Antony performed wonderful feats in battle, when indeed even his eyes were like those of "plated Mars." Caesar, waiting in Rome for Antony's return to the urgent demands of public action, condemns his "lascivious wassails" in Egypt and immediately recalls, in contrast, the magnificent Antony of the past, who, when beaten from Modena, had the fortitude to endure even more hardships than savages. Vividly evoking from the past a superhuman Antony, Caesar addresses him as if present:

> Antony,
> Leave thy lascivious wassails. When thou once
> Was beaten from Modena, where thou slew'st
> Hirtius and Pansa, consuls, at thy heel
> Did famine follow; whom thou fought'st against,
> Though daintily brought up, with patience more
> Than savages could suffer. Thou didst drink
> The stale of horses and the gilded puddle
> Which beasts would cough at; thy palate then did deign
> The roughest berry on the rudest hedge;
> Yea, like the stag, when snow the pasture sheets,
> The barks of trees thou browsed'st; on the Alps
> It is reported thou didst eat strange flesh,
> Which some did die to look on; and all this —
>
> (I.iv.55)

whereupon Caesar suddenly breaks off his vision in remembering the figure that Antony now cuts in the world, forcing the contrast between Antony's past and present to stand out even more sharply:

> It wounds thine honour that I speak it now —
> Was borne so like a soldier, that thy cheek
> So much as lank'd not.
>
> (I.iv.69)

While the description of Antony's Spartan endurance in his flight from Modena is taken from Plutarch, consider Shakespeare's omissions. Here is Plutarch's account:

Cicero on the other side being at that time the chiefest man of authority and estimation in the city, he stirred up all men against Antonius: so that in the end he made the Senate pronounce him an enemy to his country, and appointed young Caesar Sergeants to carry axes before him, and such other signs as were incident to the dignity of a Consul or Praetor: and moreover sent Hirtius and Pansa, then Consuls, to drive Antonius out of Italy. These two Consuls together with Caesar, who also had an army, went against Antonius that besieged the city of Modena, and there overthrew him in battle: but both the Consuls were slain there. Antonius, flying upon this overthrow, fell into great misery all at once: but the chiefest want of all other, and that pinched him most, was famine. Howbeit he was of such a strong nature, that by patience he would overcome any adversity, and, the heavier fortune lay upon him, the more constant shewed he himself. . . . And therefore it was a wonderful example to the soldiers to see Antonius, that was brought up in all fineness and superfluity, so easily to drink puddle water, and to eat wild fruits and roots: and moreover it is reported that, even as they passed the Alps, they did eat the barks of trees, and such beasts as never man tasted of their flesh before.[11]

In *Antony and Cleopatra,* Caesar mentions that Antony was "beaten from Modena," but it is a brief reference, of no consequence in a speech whose main purpose is to glorify Antony's former actions. Shakespeare omits all information presented by Plutarch which might reduce Antony's greatness before coming to Egypt. Caesar's remembrance of Antony's past — as Philo's opening speech of the play — is calculated to present that past as honorable and heroic; its evocation is designed to highlight the sordidness of Antony's fall from greatness.

This juxtaposition of heroic past and decadent present for the purpose of heightened contrast is not confined to the speeches of Philo and Caesar. As Pompey surveys his military position in Messina, word is brought that Antony is momentarily expected at Rome, whereupon Pompey recalls Antony's greatness as a soldier, and we again have a contrast between a once glorious Antony and an Antony so fallen into debauchery that he is but a shadow of his former greatness:

> Menas, I did not think
> This amorous surfeiter would have donn'd his helm
> For such a petty war. His soldiership
> Is twice the other twain; but let us rear
> The higher our opinion, that our stirring
> Can from the lap of Egypt's widow pluck
> The ne'er lust-wearied Antony.
>
> (II.i.32)

Or consider the summarizing comment of Canidius when Antony shamefully follows after Cleopatra "like a doting mallard" and leaves the battle of Actium:

> Had our general
> Been what he knew himself, it had gone well.

(III.x.26)

Certainly it is significant that continually remembered in the midst of crisis or defeat is an almost legendary Antony, a matchless soldier who, as Canidius suggests, would doubtlessly have triumphed had he only been what he knew himself to be. Always when Antony's past is remembered it serves as contrast to an ignominious present.

The association of valor and virtue is to be found in the opening section of Plutarch's life of Coriolanus and has relevance to Antony as well: "Now in those days, valiantness was honoured in Rome above all other virtues: which they call *Virtus,* by the name of virtue self, as including in that general name all other special virtues besides. So that *Virtus* in the Latin was as much as valiantness." [12] In being the greatest of soldiers Antony fulfilled himself as man, became, indeed, the paragon of men. This is what is stressed by those who remember his former days. In his own being Antony has no real worth; he can have value, he can be his true self, only in so far as he performs valorously, for this constitutes virtue, the ideal.

When *Antony and Cleopatra* begins we see Antony fallen away from that role which gave him nobility; he has abandoned what had been his life's work to build; he has lost his identity. "His taints and honours/ Wag'd equal with him" (V.i.30) is the judgment which Maecenas pronounced upon hearing of Antony's death. His honors, it is to be observed, are wholly in the past; his taints, in the present. To gain great stature Antony must plunge back to an old life rather than remain in his present one.

Preventing Antony from fulfilling his soldierly role, from again being the man he once was, is Cleopatra. Now if we view her as cutting Antony off from his goal in the world, which is to fulfill his destiny to be a man above all men, then she takes on the role of temptress, or even sorceress. If perfection is cankered because of her, then no equivocation can possibly save her from being maligned. It is concerning her role in the play that so many critics have put forth so many interpretations. Cleopatra has been called the eternally feminine, the lass unparalleled who is forever baffling, who cannot be reduced and confined by the cavils of criticism. A. C. Bradley would have us accept her vices as her chief glories: "Many unpleasant things can be said of Cleopatra; and the more that are said the more wonderful she appears." [13] E. E. Stoll, not usually prone to romanticizing, was so entranced by Cleopatra that she became for him a transcendent creature: "Caprice, conscious, and unconscious, is her nature, as to be queen and coquette is her station in life. *La donna è mobile*, and she is quintessential woman." [14] More and more names and adoring statements might be cited; numerous eminent Shakespearian scholars have humbled themselves before Cleopatra's charms. We must content ourselves with only one further reminder of Cleopatra's bewitchery, Harley Granville-Barker's positive assertion that she defies all moral standards: "It is futile, we know, to apply the usual moral tests to her, of loyalty, candor, courage." [15] But other commentators, less enraptured, have insisted that moral tests should be applied, and in doing so have sternly pronounced Cleopatra guilty, called her whore and snake of the Nile. Those who treat the Egyptian queen with tart discourtesy are less numerous than her admirers, but no less emphatic. Coleridge, though a romantic, was firm in his assertion that her passion "springs out of the habitual craving of a licentious nature"; [16] George Bernard Shaw harshly called her a "typical wanton"; [17] and Lord David Cecil, measuring her actions in terms of morality, found Cleopatra "by a strict moral standard, a vain, worthless, capricious coquette who does not care in the least about the true interests of her lover, and who is so dominated by the desire to attract that she cannot be faithful to him for half-an-hour." [18]

To indulge in a highly personal reaction to Cleopatra too

often results in uncovering not Shakespeare's intent but one's own prejudices or inclinations. We come to a more objective rendering of her character by applying not personal or moral standards but dramatic tests, by analyzing her role as it relates to the play's developing action. What the *dramatis personae* say of Cleopatra's past is as revealing as what they say of Antony's previous life. While no one ever reproaches Antony for his past, no one ever glorifies Cleopatra's. Whether it is Cleopatra remembering her former days, or whether another character in the play recalls the life she led before meeting Antony, in all instances one characteristic is emphasized: her magnetic sensuality which never fails to catch men in her strong toil of grace. Examining this evocation of her past helps determine her dramatic relation to Antony and to the main action of the play.

Reconstruct, first, what Cleopatra reveals of her own past. When, in Act I, after Antony has left Egypt to return to his duties in Rome, she begins to question what her Antony is doing without her, and wondering whether he is thinking of her, she recalls the power she formerly wielded over men:

> Broad-fronted Caesar,
> When thou wast here above the ground, I was
> A morsel for a monarch; and great Pompey
> Would stand and make his eyes grow in my brow;
> There would he anchor his aspect and die
> With looking on his life.
>
> (I.v.29)

Later, before the messenger from Rome has an opportunity to reveal Antony's marriage to Octavia, Cleopatra tells him that if he brings good news,

> there is gold, and here
> My bluest veins to kiss; a hand that kings
> Have lipp'd, and trembled kissing.
>
> (II.v.28)

In each instance Cleopatra, in referring to her past, calls attention to her captivating sensuality. And she evokes the same thought when Thyreus, sent by the triumphant Caesar to impose his demands on her, would kiss her hand:

> Your Caesar's father oft,
> When he hath mus'd of taking kingdoms in,
> Bestow'd his lips on that unworthy place,
> As it rain'd kisses.
>
> (III.xiii.82)

Each time Cleopatra recalls her past it is to exult in her power to entrance men. For Antony the past is an ideal manhood to be regained; its remembrance measures his fall. Cleopatra's past is a mirroring of her present character. She is now what she was before, passionate, seductive, a woman who revels in her power to entrance men.

Nor is this characteristic altered when others talk of her past. On such occasions, however, the tone is sarcastic or amusingly derisive. After Enobarbus' celebrated description of the first meeting between Antony and Cleopatra, Agrippa makes this jolting comment:

> Royal wench!
> She made great Caesar lay his sword to bed.
> He plough'd her, and she cropp'd.
>
> (II.ii.232)

What a magnificent earthy wench! is Agrippa's view of the queen. He does not idealize her; he praises her sensuality in a realistic manner, and we have no illusions about her character. The same tone prevails when, in the Roman camp at Misenum, Pompey alludes to her past. Bantering with Antony, he praises Egyptian cookery, says he heard Caesar grew fat with feasting there; and then he says of Cleopatra's past, "And I have heard, Apollodorus carried — " which Enobarbus completes, "A certain queen to Caesar in a mattress" (II.vi.71).

Antony's own remembrance depicts Cleopatra in an even more uncomplimentary fashion. To be sure, he is speaking in a rage, having caught Cleopatra entertaining Caesar's messenger; moreover, he is incensed that she would allow the messenger to kiss her hand. Nevertheless, this is the only time we receive from Antony a disclosure of how, before succumbing to her charms, he first regarded her:

> I found you as a morsel cold upon
> Dead Caesar's trencher; nay, you were a fragment
> Of Cneius Pompey's; besides what hotter hours,
> Unregist'red in vulgar fame, you have
> Luxuriously pick'd out; for, I am sure,
> Though you can guess what temperance should be,
> You know not what it is.

> (III.xiii.116)

Nobody has illusions about the queen's character. In mentioning Cleopatra's past, Agrippa, Pompey and Antony deprive her of all radiance and mystery and reduce her to a morsel for men. Thinking of her own past, Cleopatra reveals the motives which still control her actions: fully aware of her attraction, she is the coquette fascinated with her ability to bend great men. What Agrippa and Pompey and Antony say of her former days in no way contradicts what she says of herself.

There would be little value in presenting isolated references to Antony and Cleopatra's past were these not so consistently formulated. Antony must choose between his past and the temptress who would bind him to the present. This collision of opposites gives the play its structure.[19]

While it was once customary to consider *Antony and Cleopatra* a collection of distinctive scenes that had richly textured poetry but were, nonetheless, episodic, shifting haphazardly from one locale to another, recent critics have sought to demonstrate that the play does have unity, and that its structure derives from the opposing values of Rome and Egypt. At this point a brief rehearsal of these views is useful since one critic often contradicts another, and it is essential that we settle the problem of the play's structure, and most of all, the manner in which we go about determining a play's structure.

Harley Granville-Barker, countering Dr. Johnson's assertion that scenes were presented "without any art of connection or care of disposition," has had the greatest influence in formulating the most popularly held view of the action, that "Roman and Egyptian are set against each other; and this opposition braces the whole body of the play, even as conflict between character and character will sustain each scene." [20] Other interpreters of Shakespeare, proceeding from Granville-Barker's perceptive observations on how Rome and Egypt are contrasted in the staging of scenes, have built up an elaborate set of opposing attitudes and values. There are the conflicts between West and East, Mars and Venus, empire and love, duty and love, restraint and indulgence, reason and intuition, earth and heaven, the public world and the private world. Octavius Caesar has been taken to represent Roman stoicism, Cleopatra, Egyptian naturalism, and Antony, of course, the man torn between these two ways of life. Or another variation: Caesar as death, Cleopatra as the life force, and the union of Antony and Cleopatra as love triumphant over death. Cleopatra, as supreme representative of Eastern values, immoral and passionate, has her contrast in the representative of Western woman, Octavia, who is "of holy, cold, and still conversation" (II.vi.131). One of the most thorough presentations of these contrasts is a study by John F. Danby, who views *Antony and Cleopatra* as "an account of things in terms of the World and the Flesh, Rome and Egypt, the two great contraries that maintain and destroy each other. . . ." [21] Mr. Danby does not see the love of Antony and Cleopatra asserted as a "final value"; of the play's ending he has this to say: when the two representatives of vying world values meet, the duplicity of Caesar is pitted against the duplicity of Cleopatra; the World triumphs over the Flesh.[22]

In building such patterns, often provocative and illuminating, the critic misplaces emphasis, warping the proper effect of drama: background is pushed forward to displace the foreground; attention is directed to metaphysical rather than dramatic tensions; complexities of character and action are disfigured in striving for the unity of neatly defined abstractions. "Shakespeare's tragedies," Harry Levin cautions us, "are dramas of physical action and psychological conflict, not ballets of bloodless images or ceremonials for a dying god." [23] If critics can extract from *Antony and Cleopatra* quotations which support all kinds of thematic contrasts, how are we to assess violently opposing judgments of the protagonists and of the play's ending? If, for example, we accept Danby's reading of the play, Caesar impersonates the World; Cleopatra incarnates the Flesh; the World is triumphant; and there is no redemption in the love and death of the two lovers. But S. L. Bethell, presenting his set of contrasts, also draws quotations from the play to substantiate his position and arrives at an entirely different judgment. He presents Caesar as incarnating "the practical reason, or worldly wisdom, with which are closely linked the notions of restrictive morality and political order (Stoicism and the Roman law)" while standing opposite is Cleopatra, "incarnating 'intuition,' the life of the spontaneous affections, with which are linked the notions of expansive morality and aesthetic order. . . ." [24] For Bethell the ending of the play *is* redemptive because Shakespeare, he argues, shows us that "the good life may be built upon the Egyptian, but not upon the Roman." [25]

It is a mistake to seek out the structure of drama in the same way as we trace patterns in a tapestry. The movements of a play, the arrangements of incidents, unfold in time; they are not unalterably fixed in space. Aristotle still provides a most judicious basis for analyzing tragedy, for he stresses unfolding action, properly subordinating elements which reinforce and enhance what is primary, the play's controlling design. His most general definition of tragedy is "the imitation of an action." "The plot," Aristotle tells us, "is the imitation of the action: — for by plot I here mean the arrangement of the incidents. . . . But most important of all is the structure of the incidents. For tragedy is an imitation, not of men, but of an action and of life, and life consists in action, and its end is a mode of action, not a quality." [26] "The plot, then, is the first principle, and, as it were, the soul of a tragedy." [27] By concentrating on what was said of Antony's past and Cleopatra's past, we have already suggested that the plot deals with Antony's endeavor to escape the domination of Cleopatra so that he might regain his glory and once again be the most noble of men. We have not yet considered in detail the structure of the play's incidents, what Aristotle calls "the soul of a tragedy."

3

There are three separations of the lovers in the play, three reunions, and as many indecisive moments when Antony inclines now to Rome, duty, and honor, now to Cleopatra and love. In each crisis Antony alternately rejects and embraces Cleopatra; he realizes his need to renounce her, but each time finds this impossible. Leaving Cleopatra, in the first instance to journey to Rome (I.iii), Antony, it is suggested, does so not because of a strong sense of patriotism, but because Sextus Pompeius, in commanding the sea, has become a threat to his personal power, because there is the danger that the slippery Roman people might at any moment shift their favors to Pompey. We have no great illusion about his enterprise; nor have we any illusion about his ability to regain the past by breaking away from Cleopatra. Shakespeare constructs a succession of scenes culminating in what seems to be Antony's recovery of political power and prestige: reconciliation with Caesar; an expedient marriage with Octavia, its sole purpose to hold the two leaders together; and, finally, a banquet which supposedly celebrates personal amity and political unity. But throughout these events Shakespeare continually exposes to the audience the weakness and imminent collapse of political union, and the inevitability of Antony's return to Egypt. While the scenes range over the world, rapidly shifting from Rome to Egypt to Messina, they are ordered and held to a fixed center. Their unifying function is the uncovering of Roman policy, its demands upon Antony, and the presentation of an opposing claim for Antony's allegiance, Cleopatra's appeal, which we are never allowed to forget or minimize.

The main drama lies in the exposure of vying demands upon Antony; and Shakespeare dispels all illusions about these conflicting interests. Fidelity to Rome involves few ideals. The health of the Roman state, the lives of many depend upon Roman leaders who are shown to be neither good nor just nor heroic. Caesar is grimly politic; he readily agrees to Agrippa's scheme to insure peace with Antony by bartering his dearly beloved sister Octavia. Lepidus is an unthinking fool. Pompey is a man of honor: he would have rewarded Menas for slitting the throats of his three guests and rivals; being done unknown, the deed would have afterwards been found well done, but now Pompey can only condemn such a plan. When Menas determines to quit Pompey's cause, he reveals the hollowness of a world struggle based not on a concern for the state's welfare but personal gain: "Who seeks, and will not take once 'tis offer'd, / Shall never find it more" (II.vii.88).

In the scene aboard Pompey's galley, only Caesar, always resolutely detached from the pressures of the moment, retains a semblance of self-control. Lepidus, a third part of the world, is carried off drunk; Antony calls upon conquering wine to steep them all in soft and delicate Lethe. Finally, the glorious leaders of the world join hands to sing their drunken paean. Around and around go the leaders of the Roman world; and their intemperance, we are made to see, approaches that of the Egyptians. "This is not yet an Alexandrian feast" (II.vii.102), says Pompey. "It ripens towards it," replies Antony. The destiny of Rome is in the hands of the shrewdly politic, the fool, the self-seeking pirate, the weak. Purportedly signalizing harmony, the banquet presages, instead, treachery and disorder.

Shakespeare also presents Antony in such a way that the audience entertains no illusions about his progress away from Cleopatra and back to what he should be. Antony is torn by a dilemma that yields no resolution. With Cleopatra he cannot live as he knows he should; without her, he cannot live at all. The price of love is high; it involves the ruin of strength and the fall of valor. Antony's reason tells him this; but his passions overrule acceptance and he wavers between two worlds, making the worst of both.

To live wholly in the Egyptian world of revels, debauchery and all-consuming love, Antony shuts out the demands of duty and honor. When the practical world threatens to intrude upon his great love and compromise his total absorption, he would, together with Cleopatra, sacrifice all to passion and, if need be, transfer their world to another universe or intone world destruction. "Let Rome in Tiber melt, and the wide arch/ Of the rang'd empire fall!" (I.i.33) is his impassioned answer to a life without Cleopatra. And later, when Cleopatra learns of his marriage to Octavia, she echoes his apostrophe, "Melt Egypt into Nile" (II.v.78), for she faces oblivion without her love. Neither can accept the possibility that a tawdry world can keep them apart, and when all else crumbles, they look to love as refuge, transporting it and themselves out of time and place. Ecstasy or "ex-stasis" is literally the state of being outside oneself and the world. Only new heaven and new earth can measure their love, Antony tells Cleopatra (I.i.17). And like the world's greatest lovers who obliterate logic in the endeavor to achieve through love a transcendental state that defies ordinary human standards, Cleopatra describes her experience with Antony as beyond time and change, associated with all that is perfect and infinite:

Eternity was in our lips and eyes,
Bliss in our brows' bent; none our parts so poor
But was a race of heaven.

(I.iii.35)

While Antony lived, insists Cleopatra, their world did equal the world of the gods (IV.xv.77).

However, when Antony most loves Cleopatra, he is most in chaos. To be free, he must renounce a private experience that hollows his life; he must rebuild his world, repair the damage wrought by Cleopatra, and again be the renowned Antony of the past. Even at the play's beginning, when he learns of the wars brought on by his absence from Rome, he knows the consequences of his continued sojourn in Egypt:

These strong Egyptian fetters I must break,
Or lose myself in dotage.

(I.ii.120)

"Dotage" was the epithet Philo used to describe Antony in the first line of the play. Antony now sees himself as the world sees him; his revulsion equals that of Philo and Demetrius.

When a second messenger arrives to announce the death of his wife Fulvia, Antony repeats his resolve to free himself. And once again he uses the verb "break" which conveys the tremendous effort required for liberation:

I must from this enchanting queen break off;
Ten thousand harms, more than the ills I know,
My idleness doth hatch.

(I.ii.132)

Antony's predicament is much like that of Odysseus who, in his seventh year on Calypso's island, was so torn between the equally powerful demands of judgment and passion that he could not remain on the island, yet could not depart homewards. But freedom, Antony here realizes, exists only in engagement with the world. Unless he regains his manhood and virtue, those qualities which distinguish him above all men, he will be subject to the same judgment Milton's Abdiel rendered to Satan, who would not give himself over to life's highest value: "Thy self not free, but to thy self enthrall'd."

In Antony's speeches of rebellion against Cleopatra he shows that he understands himself and his world. He is not like Lear, a man who had to make a painful journey to discover his true identity. In the exchange with the messenger from Rome Antony appraises his own situation, and his evaluation agrees with that of Philo and Demetrius. He recognizes that his love affair with Cleopatra is not noble and profound — as he maintained in the opening scene — but cowardly and ignoble, an escape from himself and the world. Shakespeare masterfully conveys Antony's searing sense of shame. When Antony asks of the messenger his worst news and is told, "The nature of bad news infects the teller," he quickly replies, "When it concerns the fool or coward" — a judgment he seems to apply to his former self, for he immediately proceeds to renounce his former life, determined, in the future, to face truth:

> On:
> Things that are past are done with me. 'Tis thus:
> Who tells me true, though in his tale lie death,
> I hear him as he flatter'd.
>
> (I.ii.100)

And when the messenger proceeds with his stiff news, relating how Labienus

>   with his Parthian force
> Extended Asia from Euphrates,
> His conquering banner shook from Syria
> To Lydia and to Ionia,
> Whilst —
>
> (I.ii.104)

Antony impetuously breaks in with an unexpected condemnation of himself:

Antony. Antony, thou wouldst say, —
Messenger.   O, my lord!
Antony. Speak to me home; mince not the general tongue.
Name Cleopatra as she is call'd in Rome;
Rail thou in Fulvia's phrase, and taunt my faults
With such full license as both truth and malice
Have power to utter. O, then we bring forth weeds
When our quick minds lie still; and our ills told us
Is as our earing. Fare thee well a while.

(I.ii.108)

Antony's indictment of himself is not called forth by the
messenger's words; it is Shakespeare's way of revealing a mind
so beset with guilt that guilt must be vented at the most op-
portune provocation. Antony, here, has an intellectual understanding of his situation; he knows the debilitating effect of
Cleopatra. But self-knowledge does not guarantee that reason will control the passions. Like Milton's Adam in the
presence of Eve, when Antony approaches the person or the
remembrance of Cleopatra, so absolute she seems, so complete in herself, that authority and reason wait upon her,
and all knowledge falls degraded. Though Antony has resolved to free himself of the queen and return to Rome,
when Cleopatra appears his determination melts. Three times
he acknowledges his subjection to her; each time his capitu-
lation becomes more complete (I.iii.43,68,102).

While duty forces Antony to Rome, even there he is bound
to Cleopatra. In Egypt he attempted to face the opposing
demands of a glorious past and the temptations of Cleopatra;
the conflict ended in the collapse of his will. In Rome he
goes through the same struggle, but makes no progress in
conquering himself or in striving towards his ideal. When
Caesar belligerently condemns his riotous life in Egypt, com-
plaining that this caused Antony's wife and brother to make
war, when he further berates Antony for pocketing his mes-
sages and jeering his messenger out of audience, Antony con-
fesses neglect of his oath to lend arms and aid when required.
He recognizes and judges the consequences of his Egyptian

life: "poisoned hours had bound me up / From mine own
knowledge" (II.ii.90). In response to Pompey's surprise at seeing him in Rome, Antony again spurns his Egyptian life and
hints at a change of allegiance:

> The beds i' th' East are soft; and thanks to you,
> That call'd me timelier than my purpose hither.
> For I have gain'd by't.
>
> (II.vi.51)

But history repeats itself. Just as in Egypt Antony's denial
of Cleopatra swiftly turned to fervent vows of allegiance, so
in Rome renunciation gives way to headlong acceptance.
Admonished by the Egyptian soothsayer that if he stays by
Caesar's side he will doubtlessly lose his spirits and fortune,
for near Caesar he is constantly being overpowered, Antony
suddenly resolves, on impulse, to return to Egypt, though
moments before he vowed to his wife Octavia, "I have not
kept my square; but that to come / Shall all be done by th'
rule" (II.iii.6). The soothsayer's warning is all the excuse
Antony needs:

> I will to Egypt;
> And though I make this marriage for my peace,
> I' th' East my pleasure lies.
>
> (II.iii.38)

By summoning Ventidius and sending him off to take command of the Parthian war, Antony signalizes his withdrawal
from public duties and the abandonment of a military code
whose fulfilment had, in days gone by, earned him world
honor.

In the first episode of separation from Cleopatra and reunion with her, Shakespeare gives Antony the role of im-
potent observer of his own affairs; he is a man who seems to
know what is happening and how his fate is affected, but he
does not articulate that awareness fully. Powerless to act in
a forthright manner, Antony sways with the demands of different occasions; and when he decides to return to Egypt,
that action is really an escape. His point of view does not pre-

vail in these scenes; it is taken over by sentient observers who lend perspective and judgment to his experience; they, instead of Antony, mirror the conflict between East and West, between Cleopatra's charms and the requirements of a soldier's duty. Indeed, before Antony's arrival in Rome we are given two extended appraisals of his current reputation, the first by Caesar, who longs for his return, for he needs his aid, the second by Pompey, who hopes that Antony will remain in Egypt lest he add great strength to Caesar and Lepidus, for "his soldiership," says Pompey, "is twice the other twain." Though rivals, Caesar and Pompey render identical views of Antony. Both praise his past performance as soldier; both judge him according to martial standards and deride his fall from heroic virtue. Caesar castigates the unmanly acts of an Antony who in Egypt wastes the lamps of night in revel, who tipples with slaves and reels the streets at noon (I.iv). Pompey gives a similar picture: of Egypt as a field of feasts where Epicurean cooks and debilitating love tie up the libertine Antony and keep his brain fuming (II.i). Both Caesar and Pompey depict Cleopatra as pulling Antony into ruin; and Pompey prays that "witchcraft join with beauty, lust with both!" (II.i.22) so that Egypt and its surfeitings might hold Antony and "prorogue his honour / Even till a Lethe'd dulness!" (II.i.26).

The repeated framing of Antony's character and actions is the dominant mode of characterization in the first part of the play. Our view of Antony's life depends, for the most part, on the reflections of others. From Enobarbus, that cynical and realistic commentator who constantly sees through people and events, we get a more detailed and convincing analysis of Antony's impulse to return to Cleopatra than we do from Antony himself. His engrossing accounts of the wonderful abandon of Egyptian life, his celebrated description of the first meeting between Antony and Cleopatra and of her immediate conquests, his breathless description of the queen — all these have an important function: they build a vision of a marvelous life which only the insensate would exchange, and of a woman, magnificent and incomparable, whom no man could possibly desert — for long. The dramatic context of Enobarbus' superlatives should be kept in mind, for they are strategically placed immediately after Antony's acceptance of Octavia as his wife, a coldly politic marriage which is openly regarded as the hoop necessary to hold the two leaders together. We get no indication of inner conflict from Antony; but because of Enobarbus' celebration of Cleopatra's charms we do not need an Antony to explain why a man would return to her. And when Maecenas says, "Now Antony must leave her utterly," Enobarbus makes explicit what his previous descriptions have implicitly argued:

> Never; he will not.
> Age cannot wither her, nor custom stale
> Her infinite variety. Other women cloy
> The appetites they feed, but she makes hungry
> Where most she satisfies; for vilest things
> Become themselves in her, that the holy priests
> Bless her when she is riggish.   (II.ii.239)

While Enobarbus' idealization of Cleopatra is not wholly in keeping with the bluff, realistic person he normally shows himself to be, the functional value of his words is here more important than strict adherence to the decorum of character.[28] His presentation of Cleopatra's captivating charms, it should be noted, immediately precedes Antony's decision, in the next scene, to return to Egypt. Shakespeare substitutes external observations for inner conflict. He does this once again, after Antony tells Pompey that he has profited in being recalled to Rome (II.vi.51), and Enobarbus supplies what Antony does not himself unfold, precise motivation for the subsequent return to Egypt. "Octavia," says Enobarbus to Menas, "is of a holy, cold, and still conversation" (II.vi.130); Antony is not; and Enobarbus accurately anticipates the next scene and its outcome: "He will to his Egyptian dish again."

Sympathy involves the projection of ourselves into another person's experience. In having intermediaries interpret and judge Antony, Shakespeare keeps his protagonist at a distance. Since we rarely share Antony's thoughts and reactions, we cannot feel at one with him. Certainly it is strange that Shakespeare chooses to block the direct communication between protagonist and audience, and we can only offer tenuous suggestions to explain the matter. Perhaps it is because the dramatist wants to impart the feeling that in Rome Antony is out of his element, that near Caesar, as the Egyptian soothsayer warned, he loses all vitality. But since the commentaries on Antony's actions continue in Egypt, we are led to infer that Shakespeare is intent on exposing the illusory life Antony would build about himself. Or perhaps, in presenting Antony as a man who has a glimpse into the forces besetting him, but does not as yet understand himself fully, Shakespeare draws away from him to make use of those who can interpret his experience for us and put it in perspective. Whatever the reasons, the repeated analysis of Antony's life by others greatly influences our point of view towards him.

While choric commentators on Antony's actions provide a series of illuminations into his public conduct, stressing that he is not master of himself but bound to the powerful influence of Cleopatra, the alternations of scenes between Rome and Egypt have the same purpose, for they give such dramatic shape to Egyptian attractions as to make Antony's subjection understandable. In the first Egyptian scene, after Antony's departure from Cleopatra, we come to see the volatile appeal of the woman who draws Antony away from honor and empire. Her love is an overwhelming force; without Antony, experience is so meaningless she wishes she might drink mandragora to "sleep out this great gap of time" (I.v.5). She can think only of her Antony; nor will she let him forget her. "Met'st thou my posts?" she asks Alexas; and he replies, "Ay, madam, twenty several messengers./ Why do you send so thick?" (I.v.62) From the numerous messengers who stream back from Rome, having brought her greetings to Antony, she must have continual reports of his every mood and action, even if it means depopulating Egypt to provide enough men for this private enterprise. The love of Cleopatra, we are made to see, cannot be confined; it will reach out for Antony wherever he goes, binding him always to Egypt.

Juxtaposed with Roman scenes dealing with a public duty which can be measured and defined are Egyptian scenes presenting intense private feelings, expansive love which would transcend the shackles of time, place, duty. In setting Egypt against Rome, Shakespeare intensifies an audience's awareness of clashing worlds and values, and dramatizes Enobarbus' conviction that Antony can make no easy or lasting return to public life. Furthermore, Shakespeare externalizes the struggle between Antony's private love and public duty through the contrasted personalities of the tempestuous Cleopatra, a woman of "infinite variety," and the dignified but impotently virtuous Octavia. When Egyptian scenes unfold, the energy of Cleopatra compels admiration. Incomplete without Antony, she chafes at humdrum existence, seeks in nervous despair for diversions — music, billiards, fishing — impatiently dismissing these to dream of Antony. Her actions and words translate her sensual qualities: never at rest, she is always at the height of intense emotion, whether she thinks of Antony, the "demi-Atlas of this earth," or dreams of her past, or, forsaken for Octavia, is the passionate woman, deceived, outraged, led to extremities of violence and sorrow. When Shakespeare presents Egypt and the tumultuous Cleopatra in one scene and immediately follows this with a view of the modest Octavia, there can be no doubt which woman will attract Antony.

4

For many critics Antony's greatness derives from his rebellion against restrictive Roman life: in embracing Cleopatra's love, he rises beyond society, beyond good and evil.

Antony, it is contended, is finally transfigured, as is Cleopatra; he creates through his love a value and a vision which the world is too small to allow.[29] Those who exalt Antony in this manner tend to espouse the cult of love and the sanctity of passion; they point to the lovers' ardor as sufficient justification of all misdeeds. But there are those who do not sympathetically embrace Antony. A. C. Bradley and Arthur Sewell are dissatisfied with him because little rapport exists between protagonist and audience. Bradley does not include *Antony and Cleopatra* with Shakespeare's four great tragedies because the two protagonists do not command unreserved admiration or love; moreover, the play does not satisfy the other condition which Bradley expects of tragedy: that forces which move the protagonists, and the resulting conflict, be of terrifying and overwhelming power.[30] Arthur Sewell, arguing that the basis of identification with characters in a tragedy is moral rather than psychological,[31] asserts that vision "is not discovered by our looking at the world through Antony's eyes," and further, that we do not feel the sins or sufferings of Antony to be ours as well as his, that our reckoning of his character "involves no 'going out of ourselves,' no becoming in and for some other 'being.' " [32]

Pitting one critic against another not only shows widely divergent opinions about the same play but emphasizes the fact that drama is the most social of the arts, that it cannot help but bring into play individual bias and personal moral judgments. While an understanding of the moral vision of drama is important, since systems of value contribute to the binding together of audience and protagonist, we also need objective grounds for subjective predilections, otherwise how can critical judgments be more than arbitrary personal opinions? Dramatic construction, the way the playwright presents his characters, does afford precise knowledge of why audience and protagonist are brought closely together, psychologically, spiritually; or why, on the other hand, rapport between the two might not prevail.

Shakespeare so arranges events that Antony's personality is continually distanced in perspective: his interior life, the revelation of inner being through soliloquy, is rarely the focal point of a scene; instead, we have recurring choric, denunciatory analyses of his actions and his personality. Philo, Demetrius, Caesar, Pompey, and Enobarbus are among those who supply an audience with information about Antony which he himself either discounts or does not fully comprehend; they subject the lovers to incessant comment, constantly directing us to guide our emotions away from them, reminding us, at significant moments, of the judgment we should make. Continually seeing the protagonists from the outside, through the eyes of those who describe their lives, reproduce their dilemmas, define the quality of their actions, we are — until the death scenes toward the end of the play — blocked for the most part from being intimately caught up in their personalities.

The framing of Antony's character and actions, so prevalent in the opening scenes, continues to be of primary importance in the rest of the play. Even before we witness Antony's return to Egypt, we have his character prefigured in much the same way that Philo interprets Antony's actions just before his first entrance in Act I. From Caesar's words (III.vi.1) we are led to anticipate an insolent Antony who has lost all sense of propriety; in Alexandria he has flaunted in the "common show-place, where they exercise" (III.vi.12) his disregard for Rome and for private morality by publicly enthroning himself and Cleopatra, displaying all his illegitimate children, and handing over to them and Cleopatra rule over many lands. When, in this same scene, Octavia appears, more derogatory judgments are hurled at Antony. Believing her husband to be in Athens, Octavia is told by Caesar how wrong she is:

> Cleopatra
> Hath nodded him to her. He hath given his empire
> Up to a whore; who now are levying

The kings o' th' earth for war.

(III.vi.65)

Maecenas reinforces Caesar's judgments as he too denigrates Antony and calls Cleopatra whore. "Each heart in Rome does love and pity you," he tells Octavia,

> Only th' adulterous Antony, most large
> In his abominations, turns you off,
> And gives his potent regiment to a trull.
> That noises it against us.

(III.vi.92)

Because Caesar and Maecenas preview Antony and Cleopatra's Egyptian character the audience has been prepared to compare that view with the actual behavior of the two lovers when the next scene shifts to Egypt. This comparison, whether conscious or not, forces an audience to assume the role of judge, to evaluate the trustworthiness of the prejudiced Caesar and Maecenas.

When the Egyptian scene unfolds, Antony and Cleopatra conform to a behavior already determined for them by Caesar and Maecenas, who stressed the same view: that Antony had given over to Cleopatra all command. This is what Enobarbus says at the scene's opening as he objects to Cleopatra's going to the wars:

> Your presence needs must puzzle Antony;
> Take from his heart, take from his brain, from's time,
> What should not then be spar'd. He is already
> Traduc'd for levity; and 'tis said in Rome
> That Photinus an eunuch and your maids
> Manage this war.

(III.vii.11)

The speech is another anticipation of Antony's character; and when Antony enters, insisting that he will fight only by sea because Caesar has so dared him, his complete loss of judgment, to which Enobarbus has already alluded, is shown to be an actuality. Enobarbus offers reasonable arguments against the sea fight, pointing out that Egyptian ships are heavy, and badly manned, while on land Antony has experienced infantry at his command: to fight by sea is to throw away the best part for the worst. Against the logic of such arguments Antony has no reasoned answer; his impetuosity is immediately conveyed. To Enobarbus' first appeal to reason, he says only, "By sea, by sea" (III.vii.42); to the second, he answers curtly and obstinately, "I'll fight at sea" (III.vii.49).

While Antony shows no understanding of himself, the men about him clearly expound his situation in chorus-like fashion. Their opinions are to be taken as representative, for they include a general, Canidius, a trusted companion-in-arms, Enobarbus, and finally, a common soldier. Each associates Antony's renown with the glory he gained on land. Enobarbus and the common soldier plead with Antony: to venture into the yielding and untrustworthy sea is to renounce the "firm security" of land and reputation and give himself over to "chance and hazard." Antony's impending military defeat, like his moral decline, results from abandoning the heroic virtue of his past to plunge into an unfamiliar element; and Shakespeare brings this into sharp focus by having a common soldier implore his general to follow sage military procedure:

> O noble emperor, do not fight by sea;
> Trust not to rotten planks! Do you misdoubt
> This sword and these my wounds? Let the Egyptians
> And the Phoenicians go a-ducking; we
> Have us'd to conquer, standing on the earth
> And fighting foot to foot.
>
> (III.vii.62)

Antony has so lost his judgment that a low-ranking soldier is impelled to step forward to present a correct military plan. This episode is reversed in the next scene, a brief one, as Caesar, the general, shows complete command of himself and others. Where a common soldier tells Antony what to do, the ensuing scene affords a telling contrast: not a dissenting voice is heard when Caesar shrewdly directs his men not to provoke battle until they have finished the war at sea (III. viii.3).

It is almost as if Shakespeare will not trust an audience to look at an occasion and arrive at independent evaluation; he must reflect its significance in the reasoned judgment of percipient observers. So, at the retreat from Actium, the dissection of Antony's plight by his soldiers guides an audience into judging him and Cleopatra before they arrive on stage. Scarus complains that the world has been lost because of ignorance; and he uses a verb which is wonderfully appropriate for conveying the precise cause of defeat: "we have kiss'd away / Kingdoms and provinces" (III.x.7). He calls Cleopatra "nag of Egypt," likens Antony to a "doting mallard," and gives his final assessment to the whole affair:

> I never saw an action of such shame;
> Experience, manhood, honour, ne'er before
> Did violate so itself.
>
> (III.x.22)

Canidius also serves as chorus to Antony's pursuit of the retreating Cleopatra and the consequent defeat: "Had our general / Been what he knew himself, it had gone well" (III.x.26). But no one can show Antony the way to regain his lost virtue. Those who see his dilemma clearly are but helpless commentators, unable to communicate their knowledge to him; they can only reflect and interpret his blindness, and chronicle his fall. At the end of the scene there is another brief résumé of general significance, Enobarbus' decision,

> I'll yet follow
> The wounded chance of Antony, though my reason
> Sits in the wind against me.
>
> (III.x.35)

Canidius has decided to desert to Caesar, as have six kings; Enobarbus, highly rational — the terms "reason" and "judgment" recur in his speeches — will remain with his Emperor, though all have testified that Antony is not the man he used to be: in the past he shaped his triumphs through his heroic character; he controlled himself and others. What he is now, he is by chance.

Shakespeare repeatedly prefigures and analyzes his protagonists; only afterwards do we see them in the flesh. And when they appear, what they do coincides precisely with what has been previously suggested. At the defeat at Actium, for example, first Antony's character is set in perspective because of the caustic remarks of his men. Then the next scene moves to a close-up view and we hear Antony's own recognition of guilt and despair. Remembering the man he once was, he thinks of the now triumphant Caesar who in the past had no practice in "the brave squares of war," who at Philippi kept his sword "e'en like a dancer" while Antony struck down Cassius and ended the mad Brutus. Thoughts of his former valor and decisiveness make his present ignominy all the more humiliating. And while the horror of his subjection to Cleopatra breaks forth as he berates himself for losing command, offending reputation, and ending in shameful dishonor, his recognition brings no resilient, lasting opposition to the woman who has gained full supremacy over his spirit. Though he realizes, as he has before, his need to renounce Cleopatra, again he succumbs, vindicating the judgments of those who anatomized his character and situation in the previous scene. In a speech which brings the scene to its conclusion, he shows himself hastening back to the sensual Egyptian life in which he is bound to lose himself further:

> Fall not a tear, I say; one of them rates
> All that is won and lost. Give me a kiss.
> Even this repays me. . . .
>   Love, I am full of lead.
> Some wine, within there, and our viands! Fortune knows
> We scorn her most when most she offers blows.
>
>   (III.xi.69)

Surely it is not by chance that Antony's appeal to wine or food recurs in the play, always at a revealing moment. During the banquet aboard Pompey's galley, he calls for more and more wine to steep the senses in "soft and delicate Lethe" (II.vii.115), while Caesar will not give himself over completely to its effects. Never yearning to escape the world, Caesar puts an end to the revels before all make complete fools of themselves. For Antony, food and wine provide escape from tension or constraining duty or the bitterness of defeat. His appeal to wine becomes a characteristic gesture; it offers him a release from his degrading defeat at Actium; and when next he calls for a night of revelry, it too is at a time when he has lost his self-esteem. Having discovered Cleopatra entertaining Caesar's messenger, Antony has the messenger whipped; he rages at Cleopatra for her familiarity; then, attempting to regain his stature, he announces his resolve to regroup his forces and attack Caesar at Alexandria. And he ends with his characteristic proposal:

> Let's have one other gaudy night. Call to me
> All my sad captains; fill our bowls once more;
> Let's mock the midnight bell.

(III.xiii.183)

Before the battle, after moving his men to tears with sad thoughts of death, again he calls out his invitation, "Let's to supper, come, / And drown consideration" (IV.ii.44).

At the beginning of the play Caesar and Pompey criticize Antony's Egyptian revelry because such indulgence is abhorrent to Roman generals who idealize the austerity associated with military bearings. However, in Egypt, where drinking and feasting are taken for granted, such criticism is not levelled against Antony. Only when we see the repetition of his self-indulgence at moments when this constitutes retreat from jarring reality do we recognize that Shakespeare is emphasizing the protagonist's weakness of character. Several references to Antony's excessive drinking are to be found in

Plutarch's *Life;* there is, for example, the statement that "he followed Bacchus: and therefore he was called the new Bacchus." [33] But nowhere does Plutarch suggest that Antony's self-indulgence is an escape from the self. Shakespeare develops such a trait, for it fits the personality of an Antony who knows himself but slenderly. When we read Plutarch's account of Antony's life we see how Shakespeare alters incidents in his primary source to build up Antony's weaknesses in detail, putting more blame on him than on Cleopatra, whom Plutarch continually castigates in the manner of a scourging moralist. Shakespeare makes Antony fully responsible for allowing Cleopatra to go to the wars; Plutarch, on the other hand, removes the onus of blame from Antony by stressing that the Egyptian queen's machinations lead him into following her will. At first Plutarch relates that Domitius persuaded Antony to command Cleopatra's return to Egypt (this is not found in Shakespeare's presentation); then he describes the turning point, which Shakespeare completely changes. Cleopatra, fearing that Octavia would re-establish a friendship between Antony and Caesar, plies Canidius with money so that he will argue her cause with Antony; and because of this strategy, she prevails and participates in the war.[34] In Shakespeare's play Antony alone decides, in a fit of pique, to battle Caesar on sea rather than on land. In Plutarch's account, the responsibility for this decision is attributed to Cleopatra.[35] And while Shakespeare shows Antony as stubborn and thoughtless in replying to those who rationally argue against his plan to battle on sea, Plutarch has a different version, for he places complete blame on a selfish, insidious Cleopatra.[36]

Shakespeare's departures from Plutarch support a view which the play's developing action makes clear: that Cleopatra's overt influence over Antony is less responsible for determining events than Antony's own deterioration of will-power and judgment. "Is Antony or we in fault for this?" (III.xiii.2) Cleopatra asks of Enobarbus after the defeat at

Actium, and he replies, "Antony only, that would make his will / Lord of his reason." The techniques that Shakespeare employs to make Antony's weaknesses transparent explain Arthur Sewell's criticism that the personalities of Antony and Cleopatra "do not lead us beyond themselves." [37] First, there is the prefiguring of characters. In *Antony and Cleopatra,* as in *Coriolanus,* the device of having *dramatis personae* accurately analyze and predict future actions is extensively used. When, in both plays, the protagonists proceed to act according to predetermined judgments, they lose stature, for they are unchanging; they display little freedom to be different from what we have been led to presume. Whether in literature or in life, the possibility of man's change and growth engages sympathetic attention; the glory of man is his capacity to adapt and develop, to confront entirely new situations and in a trial of strength exhibit maturity which excites admiration.

Antony does not confront an occasion which forces him to see himself anew, change, and come to terms with himself and his world. He has so little insight that Shakespeare transfers awareness of personality and events to others, who subject him to choric comment and analysis. This repeated use of external description also accounts for that mechanical, confining quality which Arthur Sewell found to be characteristic of the play's lovers. We see the effect of choric commentary most clearly in scene xiii of Act III where Enobarbus relentlessly expatiates on Antony's actions. From the beginning of the scene, where he serves as *raisonneur,* condemning Antony for allowing the "itch of his affection" to nick "his captainship," until the final speech, where he decides to desert an Antony who has lost all reason, we look at the protagonist's every move from Enobarbus' point of view.[38] In this scene Antony attempts to regain his reputation. Made to feel insignificant in a succession of degrading events, he recalls, in the midst of despair, what he was in the past. Memory gives him strength and dignity, and he tries to hold on to the image of the powerful man he once was. When he is told that Caesar will treat Cleopatra with courtesy if she will only betray her lover, Antony would belie his impotence: he calls Caesar, "boy," and challenges him to personal combat, "sword against sword,/ Ourselves alone" (III.xiii.27). He may delude himself, but Shakespeare does not want an audience to be taken in; and it is Enobarbus who punctures the illusion with taunting asides designed to present the reality which Antony violates by his vain imaginings:

> That he should dream,
> Knowing all measures, the full Caesar will
> Answer his emptiness! Caesar, thou hast subdu'd
> His judgement too.
>
> (III.xiii.34)

The same kind of situation is repeated when Antony discovers Cleopatra entertaining Caesar's messenger. "Authority melts from me," he cries, and he tries to retrieve his worth by invoking his former figure:

> Of late, when I cried "Ho!"
> Like boys unto a muss, kings would start forth
> And cry, "Your will?" Have you no ears? I am
> Antony yet.
>
> (III.xiii.90)

In having the messenger soundly whipped, he would have us believe that he is the mighty Antony of old, commanding himself and others. "Get thee back to Caesar," he tells the messenger,

> Tell him thy entertainment. Look thou say
> He makes me angry with him; for he seems
> Proud and disdainful, harping on what I am,
> Not what he knew I was.
>
> (III.xiii.140)

Antony, who was reared to valor, thinks of a time when his commands were unquestioned, when no man dared cross him, and he tries to speak with his former voice, but it is strangely altered, strident, empty-sounding. Enobarbus will not allow us to believe his utterances, but forces us instead to observe him with detachment. When Antony orders Caesar's messenger to be whipped, Enobarbus' caustic aside, " 'Tis better playing with a lion's whelp / Than with an old one dying," shows us how we must view and judge him at this moment. And though Antony loudly resolves to Cleopatra that he will again be himself, though he boasts of earning their chronicle with his sword, and glories in a vision of being "treble-sinew'd, hearted, breath'd," of setting his teeth and sending to darkness all who would stop him, there is no audience rapport with him, for in the scene's concluding speech Enobarbus exposes these lofty heroic claims as the hollow vauntings of a fool:

> Now he'll outstare the lightning. To be furious,
> Is to be frighted out of fear; and in that mood
> The dove will peck the estridge; and I see still
> A diminution in our captain's brain
> Restores his heart. When valour preys on reason,
> It eats the sword it fights with. I will seek
> Some way to leave him.
>
> (III.xiii.195)

All the techniques of character portrayal circumscribe Antony's personality and destiny; he becomes, not a dynamic figure, but a caricature whose features Enobarbus etches, constantly framing him for our proper assessment. He prefigures Antony at the beginning of the scene, telling us how we should view him when he comes on stage; at every turn he mocks Antony's heroic posturings; and he summarizes, at the end, the import of Antony's every endeavor. All is sham, he tells us; it is impossible to correct Antony's irredeemable folly; and so the wisest act is to leave him to his ignorance and self-destruction. The dramatist freezes Antony in a set of actions which reflect not freedom but paralysis.

Antony does confront conflict: to regain his heroic stature he must overcome Cleopatra's debilitating influence. But only in reverie does he recapture the image of the man he once was. The world to which he nostalgically returns in his memory is the world of absolute manhood; virtue is associated with military prowess; the sword is the means of gaining honor and reputation. Recalling how in the past he cut down Cassius and Brutus, Antony speaks contemptuously of Caesar, who did not manfully wield his sword at Philippi (III.xi.35). The sword is a manifestation of man's ability and worth: "I and my sword will earn our chronicle" (III.xiii.-175), Antony tells Cleopatra. Before his suicide, Antony gathers together remembrances of the wonderfully heroic things he did in the past, and of a world he conquered and established: "I, that with my sword / Quarter'd the world, and o'er green Neptune's back / With ships made cities . . ." (IV.xiv.57).

The repetition of sword imagery also suggests a conflicting force which brings on the loss of manhood, virtue, reputation. In gaining mastery over Antony's sword, Cleopatra destroys his manhood. She corroborates Caesar's indictment that Antony "is not more manlike / Than Cleopatra, nor the queen of Ptolemy / More womanly than he" (I.iv.5), when, Antony away in Rome, she reminisces:

> I laugh'd him out of patience; and that night
> I laugh'd him into patience; and next morn,
> Ere the ninth hour, I drunk him to his bed;
> Then put my tires and mantles on him, whilst
> I wore his sword Philippan.
>
> (II.v.19)

Cleopatra's exchange of garments with Antony and her appropriation of his sword, symbol of manliness and soldierly virtue, signify more than playful hilarity; they point to her dominance over him, and this is made explicit on many occasions. When, before the defeat at Actium, Antony refuses to alter his senseless plan to fight on sea, Canidius delivers this estimation: "So our leader's led, / And we are women's men" (III.vii.70). After the defeat, Antony painfully declares that he has offended reputation, and in his desperation acknowledges the cause: "You did know," he tells Cleopatra,

> How much you were my conqueror, and that
> My sword, made weak by my affection, would
> Obey it on all cause.

(III.xi.66)

And when Cleopatra's fleet yields to the foe at the battle of Alexandria and brings on Antony's defeat, once again he associates his sword with manly virtue and reputation as he calls out to Mardian, "O, thy vile lady! / She has robb'd me of my sword" (IV.xiv.22).

Antony's life becomes a repetition of recurring mechanical gestures. Three times he recognizes that Cleopatra prevents him from fulfilling himself as a soldier; each time, though he knows he should cast her off, he capitulates and embraces her. In Rome he voices thanks for being called from Egypt where poisoned hours bound him up from his own knowledge (III.ii.90); yet he quickly hastens back to Cleopatra. After the defeat at Actium he blames the Egyptian queen for leading him into dishonor, but one kiss from her is sufficient repayment for disgrace (III.xi.70); and when she humiliates him by entertaining Caesar's messenger, though he rails against her intemperance, accuses her of being "a boggler ever" (III.xiii.110), and seems on the point of leaving, her one speech, rhetorical and most unconvincing, completely changes his mind. Again, after his Alexandrian defeat, Antony turns against her, vehemently proclaiming: "This foul Egyptian hath betrayed me" (IV.xii.10). Violent in his condemnation, he calls Cleopatra, "Triple-turn'd whore" (IV.xii.13), "false soul of Egypt" (IV.xii.25), "most monster-like" (IV.xii.36), "witch" (IV.xii.47), "vile lady" (IV.xiv.22). But once again renunciation gives way to reunion.

Each conflict is resolved by the collapse of Antony's willpower; and this characteristic also affects an audience's attitude towards him. In confronting his world, Antony undergoes no change or development; no new possibilities are opened to him, and through him, to the community which is the audience. It is significant that Enobarbus, the *raisonneur*, not Antony, experiences the only conflict which leads to a definite resolution; his self-recognition is the most poignant; and only his death entails moral judgment.

5

The language of *Antony and Cleopatra* is a miracle of the imagination. It can sound the complete range of emotions and impart boldness and strength to the turmoil of passion as well as to the profound mysteries of love. But the rich texture of the poetry opposes the dramatic structure; Shakespeare lavishes his imaginative splendors not upon military values and the ideals which Antony must attain, but upon Cleopatra, love, and the Egyptian attractions he is called upon to renounce. Consequently, those who are dazzled by the incomparable language often celebrate its paean of love and minimize or disregard the unfolding events that chronicle a man's fall.

Cleopatra is repeatedly described in the language of magical wonder; she excels, Enobarbus tells us, even the delights of art, "O'er-picturing that Venus where we see / The fancy outwork nature" (II.ii.205). So it is that the exciting drama inherent in the poetry surrounding Cleopatra competes with the more mundane drama of the play's action: when Cleopatra demonstrates most forcefully the power of her attraction, Antony is at his weakest, he is a woman's man, stripped of the judgment he must have to be his heroic self. While acknowledging the imposing beauty of the language associated with love, we should remember the consequences of the play's action. Antony sees his world demolished; he suffers the betrayal of faith and love; he perceives, however dimly, that he has dishonored Octavia, his loyal soldiers, himself. His fortunes have "corrupted honest men," and his own revulsion is as important to the play's central meaning as the alternative judgment, Dryden's version of a world well lost for love.

Antony and Cleopatra is a puzzle to many because Shakespeare sustains things in perilous balance, so much so that critics have recurringly used the terms "paradox," "duality," and "ambiguity" to describe the complexity of emotions and events. Shakespeare's play world is not unlike the real world. It is a tangled skein; white and black merge; good grows up together with evil almost inseparably. What people do is not always what they know they should do, and there is neither the illusion that the traditional currency of virtue will find conventional reward nor the delusion that evil will of necessity meet with retributive punishment. Opposing values and beliefs are very often held in tenuous balance because they are presented as having equally compelling merit. Shakespeare's unparalleled strength comes not only from the marvels of language but also from his penetration into the bewildering incongruities and possibilities of human experience. Enobarbus, for example, is a cynic who rules his imagination with a soldier's firm logic and practicality, yet he is the one who garbs Cleopatra in the imaginative and lavish language of hyperbole. To serve a master who has lost his wits is folly, Enobarbus argues with himself; but to leave him in such straits is knavery. Enobarbus forsakes his lord because folly is indeed against all reason; unlike Antony, he dutifully follows the path of reason — but his heart bursts. The foolish man of passion proves worthier than the practical man of reason; Antony "continues still a Jove" (IV.vi.28); he is magnanimous.

Contradictions are to be found everywhere in this drama of world power and love; opposites play against one another to form a monumental life-resembling work of art. There is the seeming contradiction of loving one's nemesis, of hating and loving the same person at the same time. There are strange occurrences to be reckoned with: that spiritual grandeur rises out of destruction, that life at its greatest moment is not a thing of joy but of sorrow, that happiness is the state of being well-deceived. And then there is the volatile Cleopatra who is both childish shrew and dignified queen.

"If Cleopatra kindles, she also quenches." This observation by W. B. C. Watkins [39] helps explain, with disarming clarity, why so many people disagree in their estimation of the play's lovers. Pursuing Cleopatra, Antony rushes towards his destruction; yet only in Cleopatra can he find fulfillment. There is the maddening paradox of running for a joy which, being found, torments. And in sonnet 129 Shakespeare depicts an experience that might serve as an epigraph, for the same feelings are made to jostle each other, the sense of passion's enormous vitality, and cutting through this, the savage indignation at its destructive fury:

> Enjoy'd no sooner but despised straight,
> Past reason hunted, and no sooner had
> Past reason hated, as a swallow'd bait
> On purpose laid to make the taker mad;
> Mad in pursuit and in possession so;
> Had, having, and in quest to have, extreme;
> A bliss in proof, and prov'd, a very woe;
> Before, a joy propos'd; behind, a dream.

Shakespeare dramatizes; he does not unknot inextricable strands of experience and separate them to provide a moral lesson that will serve as a practical guide for living. His sonnet ends with the reminder, "All this the world well knows; yet none knows well/ To shun the heaven that leads men to this hell."

The Egyptian queen rouses in Antony a passion that consumes him in frenzy. Like Eve, she embodies the temptation that imperils human destiny. Torn between two contraries — by Cleopatra who paradoxically threatens his manhood, and by military achievement which affords the only means of regaining honor and integrity — Antony recognizes the pos-

sibility of a tragic fall: "If I lose mine honour,/ I lose myself"
(III.iv.22). But he is powerless before Cleopatra; he has neither
the strength to dominate her nor the wisdom to understand
her nature. She is, he acknowledges, "cunning past man's
thought" (I.ii.150), and audiences agree. Few women in literature have called forth so intense and personal a response.
Cleopatra is either adored or vilified. No one treats her with
indifference.

Cleopatra generates enormous excitement, and this accounts for her great appeal. Never passive, her energy is as
boundless in grief as in love. Mistress of infinite variety, she
commands a tremendous repertoire of emotions and moods
to suit all occasions. At one moment her sincerity can be over-
whelmingly poignant — as when she faces the inevitability of
Antony's departure from Egypt. Trying to find words that
will make her tangled emotions felt and understood, she
begins with facts — parting and loving — but facts are hopelessly inadequate:

> Sir, you and I must part, but that's not it;
> Sir, you and I have lov'd, but there's not it;
> That you know well. Something it is I would, —
>
> (I.iii.87)

she breaks off; and groping for that which would explain all,
she reaches truth that is both poetry and illumination: "O,
my oblivion is a very Antony, / And I am all forgotten." Her
"oblivion" is the loss of Antony as well as of speech; without
him life is a senseless void.

But there are other moments when her sincerity is feigned,
when calculation leads her into enacting every kind of pose.
Again and again she becomes the incomparable actress, pro-
ficient in emotional acrobatics. Shakespeare calls attention
to her dominant characteristic in the repetition of "play-
acting" images and allusions. Her predilection for dazzling
show is made quite explicit at the play's beginning when
Antony decides to return to Rome. Enobarbus anticipates

the poses that can be expected from Cleopatra, who "catching but the least noise of this, dies instantly; I have seen her die twenty times upon far poorer moment" (I.ii.144). Nor does her appearance upset his prediction, for we see her direct Charmian to seek Antony and act out a role appropriate to the occasion:

> If you find him sad,
> Say I am dancing; if in mirth, report
> That I am sudden sick. Quick, and return.

> (I.iii.3)

As soon as Antony enters, Cleopatra begins her performance: "I am sick and sullen" (I.iii.13); and she continues to dramatize herself and her emotions, passing from despair to joy, or balancing the two extremes ("I am quickly ill and well, / So Antony loves"), always with enormous presence, always with poetry that presents the exact curve of feeling.

Sometimes it is difficult to determine whether Cleopatra is merely playing a superb role, or whether she is completely truthful; and perhaps one should not make the distinction, for her personality is such that she always gives the impression of playing at life, of being intensely aware of every stance, as if she cannot help but live and die before a mirror. Acting is so much a part of her that at a time of great crisis, when after the Alexandrian defeat Antony seeks her, raging, "The witch shall die," she still attends to the staging of dramatic effects. Accepting Charmian's advice to feign death, she instructs her servant in the precise manner of speaking her lines:

> To th' monument!
> Mardian, go tell him I have slain myself;
> Say that the last I spoke was "Antony,"
> And word it, prithee, piteously.

> (IV.xiii.6)

Finally, her act of suicide is at once the consummate escape from the world and her most accomplished self-dramatization. She carries off her last performance with perfect artistry,

robing and crowning for death, speaking magnificent poetry
in her farewell address.

In Act II, scene v, the repeated allusion to "playing" illuminates Cleopatra's character as well as her relationship
to Antony. While Antony plays at world politics in Rome,
Cleopatra whiles away her time in Egypt. At first she thinks
of playing at billiards, but Charmian is tired; then she would
play with the eunuch Mardian, but foregoes this to play, in
reverie, at catching Antony again:

> Give me mine angle, we'll to th' river; there,
> My music playing far off, I will betray
> Tawny-finn'd fishes; my bended hook shall pierce
> Their shiny jaws; and, as I draw them up,
> I'll think them every one an Antony,
> And say, "Ah, ha! you're caught."
>
>   (II.v.10)

The joy of knowing her own attraction is like no other joy
that life can give; and this explains why, in remembering her
past, she always sees herself captivating men.

When Cleopatra recalls how she playfully exchanged her
tires and mantles for Antony's sword (II.v.22), she makes an
oblique commentary on the drama's central action. The
"playing" incident points to the reversal of sexual roles. In
the past, Antony fulfilled himself by dominating other lands
and people; now, a woman's man, he surrenders himself
completely to another. It is the woman who feels the mas-
culine desire to take possession, and Cleopatra employs all
sorts of stratagems and violence to impose her will on people
and events. While Charmian advises her to give in to Antony,
"cross him in nothing" (I.iii.9), Cleopatra has her own device, "Thou teachest like a fool: the way to lose him." She
knows how to keep Antony bound to her; she knows the
effects a woman can produce with the skilful maneuver of
attraction, followed by sudden disdain. This is made most
apparent after the battle of Actium when Antony loses the
respect of his men and his own self-esteem. His shame turns

to gall at the sight of the queen's subservient behavior toward his enemy's messenger; and yet, no matter how low Cleopatra brings him, he cannot dismiss her. Inevitably the torments of dishonor fall away and rage dissolves into the fearful apprehension, "Cold-hearted toward me?" (III.xiii.158). The thought of losing Cleopatra makes him sweat for her.

However great Cleopatra's appeal, we must question the popular view that Shakespeare advocates the romantic notion of passion's nobility and its power to absolve man from all duty. If we were to concentrate only on the imagery of love, neglecting dramatic context, there would be the danger of extracting Cleopatra's heightened vision of love, so magnificently phrased, to argue that the playwright presents it as life's highest value, more real than society or morality. Shakespeare's dramatic technique in portraying Cleopatra provides substantial evidence that this is not so. The general conclusions about the point of view established towards Antony have equal relevance for Cleopatra, whose actions are also framed by choric commentary: she too is subjected to prefiguring and to analysis by intermediaries. This mode of characterization is designed to make vivid and understandable Cleopatra's tremendous power to influence Antony's decisions. It explains why Enobarbus analyzes Cleopatra's charms and prefigures her wiles. It also explains why Cleopatra indulges in self-exposure, openly revealing to an audience that she will act out a pose to keep Antony bound to her. Because Shakespeare is primarily interested in having an audience understand the conflicting demands upon Antony, we do not become emotionally involved with the protagonists. Cleopatra, we know, is acting, rising, it is true, to magnificent heights, but we become more involved with the effect she has and will have upon Antony.

6

So dazzlingly impressive are Cleopatra's final moments in the play that they have always brought forth excited bravos from spectators and panegyrics from critics. Indeed, many commentators have been so overwhelmed by the ending that they read the play backwards, attempting to reconstruct a consistent characterization so that the final glory of Cleopatra may prevail. Such a reading would maintain that Cleopatra recovers full innocence at her death; that she and Antony are transfigured; therefore, Shakespeare's play is not about corruption and human weakness but the exaltation of love and its final triumph over death and the world. To interpret the ending this way, however, is to distort what we have seen to be the developing action of the play, Antony's attempt to regain his heroic past. It is to reconcile the irreconcilable, for we cannot gloss over Cleopatra's role as temptress, nor minimize the consequences of her preventing Antony from regaining his virtue to become again the wonder of the world, ideal man. Nor can we expunge the treachery she contemplated, her resolve to forsake Antony and yield to the triumphant Caesar (III.xiii.60). Furthermore, even her conduct at the time of Antony's death is hardly exemplary. Indeed, the events approach the point of being ludicrous. Antony bungles his suicide. He is carried to the queen, who looks down at him from the height of her monument. While she laments the misfortune and calls on the sun to burn itself out and cast the world in darkness, she refuses to come down to her lover, lest she be captured. Hoisted up to her, the dying Antony tries to speak a few words of comfort and advice: "I am dying, Egypt, dying./Give me some wine, and let me speak a little" (IV.xv.41). But Cleopatra breaks in forcefully, "No, let me speak"; and what she says is merely the empty and shrill sounding of Senecan hyperbole:

> and let me rail so high,
> That the false housewife Fortune break her wheel,
> Provok'd by my offence.

(IV.xv.43)

In having Cleopatra enact this stock pose of tearing a passion to shreds, Shakespeare is certainly not intent on glorifying her. He makes the queen appear even more vain and self-determined in the final exchange with her lover. In great pain, gasping his dying words, Antony tries to give advice:

> *Antony.*   One word, sweet queen:
> Of Caesar seek your honour, with your safety. O!
> *Cleopatra.* They do not go together.
> *Antony.*   Gentle, hear me:
> None about Caesar trust but Proculeius.
> *Cleopatra.* My resolution and my hands I'll trust;
> None about Caesar.
>
> (IV.xv.45)

Each time Cleopatra sharply contradicts Antony, a departure from Plutarch's *Life*, for there she is persuaded by his speech: "When he had drunk, he earnestly prayed her, and persuaded her, that she would seek to save her life, if she could possible, without reproach and dishonour: and that chiefly she should trust Proculeius above any man else about Caesar." [40]

When Antony dies, Cleopatra is overcome with genuine grief. Because the language of her lament is so beautiful, no one could possibly be insensitive to her despair:

>   Young boys and girls
> Are level now with men; the odds is gone,
> And there is nothing left remarkable
> Beneath the visiting moon.
>
> (IV.xv.65)

She even decides to join Antony in suicide "after the high Roman fashion" (IV.xv.87). But in the next act she is still importuning death in beautifully shaped language, falling rather awkwardly from tragic heights when her treasurer reveals to Caesar her deceit in holding back her wealth. Clearly she entertains the possibility of living on, though Antony is dead.

Cleopatra's shifting moods and emotional acrobatics may testify to her infinite variety, but they do not lend great support to the view that her last moment, magnificent as it is, transfigures her and provides the key to the entire play: the assumption that Shakespeare's final vision is of a love which glorifies man and woman and ultimately redeems them. This judgment is based on a consideration of the play's structure and events. While a change seems to come over the protagonists towards the drama's end,[41] does this result from inner transformation, or is it to be explained by the sudden shift in character presentation and an attendant shift in point of view?

When Antony approaches his death, for the first time in the play all *raisonneurs* fall away; there is neither derogatory framing of his deed nor critical analysis. We see Antony directly, not through intermediaries who would alienate an audience by exposing discrepancies between what he says and what he does or should do. The irony, which has continually been directed at Antony's affirmations and aspirations, fades away; judgment, therefore, is held in abeyance. What Antony now says, we accept at face value. Furthermore, there is no ignominy to tarnish his end. He confronts death with stoic honor and dignity; and those who chorus on his imminent death invest it with solemnity and awe. "The star is fallen," the Second Guard intones. "And time is at his period," mourns the First Guard. "Alas and woe!" is the communal lament. Until this scene, choral commentary, whether individual or communal, provided a commonsense norm to measure Antony's actions. Now the chorus grieves the loss of a great public figure and elevates his stature.

There is a significant change in the way an audience sees Antony; there is no transfiguration. Antony's death does not glorify his love nor make of it the play's transcendent value. His final thoughts do not in any way extenuate his decline and fall; nor do they celebrate his love for Cleopatra. He tells her:

> The miserable change now at my end
> Lament nor sorrow at; but please your thoughts
> In feeding them with those my former fortunes
> Wherein I liv'd, the greatest prince o' th' world,

> The noblest; and do now not basely die,
> Not cowardly put off my helmet to
> My countryman, — a Roman by a Roman
> Valiantly vanquish'd. Now my spirit is going;
> I can no more.
>
> (IV.xv.51)

To have an honorable reputation — this is what matters most. Antony dies with a vision of his best self before him. At the end of his life he does not invoke remembrances of a life with Cleopatra, but a time before, when he was the greatest of men. And he dies with the comforting thought that in taking his own life he shows himself strong and valiant, worthy of the virtue and nobility associated with his former fortunes.

It cannot be said, therefore, that Antony changes. He does not confront an experience that brings about a resettlement of his being. In drawing comfort and dignity from memory, he only repeats what he has previously done on many occasions. What Antony is at his death, he was before. There is this important difference, however: for the first time in the play we are not called upon to judge him; and we are asked to remember his public greatness — but this greatness, we should keep in mind, was of an Antony who flourished before the play began.

Cleopatra also faces death with royal dignity. The fear of a Roman triumph prevails over her fear of death and convinces her to escape the world's great snare. "Know, sir," she tells Proculeius,

> that I
> Will not wait pinion'd at your master's court;
> Nor once be chastis'd with the sober eye
> Of dull Octavia. Shall they hoist me up
> And show me to the shouting varletry
> Of censuring Rome? Rather a ditch in Egypt
> Be gentle grave unto me!
>
> (V.ii.52)

Dolabella confirms her misgivings: Caesar will indeed lead her in triumph, make of her a public spectacle. She thinks of the degrading horror, of mechanic slaves with greasy aprons uplifting her to common view, of being enclouded in the stinking breath of the multitude. And she tells Iras:

> Saucy lictors
> Will catch at us like strumpets, and scald rhymers
> Ballad us out o' tune. The quick comedians
> Extemporally will stage us, and present
> Our Alexandrian revels; Antony
> Shall be brought drunken forth, and I shall see
> Some squeaking Cleopatra boy my greatness
> I' th' posture of a whore.
>
> (V.ii.214)

The words describe what we have already witnessed in the play; we have heard Cleopatra called whore, we have seen Alexandrian revels and a drunken Antony. Her words even describe the present moment, for they are being delivered to Shakespeare's audience by a squeaking boy. The Egyptian queen creates a wonderful illusion: all the play, she would persuade us, has been fictional and cheap; what we are witnessing at this heightened occasion is more real than the play-world. In embracing her own illusions, Cleopatra would have us imagine that she transcends the unreality of fiction, just as she would have Dolabella accept her dream of Antony as fact. "I dream'd there was an Emperor Antony," she tells him: his face was as the heavens, his legs bestrid the oceans, in his livery walked crowns and crownets. "Think you there was or might be such a man" she asks him; and he replies, "Gentle madam, no" (V.ii.94).

For Cleopatra illusions are real and the real enactments of the play are but shadows. Dolabella's gentle rebuke has little effect upon her. Nor does it have too great an effect upon an audience because in these final scenes we become one with Cleopatra, seeing events through her eyes. There is no sharp discontinuity between the Cleopatra of the early scenes and the Cleopatra of the play's finale; she has not undergone any great change in vision or personality. But now there are no caustic commentators who stand about her to prefigure action, guide judgment, or tear aside illusions to uncover hypocrisy or self-deception. It is the radical shift in the point of view established towards Cleopatra that brings about audience rapport with her and helps explain why so many critics have insisted that an entirely new Cleopatra emerges in these last scenes.

Cleopatra's speeches before her death are incomparable self-dramatizations. In commenting on the self-dramatization of Shakespeare's heroes at moments of tragic intensity, T. S. Eliot has suggested that the death speeches of Othello, Coriolanus, and Antony are instances where "*bovarysme*, the human will to see things as they are not," [42] clearly prevail. I would offer a slightly different interpretation: that in general, when Shakespeare's tragic heroes face death, they render their final and best estimate of themselves; they embrace what is most meaningful in their lives. To lose one's meaning, one's status in life, is to be reduced to nothingness — this is the anguish felt by Richard II who, losing his crown, calls for a mirror to see how changed is a face that is bankrupt of majesty. He dashes the glass to pieces because, in losing his status, his face has lost its meaning.

At the moment before death, Antony seeks what is most noble in his life; once again he is in love with his honor, and he finally achieves integrity not through private love but the remembrance of his public worth. Antony's final commitment is to his reputation and his honor. At her end, Cleopatra strives for a comparable vision. She sees herself as wife. Robing and crowning for death, she embraces, with complete sincerity, a self-created dream and is overpowered by it. "Methinks I hear / Antony call," she exclaims; and immediately she translates vision into fact: "I see him rouse himself / To praise my noble act." With self-conscious awareness, as if acting before Antony, seeking his approbation, she terms her deed "noble." "Husband, I come!" Cleopatra calls to him, and then, as if realizing the significance of her utterance, she would consciously elevate herself to noble thought and deed that she might be worthy of the name she has just taken: "Now to that name my courage prove my title!" Whereupon she proceeds to verbalize her determined ascent: "I am fire and air; my other elements / I give to baser life."

An audience, awed by spectacle and superb language, can imagine a Cleopatra suddenly changed in personality, though her own words reveal that step by step she is convincing herself of the role she must enact before Antony. But unlike Antony, she cannot sustain the vision; hers is inspired by a dream; Antony's is the recall of an actual past. When Cleopatra forgets that Antony is watching, she breaks her own tragic spell. Seeing that Iras has died, she hastens to apply another asp, lest Antony "spend that kiss / Which is my heaven to have." The spell broken momentarily, she descends even further from tragic heights as she gloats that her action will thwart the great Caesar:

> Poor venomous fool,
> Be angry, and dispatch. O couldst thou speak,
> That I might hear thee call great Caesar ass
> Unpolicied!
>
> (V.ii.308)

Her instinct to dominate and rule prevails to the end. She made a fool of the first Caesar; she will do the same to the second.

The energy of Cleopatra's thoughts and actions, her infinite variety, compel admiration, "since things in motion sooner catch the eye / Than what not stirs." [43] It is not too surprising that many people have ambivalent feelings toward characters like Dante's Paolo and Francesca, Ulysses, or Milton's Satan. Even when these are condemned, their intensity of desire, of mind and will are often admired. There is, furthermore, the feeling in most men that a life of energy, even the satanic, partakes of nobility. Keats, in one of his letters, affirms this: "Though a quarrel in the Streets is a

thing to be hated, the energies displayed in it are fine. . . ." [44]
Consequently, there is the danger of confusing energy with
moral stature and of so mistaking admiration for approval
that Cleopatra's final moments are wrongly interpreted as a
redemption and a transfiguration which make all previous
conduct of no account. Such a view distorts character and
action in this play. Certainly Antony and Cleopatra achieve
great nobility in death; but the play, after all, is a chronicle
of their lives and an exposure of the illusions they would live.
Neither Antony nor Cleopatra changes identity. Even in
death Cleopatra looks "As she would catch another Antony
/ In her strong toil of grace." Caesar makes this observation
at the close of the play; and he says further:

> their story is
> No less in pity than his glory which
> Brought them to be lamented.

CHAPTER IV

CORIOLANUS

WHILE Hamlet is such a large imaginative creation that critics have repeatedly recast him in their own image, Coriolanus has remained unelusive, for his character is presented so neatly and systematically that very few have given radically differing interpretations. All agree that he is an unsympathetic character, and that chief of his glaring faults is inordinate pride. And yet the play has consistently puzzled critics. A. C. Bradley's insistence on something amiss can be taken as typical: "It may seem a more serious obstacle that the hero's faults are repellent and chill our sympathy; but Macbeth, to say nothing of his murders, is a much less noble being than Coriolanus. All this doubtless goes for something; but there must be some further reason why this drama stands apart from the four great tragedies and *Antony and Cleopatra.*" [1] For Bradley, among others, the source of the play, North's *Plutarch*, explains the drama's deficiencies: it so constricted Shakespeare's talents that "his whole power in tragedy could not be displayed." [2] More recently Professor Campbell has offered another interpretation: [3] that *Coriolanus* has not the structure of conventional tragedy; that Shakespeare, instead of enlisting sympathy for the central figure, deliberately alienates it; and finally, "careful analysis of the play will show how skillfully the political teaching, the central theme of every Elizabethan history play, has been fitted to the satiric form of the drama." [4]

Our concern with the point of view established towards the hero is an attempt to answer the problems posed by Bradley and others on the basis of what Granville-Barker has termed the "physics" of drama, a study of dramatic techniques and the effects produced.

2

The opening scenes of *King Lear* and *Antony and Cleopatra* end with a review of the protagonist's character; the concluding speeches foreshadow the central conflict of each play. Since the first scene of *Coriolanus* ends in a similar manner, we should investigate whether the concluding speeches of Brutus and Sicinius also indicate the themes that will shape the play's structure. At the end of the scene they review what has happened and analyze the hero's traits. Now, notice what insistently preoccupies their thoughts:

> *Sicinius.*   But I do wonder
>   His insolence can brook to be commanded
>   Under Cominius.
> *Brutus.*   Fame, at the which he aims,
>   In whom already he's well grac'd, cannot
>   Better be held nor more attain'd than by
>   A place below the first; for what miscarries
>   Shall be the general's fault, though he perform
>   To th' utmost of a man, and giddy censure
>   Will then cry out of Marcius, "O, if he
>   Had borne the business!"
> *Sicinius.*   Besides, if things go well,
>   Opinion that so sticks on Marcius shall
>   Of his demerits rob Cominius.
> *Brutus.*   Come.
>   Half all Cominius' honours are to Marcius,
>   Though Marcius earn'd them not, and all his faults
>   To Marcius shall be honours, though indeed
>   In aught he merit not.
> *Sicinius.*   Let's hence, and hear

How the dispatch is made, and in what fashion,
More than his singularity, he goes
Upon this present action.
Brutus.   Let's along.

(I.i.265)

Their concern is with Caius Marcius' pride, his worth, and above all, his future reputation. Tentatively we shall offer these observations, to be further tested: that here Sicinius and Brutus indicate the contrasting themes that will shape the drama; that setting the key for the play are not dominating symbols or images,[5] but the concern with reputation and honor, the concepts caught up in the play's reiterated words "noble" and "nobility," "worthy," "honour," "fame"; that in *Coriolanus* Shakespeare submits to searching scrutiny the problem of human integrity, its conception, its worth, how it may be destroyed. That these observations explain the central concern of the play can be shown on dramatic grounds by analyzing the point of view established towards the hero; by noting the interplay between characters, and the playing off of scenes, one against another. However, before proceeding to such a structural analysis, it is best to see how these key terms operate.

3

Troilus' question, addressed to Hector during the controversy over the advisability of retaining Helen in the Trojan camp,

What is aught, but as 'tis valu'd?
(*Troilus and Cressida*, II.ii.52)

is likewise an important concern in *Coriolanus* where opinion and value are also at odds with each other. No less than thirty-five times is the term "honour" voiced in the play, its meaning ranging from reputation, the estimation of a man by society, to be conferred or withdrawn depending upon the transitory opinion of others — to honor as abiding truth, which inheres in truth to oneself. Coriolanus is called "noble" and "worthy" more than any other Shakespearian character, and these terms also sound continuously throughout the play in a wide range of usage.

Most often associated with the terms "honour," "noble," and "worthy" are Marcius Caius Coriolanus' fame, his martial prowess, and his glorious deeds in battle. The following examples, selective rather than exhaustive, provide a partial context for this view:

Volumnia, Marcius' mother, equates honor solely with fame in battle:

> If my son were my husband, I would freelier rejoice in that absence wherein he won honour than in the embracements of his bed where he would show most love. When yet he was but tender-bodied and the only son of my womb, when youth with comeliness pluck'd all gaze his way, when for a day of kings' entreaties a mother should not sell him an hour from her beholding, I, considering how honour would become such a person, that it was no better than picture-like to hang by th' wall, if renown made it not stir, was pleas'd to let him seek danger where he was like to find fame. To a cruel war I sent him; from whence he return'd, his brows bound with oak.
>
> (I.iii.2)

To Volumnia life derives its meaning only from the honors of war:

> *Virgilia.* But had he died in the business, madam, how then?
> *Volumnia.* Then, his good report should have been my son; I therein would have found issue. Hear me profess sincerely: had I a dozen sons, each in my love alike and none less dear than thine and my good Marcius, I had rather had eleven die nobly for their country than one voluptuously surfeit out of action.
>
> (I.iii.20)

Cominius, commander of the Roman forces, would have Marcius' honors, his martial deeds, recognized by all:

> If I should tell thee o'er this thy day's work,

Thou'lt not believe thy deeds; but I'll report it
Where senators shall mingle tears with smiles,
Where great patricians shall attend and shrug,
I' th' end admire, where ladies shall be frighted
And, gladly quak'd, hear more; where the dull tribunes,
That with the fusty plebeians hate thine honours,
Shall say against their hearts, "We thank the gods
Our Rome hath such a soldier."

(I.ix.1)

Proclaiming Marcius' single combat within Corioli's walls,
the Herald calls attention to this honor:

Know, Rome, that all alone Marcius did fight
Within Corioli gates; where he hath won,
With fame, a name to Caius Marcius; these
In honour follows Coriolanus.

(II.i.179)

Officers of the army point to Marcius' honors in battle which
merit the people's unstinting gratitude:

Second Officer. He hath deserved worthily of his country;
and his ascent is not by such easy degrees as those who,
having been supple and courteous to the people, bonneted, without any further deed to have them at all into
their estimation and report. But he hath so planted his
honours in their eyes and his actions in their hearts that
for their tongues to be silent and not confess so much
were a kind of ingrateful injury; to report otherwise were
a malice that, giving itself the lie, would pluck reproof
and rebuke from every ear that heard it.
First Officer. No more of him; he's a worthy man. Make way,
they are coming.

(II.ii.26)

And Menenius would have the nation confer upon Coriolanus honors commensurate to the honors won in battle:

Having determin'd of the Volsces and
To send for Titus Lartius, it remains,
As the main point of this our after-meeting,
To gratify his noble service that
Hath thus stood for his country; therefore, please you,

> Most reverend and grave elders, to desire
> The present consul and last general
> In our well-found successes, to report
> A little of that worthy work perform'd
> By Caius Marcius Coriolanus, whom
> We met here both to thank and to remember
> With honours like himself.
>
> (II.ii.41)

In this pervading attitude honor, nobility, and worth have absolute value, the basis of which, in Volumnia's words, is "deed-achieving honour" (II.i.190). This glorification of valor is found in Plutarch, where valor is presented not only as the greatest virtue, but as that which encompasses all others: "Now in those days, valiantness was honoured in Rome above all other virtues: which they called *Virtus,* by the name of virtue self, as including in that general name all other special virtues besides. So that *Virtus* in the Latin was as much as valiantness." [6] The equation of valor and virtue, so different from Aristotle's concept of *areté* where man's virtue, his excellence or proper function was the use of reason, finds expression in *Coriolanus* at the beginning of Cominius' lengthy panegyric tracing the history of Coriolanus' martial valor:

> the deeds of Coriolanus
> Should not be utter'd feebly. It is held
> That valour is the chiefest virtue and
> Most dignifies the haver; if it be,
> The man I speak of cannot in the world
> Be singly counterpois'd.
>
> (II.ii.86)

It is this particular view of valor as the chiefest virtue that Coriolanus holds for himself. Thus, his attack upon the citizens, after they reverse their approval of him as consul, is based entirely on their lack of noble performance: they neither did service to earn corn, nor did they perform valorously in battle (III.i.119). Coriolanus has a definite code of belief, hence a standard of action and judgment. Since his chief virtue — valor — is equated with nobility, nobility is therefore bound up in his own being, an objective value which is not dependent on unstable opinion but on his remaining true to himself. It is this idea of Coriolanus' valor, his nobility, as a truly abiding objective value that informs Cominius' speech to Marcius before the assembled Roman troops after Marcius has triumphed over the Volscians:

> You shall not be
> The grave of your deserving; Rome must know
> The value of her own. 'Twere a concealment
> Worse than a theft, no less than a traducement,
> To hide your doings and to silence that
> Which, to the spire and top of praises vouch'd,
> Would seem but modest.
>
> (I.ix.19)

But now there can only be a clash between opinion and value. Since honor for Coriolanus depends upon remaining true to himself if he is not to be the grave of his own deserving, his honor must perforce be translated to public acclaim — the voices of the citizens.

While many critics have discussed the role of the citizens in this play, their efforts have been expended mainly in trying to reconstruct Shakespeare's political views.[7] Surprisingly, no critic to our knowledge has shown how Shakespeare uses the citizens dramatically, and in a very particular way — as mere opinion. Over and over Shakespeare associates shifting opinion with the citizens. They are depicted as fickle and untrustworthy; as having no judgment of their own; as incapable of molding any standards of belief or action. The tribunes, Brutus and Sicinius, manipulate the crowd's opinion at will. After Coriolanus is accepted, then rejected, as consul, Coriolanus calls attention to the citizens' incapacity for independent judgment or action when he designates the tribunes as "tongues o' th' common mouth" (III.i.22); using the same figure of speech, he rages against them, "You being their mouths, why rule you not their teeth" (III.i.36). And First Citizen, supporting the tribunes against Coriolanus, lends finality to this characterization of the citizens as incapable of independent thought:

> He shall well know
> The noble tribunes are the people's mouths,
> And we their hands.
>
> (III.i.270)

Throughout the play Shakespeare dramatizes how the citizens are continually led to think and act as others would have them. Consider the opening of the play:

> *1. Citizen.* Before we proceed any further, hear me speak.
> *All.* Speak, speak.
> *1. Citizen.* You are all resolv'd rather to die than to famish?
> *All.* Resolv'd, resolv'd.
> *1. Citizen.* First, you know Caius Marcius is chief enemy to the people.
> *All.* We know't, we know't.
> *1. Citizen.* Let us kill him, and we'll have corn at our own price. Is't a verdict?
> *All.* No more talking on't; let it be done. Away, away!
>
> (I.i.1)

Here the crowd merely picks up the leader's words, "Speak. . . . Resolv'd"; like puppets, the masses unthinkingly mouth their leader's decision. And yet, it must be pointed out that individual opinion is heard when Second Citizen raises his voice in protest. But the mob's gullibility, its habit of picking up the leader's words in mechanical, though excited, repetition, is too frequently presented to be anything but significant characterization:

> *Herald.* Welcome to Rome, renowned Coriolanus!
> *All.* Welcome to Rome, renowned Coriolanus!
>
> (II.i.183)
>
> *Sicinius.* What is the city but the people?
> *Citizens.*   True,
>   The people are the city.
>
> (III.i.199)

Brutus. There's no more to be said, but he is banish'd,
As enemy to the people and his country.
It shall be so.
Citizens. It shall be so, it shall be so.

(III.iii.117)

Aedile. The people's enemy is gone, is gone!
Citizens. Our enemy is banish'd! he is gone! Hoo! hoo!
Sicinius. Go, see him out at gates, and follow him,
As he hath follow'd you, with all despite. . . .
Citizens. Come, come; let's see him out at gates; come.

(III.iii.136)

First Senator.   Strew flowers before them!
Unshout the noise than banish'd Marcius!
Repeal him with the welcome of his mother;
Cry, "Welcome, ladies, welcome!"
All.   Welcome ladies,
Welcome!

(V.v.3)

Conspirators.   Let him die for't.
All the People. Tear him to pieces! Do it presently! — He
kill'd my son! — My daughter! — He killed my cousin
Marcius! — He kill'd my father!

(V.vi.120)

In this last example we see the workings of unstable opinion
in its most acute form. Only a few lines before, the conspirators had pictured the unbridled enthusiasm which Coriolanus engendered (V.vi.51), and now the Volscian mob, in
the wild abandon of a turning moment, effaces its former
fanatical adoration of Coriolanus and would rip him apart.

Or consider the way in which the Roman citizens' opinion
rapidly changes when they hear that Coriolanus is about to
wreak his vengeance upon the city. "When I said banish him,
I said 'twas pity" (IV.vi.140), First Citizen quailingly protests.
And the chant is taken up by Second Citizen, "And so did
I," and then by Third Citizen, "And so did I; and, to say the
truth, so did very many of us. That we did, we did for the
best; and though we willingly consented to his banishment,
yet it was against our will." When Cominius contemptuously
replies to these citizens' shifting opinion, "You're goodly

things, you voices!" (IV.vi.147) his rebuke focuses on a technique of characterization which Shakespeare masterfully employs — the reiterated association of "voices" with the citizens. This technique, so brilliantly utilized in *Coriolanus*, has hitherto been unnoticed by critics.

The initial use of the term "voices" can only be viewed as the introduction of a calculated and significant thematic design by Shakespeare. It occurs at the very moment when Coriolanus, to obtain public honor, is called upon to make an outward show of his nobility, a vulgar and humiliating display he would earnestly forego:

> I do beseech you,
> Let me o'erleap that custom; for I cannot
> Put on the gown, stand naked and entreat them
> For my wounds' sake to give their suffrage. Please you
> That I may pass this doing.
>
> (II.ii.139)

At this point, with Sicinius' reply, the carefully wrought use of "voices" begins:

> *Sicinius.*   Sir, the people
>   Must have their voices; neither will they bate
>   One jot of ceremony.
>
> (II.ii.142)

And in the ensuing scene in the forum the leitmotif of citizens' voices is sounded at the very beginning.

> *First Citizen.* Once if he do require our voices, we ought not to deny him.
> *Second Citizen.* We may, sir, if we will.
> *Third Citizen.* We have power in ourselves to do it, but it is a power that we have no power to do; for if he show us his wounds and tell us his deeds, we are to put our tongues into those wounds and speak for them; so, if he tell us his noble deeds, we must also tell him our noble acceptance of them.
>
> (II.iii.1)

For Coriolanus valor in battle had unique, ultimate value;

it constituted personal honor and nobility; and it was achieved by the individual himself, its worth was not dependent on others. But now, in the forum, public recognition of his worth, in the form of the consulship, hinges on the citizens' opinion. Coriolanus must beg that the citizens' voices give, as it were, sanction to his nobility, "As if," as he says, "I had receiv'd them [wounds] for the hire/ Of their breath only" (II.ii.153).

No less than thirty references to "voices" occur in this scene as Coriolanus goes from one citizen to another, asking, "Your good voice, sir; what say you?" until, the crescendo mounting, he addresses three citizens in a sardonic tone which they will not judge as such until later.

> Your voices! For your voices I have fought;
> Watch'd for your voices; for your voices bear
> Of wounds two dozen odd; battles thrice six
> I have seen and heard of; for your voices have
> Done many things, some less, some more. Your voices.
> Indeed, I would be consul.
>
> (II.iii.133)

Whereupon the citizens give him their voices and proclaim him consul.

Forced to traffic in voices, opinion, Coriolanus has acted out of character: bending to the citizens is repugnant to his conception of his own austere dignity and position. To belong to the world, Coriolanus must repudiate himself. A complete alteration of character is necessary to live in the world of voices and gain its plaudits. What is called for is the stance of the actor or the guile of the Machiavellian; it is to be what one is not; to seem. And Shakespeare effectively brings out this frame of mind by having Coriolanus repeatedly liken himself to an actor playing a role before the citizens. "It is a part/ That I shall blush in acting" (II.ii.148), he tells Menenius when asked to submit to the people's voices. After his elevation to consul, learning that he can now change his humble garments, the idea of acting out of character is fore-most:

> That I'll straight do; and knowing myself again
> Repair to th' Senate-house.
>
> (II.iii.155)

Again, after the people reverse their opinion, Coriolanus further reveals the torments of being false to himself:

> Would you have me
> False to my nature? Rather say I play
> The man I am.
>
> (III.ii.14)

But his mother, Volumnia, would have him adopt Machiavellian "policy," arguing that, "If it be honour in your wars to seem/ The same you are not" (III.ii.46) such policy in peace is no more dishonorable. Again Coriolanus likens himself to an actor who must feign an antic disposition in order to be accepted:

> Well, I must do't.
> Away, my disposition, and possess me
> Some harlot's spirit! My throat of war be turn'd,
> Which choir'd with my drum, into a pipe
> Small as an eunuch's, or the virgin voice
> That babies lull asleep! The smiles of knaves
> Tent in my cheeks, and schoolboys' tears take up
> The glasses of my sight! A beggar's tongue
> Make motion through my lips, and my arm'd knees,
> Who bow'd but in my stirrup, bend like his
> That hath receiv'd an alms! — I will not do't,
> Lest I surcease to honour mine own truth,
> And by my body's action teach my mind
> A most inherent baseness.
>
> (III.ii.110)

This magnificent speech suddenly lays bare Coriolanus' inner being. The contrast between the norm of his comparisons — "throat of war" . . . "arm'd knees/ Who bow'd but in my stirrup" — and what is expected of him reveals the ideal which shapes him: an austere dignity of martial valor. Ver-

bally enacting the dissimulation necessary to have private
honor publicly recognized, he utters the fierce anguish that
sears the spirit forced to play the fool to itself.

Giving meaning to Coriolanus' life is a human dignity
which cannot bend to compromise. "Must I," he cries out to
his mother, "with my base tongue give to my noble heart/ A
lie that it must bear?" And in one of the few soliloquies of
the play, Coriolanus, in dramatizing the conflict that rages
within him, reveals that clash between value and opinion,
truth and reputation, continually aware of the fatal impossi-
bility of reconciling these opposites:

> Most sweet voices!
> Better it is to die, better to starve,
> Than crave the hire which first we do deserve.
> Why in this woolless toge should I stand here,
> To beg of Hob and Dick, that do appear,
> Their needless vouches? Custom calls me to't:
> What custom wills, in all things should we do't,
> The dust on antique time would lie unswept,
> And mountainous error be too highly heapt
> For truth to o'er-peer. Rather than fool it so,
> Let the high office and the honour go
> To one that would do thus. — I am half through;
> The one part suffer'd, th' other will I do.
> Here come moe voices.

> (II.iii.119)

Having traced the general pattern of reiterated key words,
"noble" and "nobility," "worthy," "honour," "fame," we
have focused upon the play's concern with honor as reputation and honor as absolute value. If we abstract from the
main design of the play Menenius' judgment of Coriolanus —
"His nature is too noble for the world" (III.i.255) — then the
drama can be viewed as a fatal conflict between a noble hero
and an ignoble society.[8] To do this, however, is wilfully to
overlook Coriolanus' ignoble qualities which are presented
in great detail.[9] "Pattern" abstractions can be extremely
illuminating. However, in neglecting the dramatic interrela-

tions of character, and the emotions and circumstances of the dramatic moment, this technique can, in its stiff schematism, contradict or distort the meaning developed in the plot of the play. Both the concentration on pattern abstractions and the overemphasis of historical context often neglect, in Matthew Arnold's words, "To see the object as in itself it really is." It is almost uncomfortably naïve to remind ourselves that Shakespeare's drama was a public art; that the plays were written to be performed before people who crowded the Globe to be entertained. Yet such reminders keep one on guard against making too large a breach between the work of art and its medium, completely divorcing Shakespeare's plays from the stage and transferring them to the study, thus translating public art into a very private experience. Therefore, at this point we turn to the dramatic and structural techniques which establish a certain point of view towards the hero of the play.

4

In the first scenes of the Roman plays, *Julius Caesar, Antony and Cleopatra* and *Coriolanus,* the hero is unfavorably prefigured before he appears on stage — sketchily in *Julius Caesar,* more fully in *Antony and Cleopatra* and *Coriolanus.* Now first impressions are always extremely important. Even in life we seldom form a composite picture of a person on first acquaintance, but concentrate, instead, on outstanding features, a snub nose, a shrill voice, deep-set eyes, the wit or logic or silliness of conversation. If the individual we are meeting for the first time has been described beforehand, consciously or unconsciously we shall be making comparisons. These points are equally valid for an audience's first impressions of characters in a play, especially so because the dramatist establishes certain conditions, a context, to elicit a particular emotion and response. And in *Coriolanus* Shakespeare is deeply concerned with the way in which an audience is to view the hero.

The first reference to Coriolanus is striking, the strident shouting of the First Citizen to the mutinous crowd: "First, you know Caius Marcius is chief enemy to the people" (I.i.7). The voices of the citizens shout back confirmation: "We know't, we know't." Presenting Caius Marcius as the scapegoat, the tangible cause of all their troubles, the First Citizen urges his death that they might have corn at their own price and avert starvation. While First Citizen counsels violence to an angry mob, Shakespeare gives his argument understandable urgency: hunger is dramatically a more cogent cause for action than that presented in Plutarch, the oppression by usurers who were favored by the government.[10] When the Second Citizen tries to interrupt and temper the situation, "One word, good citizens," the First Citizen takes these words and juxtaposes them with effective irony: "We are accounted poor citizens, the patricians good." The antagonistic forces are sharply drawn by the First Citizen: the starving citizenry, poor in food and in the estimation of the patricians, and, in opposition, a smug and surfeited ruling class, callous to the pressing needs of the starving (I.i.16). From the almost euphuistic balance of his set prose speech a definite emotional context is established at the beginning of the play, one that is not unsympathetic to the citizens. By repeatedly comparing the desperate plight of the citizens to the unreasonable insensibility of the patricians, the First Citizen highlights the justice of their cause, for the effect of contrast is magnification. His final and disarming protest — "the gods know I speak this in hunger for bread, not in thirst for revenge" — produces sympathy for his cause.

With such a social and political background swiftly presented, attention again focuses on the hero of the play when the Second Citizen asks, "Would you proceed especially against Caius Marcius?" And in the ensuing dialogue Shakespeare sets forth, almost in the form of a debate, a balanced character sketch which previews Caius Marcius in detail.

First Citizen. Against him first; he's a very dog to the commonalty.

Second Citizen. Consider you what services he has done for his country?

First Citizen. Very well; and could be content to give him good report for't, but that he pays himself with being proud.

Second Citizen. Nay, but speak not maliciously.

First Citizen. I say unto you, what he hath done famously he did it to that end. Though soft-conscienced men can be content to say it was for his country, he did it to please his mother, and to be partly proud; which he is, even to the altitude of his virtue.

Second Citizen. What he cannot help in his nature, you account a vice in him. You must in no way say he is covetous.

First Citizen. If I must not, I need not be barren of accusations; he hath faults, with surplus, to tire in repetition.

(I.i.28)

After such a balancing of good and bad qualities an audience must, when Marcius comes on stage, discover for itself the truth about him.

Marcius appears on stage immediately after Menenius concludes his famous parable of the belly and its members to which many commentators on Elizabethan order have pointed as indicating how Shakespeare reflects the orthodox thinking of the age. One might ask, however, whether this speech has a dramatic function in this scene, or is to be regarded merely as a "set-piece" revealing, as some commentators suggest, Shakespeare's own attitude towards the common people.[11]

Menenius' fable of the belly is to be found in North's translation of Plutarch's *Lives*.[12] At this point a study of Shakespeare's source affords an insight into his dramatic technique. If we set up an assertion that whenever possible Shakespeare follows Plutarch, who provided the dramatic plot and well-defined characterizations which could be taken over with little change, then it would follow that any deviation from the source is likely to be deliberate and to reflect Shake-speare's dramatic method.

Of Menenius Plutarch says only that he was "chief man of the message from the Senate"; that he was of "the pleasantest old men and the most acceptable to the people among them"; and that "after many good persuasions and gentle requests made to the people on the behalf of the Senate, knit up his oration in the end with a notable tale." [13] Shakespeare expands such details and hints of characterization and gives Menenius a prominent role as Coriolanus' close friend. When Menenius first appears on stage the two citizens, who have just debated Coriolanus' characteristics, utter views which coincide with Plutarch's assertion that Menenius was of "the pleasantest old men and the most acceptable to the people":

> *First Citizen.* Soft! who comes here?
> *Second Citizen.* Worthy Menenius Agrippa, one that hath always lov'd the people.
> *First Citizen.* He's one honest enough; would all the rest were so!
>
> (I.i.51)

Menenius thus serves as a foil to Marcius. While Marcius is seen as a "very dog to the commonalty," Menenius is regarded, in direct contrast, as one who "always lov'd the people" and who is "honest enough." In North's *Plutarch* the fable of the belly is presented in an undramatic manner. Shakespeare breaks up Plutarch's straight narrative of the fable, converting it into a dramatic interplay between Menenius and the First Citizen so that the speech actually bears out Plutarch's reference to Menenius' "good persuasions."

Menenius' manner of handling the citizens, his wheedling humor and good nature, is calculated to serve as a marked contrast to Caius Marcius' arrogant vituperation. Compare, for example, Menenius' first words in the play:

> What work's, my countrymen, in hand?
> Where go you

With bats and clubs? The matter? Speak, I pray you.
(I.i.56)

with Coriolanus' first words. To Menenius' greeting, "Hail, noble Marcius," there is the curt reply, "Thanks," whereupon Marcius immediately turns upon the citizens and launches into an opprobrious attack, its focus in an image of sickness, conveying the speaker's disgust:

What's the matter, you dissentious rogues,
That, rubbing the poor itch of your opinion,
Make yourselves scabs?
(I.i.168)

Both Menenius and Marcius ask in their first speeches what the trouble is all about — and the particular way of asking individualizes each. Menenius, in questioning, associates himself with the citizens, calls them, "countrymen," bids them in a beseechingly friendly way, "Speak, I pray you." And the First Citizen gives him civil answer. Caius Marcius asks, "What's the matter," but waits for no answer; he immediately attacks the citizens and his language betrays judgment already formulated. Menenius aims at persuasion; Caius Marcius rails. Menenius, calmly good-humored, reasoning, friendly, addresses the citizens as "masters, my good friends, mine honest neighbors" (I.i.63) and when he protests that the patricians care for the citizens like fathers, he receives a reasoned indictment from the First Citizen (I.i.81). Marcius elicits no information from the citizens; he is not interested primarily in finding out the causes of the disturbance. The only words spoken to him are First Citizen's ironic: "We have ever your good word." And Marcius' reply, following so close upon Menenius' handling of the citizens, draws a contrast between the two attitudes towards the citizens and the differing modes of dealing with them, a contrast that will have significant prevalence throughout the play:

He that will give good words to thee will flatter
Beneath abhorring. What would you have, you curs,

That like nor peace nor war? The one affrights you,
The other makes you proud. He that trusts to you,
Where he should find you lions, finds you hares;
Where foxes, geese. You are no surer, no,
Than is the coal of fire upon the ice,
Or hailstone in the sun. Your virtue is
To make him worthy whose offence subdues him,
And curse that justice did it. Who deserves greatness
Deserves your hate; and your affections are
A sick man's appetite, who desires most that
Which would increase his evil. He that depends
Upon your favours swims with fins of lead
And hews down oaks with rushes. Hang ye! Trust ye?
With every minute you do change a mind,
And call him noble that was now your hate,
Him vile that was your garland. What's the matter,
That in these several places of the city
You cry against the noble Senate, who,
Under the gods, keep you in awe, which else
Would feed on one another? What's their seeking?
Menenius. For corn at their own rates; whereof, they say
The city is well stor'd.

(I.i.171)

For Caius Marcius there can be no communication with the citizens; he must always remain above them so long as he passes judgment without understanding or sympathy, for such an act of judgment sets one apart, isolates completely. To him the citizens are "curs," untrustworthy, their loyalty suspect; and the truly great man is deserving of their hate. He turns, characteristically, to Menenius, a fellow patrician, in asking, "what's their seeking?" — and this he does only after delivering his scathing denunciation. The citizens are first pronounced guilty; only after rendering judgment does Marcius wish to be informed.

Other important contrasts set the characters apart and accentuate their differences. Marcius would settle the disturbance with ruthless force:

Would the nobility lay aside their ruth
And let me use my sword, I'd make a quarry

> With thousands of these quarter'd slaves as high
> As I could pick my lance.
>
> (I.i.201)

Menenius has, through cajolery and humor and a fable, already taken a different course of action, and with success, as he points out to Marcius:

> Nay, these are almost thoroughly persuaded;
> For though abundantly they lack discretion,
> Yet are they passing cowardly.
>
> (I.i.205)

And yet Menenius and Coriolanus are alike in their lack of sympathy and understanding for the citizens' troubles. Menenius, like Coriolanus, feels no responsibility for the existing conditions: "For the dearth," Menenius rationalizes, shifting responsibility, "the gods, not the patricians, make it" (I.i.74). Confident in the supreme position of his class, Menenius can only see the mutinous citizens as either "malicious" or full of "folly" (I.i.91) after First Citizen explains their grievances. Moreover, his tale of the belly accomplished exactly what the First Citizen, hearing of Menenius' purpose to tell a "pretty tale," warned against: "Well, I'll hear it, sir, yet you must not think to fob off our disgrace with a tale. But, an't please you, deliver" (I.i.96). The fable has most decidedly fobbed off their disgrace: it glossed over their claims of injustice and asserted the principle that all benefits come from the nobility, that none can derive from the common citizens. In spite of Menenius' intransigent attitude toward the rights of the citizens and his attack on one of them, he never incurs their ire, as does Marcius, for he is not so proud of his patrician status that he would refuse to talk on an equal plane with them.

Even on the concept of order Menenius and Marcius hold divergent views which bring out their respective traits. Menenius had likened the belly to the patrician class; order depended on the due subordination of parts to the whole; and his class assured order and well-being because its natural function was to dispense all rights and benefits to the rest of society (I.i.134). For Marcius, order means power, whose end is not the benevolent dispensation of good but the restraint imposed upon inferior and untrustworthy beings who would otherwise destroy one another. Denouncing the mutinous citizens in his first speech in the play, he reveals this attitude:

> What's the matter,
> That in these several places of the city
> You cry against the noble Senate, who,
> Under the gods, keep you in awe, which else
> Would feed on one another?

(I.i.188)

In Plutarch we find Marcius' surly nature explicitly presented: "he was so choleric and impatient, that he would yield to no living creature: which made him churlish, uncivil, and altogether unfit for any man's conversation. . . . they could not be acquainted with him, as one citizen useth to be with another in the city: his behaviour was so unpleasant to them by reason of a certain insolent and stern manner he had, which, because it was too lordly, was disliked." [14] Shakespeare depicts Marcius as Plutarch describes him but he develops the psychology of character, providing several explanations for the protagonist's recurring snarl, his insolence and lordly aloofness. Shakespeare's Marcius is scrupulously honest but he is honest to himself alone; his sense of responsibility does not extend to others or even to the state. When, in his speeches, he openly invokes power to settle affairs, he betrays this singular concern with his own self. He looks upon the citizens' uprising as an affront both to the principle of power and his own military position, which is a manifestation of that power. When he recounts to Menenius how the citizens prevailed upon the senate to grant five tribunes to represent them, he again shows his concern for absolute power and insists on settling the matter in his own way.

The granting of the petition, he says, made "bold power look pale" (I.i.216); and he ends his account with foreboding:

> The rabble should have first unroof'd the city
> Ere so prevail'd with me. It will in time
> Win upon power, and throw greater themes
> For insurrection's arguing.
>
> (I.i.222)

Through Marcius' speech and through the comments of others, Shakespeare emphasizes the fact that personal rather than public considerations motivate his great services to Rome; indeed, the exclusive concern with personal interests is a more compelling force than national duty and helps explain Marcius' joining the Volscians to war against his own country.[15] Prefiguring Marcius at the beginning of the play, the First Citizen pointed out that Rome's hero fought not for his country but to please his mother and himself:

> I say unto you, what he hath done famously, he did it to that end. Though soft-conscienc'd men can be content to say it was for his country, he did it to please his mother, and to be partly proud; which he is, even to the altitude of his virtue.
>
> (I.i.36)

Though Marcius says he would have no one praise his deeds in battle because he fought, as the others, "for my country" (I.ix.17), the concern with country is never particularly stressed, nor is it ever foremost. Exhorting his troops to follow him into the battle at Corioli, Marcius mentions duty to country last in his catalogue of incentives:

> If any such be here —
> As it were sin to doubt — that love this painting
> Wherein you see me smear'd; if any fear
> Lesser his person than an ill report;
> If any think brave death outweighs bad life,
> And that his country's dearer than himself;
> Let him alone, or so many so minded,
> Wave thus, to express his disposition
> And follow Marcius.
>
> (I.vi.67)

And later in the play, Volumnia, incensed at her son's refusal to dissimulate before the citizens to gain the consulship,
gives support to First Citizen's judgment that Marcius' feats
in war are not for his country, but to please his mother, and
to be partly proud. To her son she bitterly says,

> Do as thou list,
> Thy valiantness was mine, thou suck'st it from me,
> But owe thy pride thyself.

>   (III.ii.128)

First Citizen's judgment of Marcius in the first scene is far
more than a descriptive introductory sketch which enables
Shakespeare to minimize direct self-explanation by Marcius.
It is part of a careful dramatic design, the use of a technique
which Henry James, describing his own devices, aptly termed
"reflector." [16] By interpreting Marcius for the audience, the
First Citizen reflects the central issue of the situation; and
when Marcius arrives on stage and speaks and acts, the situation, in turn, illuminates him. When, indeed, at the end of
the scene the interest turns to the country's defense against
the armed Volsces, Marcius vindicates the First Citizen's
condemnation that his military deeds stem from private
rather than public concern. Hearing that the Volsces are in
arms, Marcius' first response betrays this personal preoccupation.

> *Messenger.* The news is, sir, the Volsces are in arms.
> *Marcius.* I am glad on't. Then we shall ha' means to vent
>   Our musty superfluity.

>   (I.i.228)

To Marcius, then, the war affords an opportunity for personal revenge against Rome's commoners. Shakespeare reinforces and heightens this personal concern when immediately following Marcius' reply to the Messenger, First Senator brings him the same news, "The Volsces are in arms."
At this point Marcius extols the Volscian leader, Tullus
Aufidius, exclaiming that if he were not Caius Marcius, he

would wish to be Aufidius; and were Aufidius on his side in
the war, he would desert to the enemy that he might have
the opportunity of fighting such a magnificent rival (I.i.237).
War affords an occasion for settling private feuds, for en-
hancing his own personal glory. His final speech in the first
scene, a diatribe against the citizens, ill befits a general who
is to lead them in battle:

> Nay, let them follow:
> The Volsces have much corn; take these rats thither
> To gnaw their garners. Worshipful mutiners,
> Your valour puts well forth.
>
> (I.i.252)

Against a background of Rome's political, social and eco-
nomic turmoil Marcius stands forth, placed in the middle
light, the real center of interest in the scene. The emphasis
is on an objective Marcius. The multiple views of the First
and Second Citizens at the beginning, and of the tribunes
Brutus and Sicinius at the end of the scene, are part of an
elaborate and careful construction whose purpose is to frame
his character, subject him to relentless scrutiny. By prefiguring Marcius, the citizens anticipate, hence focus keen attention on, his entrance, his character and action. We first see
Marcius from the outside, as it were; then his own speech
introduces us directly to his inner self without intervening
evaluation. But evaluation takes place, dramatic involvement
is effected, when the audience is forced to relate the picture
of Marcius presented by the First Citizen — a proud hero
whose services and brave deeds result from a concern for
self — to Marcius' own speech and actions. In this way an audience must establish for itself the credibility of the initial
judgment. Finally, there are the recapitulating judgments of
Brutus and Sicinius which take place after Marcius leaves
the stage.

> *Sicinius.* Was ever man so proud as is this Marcius?
> *Brutus.* He has no equal.
> *Sicinius.* When we were chosen tribunes for the people, —

Brutus. Mark'd you his lip and eyes?
Sicinius.   Nay, but his taunts.
Brutus. Being mov'd, he will not spare to gird the gods.
Sicinius. Be-mock the modest moon.
Brutus. The present wars devour him! He is grown
   Too proud to be so valiant.
Sicinius.   Such a nature,
   Tickled with good success, disdains the shadow
   Which he treads on at noon.

                                                        (I.i.256)

As in the first scene of *Lear* where Goneril and Regan and
Kent concur in their judgments of the blind folly that is the
king's, there is in the opening of *Coriolanus* agreement on
Marcius' folly, his pride. It is to be pointed out, of course,
that the tribunes do not render impartial judgment, for
Marcius is their enemy and threatens their political position.
However, Shakespeare establishes a definite point of view
towards the hero of the play. That Marcius is inordinately
proud is a judgment rendered through prefiguring, through
contrast with Menenius, through his own speech, and through
the reactions of those about him.

5

In no other Shakespearian play do the *dramatis personae*
make so many explicit analyses and judgments about the
central figure as they do in *Coriolanus*. "Shakespeare treats
Caius Marcius himself detachedly, as a judge might, without
creative warmth," Harley Granville-Barker has observed:
"Both sides of his case are to be heard. . . . Finally, something like justice is to be done." [17] These incisive comments
illuminate not only Caius Marcius, but the dramatic construction of the play, especially the way in which scenes and
characters are played against each other to put the hero in
proper perspective.

This perspective depends on the balanced view of Marcius
presented in the first scene: a hero who is proud, and yet one
who deserves praise for his deeds in battle. These two ideas

are continually clashing in the play. "You have deserved
nobly of your country, and you have not deserved nobly," is
the way Third Citizen underscores this conflict when Coriolanus asks to be named consul. To Coriolanus' question,
"Your enigma?" Third Citizen points to the disparity between the hero's worth in war and peace: "You have been
a scourge to her enemies, you have been a rod to her friends;
you have not indeed loved the common people" (II.iii.97).
Brutus and Sicinius voice a similar judgment after Coriolanus' banishment from Rome:

> *Brutus.*   Caius Marcius was
>   A worthy officer i' th' war, but insolent,
>   O'ercome with pride, ambitious past all thinking,
>   Self-loving, —
> *Sicinius.*   And affecting one sole throne,
>   Without assistance.
> *Menenius.*   I think not so.
> *Sicinius.* We should by this, to all our lamentation,
>   If he had gone forth consul, found it so.
>
>   (IV.vi.29)

There is a gulf between the estimation of Coriolanus' worth
in war and peace. Coriolanus' own conception of himself is
wholly rooted in the values of war; and in war, where his
private values pertain, he is eminently successful. But his
private values, rigid and exclusively personal, are suspect,
ineffective in peace. In North's *Plutarch* we find in expanded
narrative form the conflict which Shakespeare developed into
a major concern of the play: a man of prowess and great
courage, the most praiseworthy in time of war, who is incapable of fulfilling the political role of "governor" in time of
peace. Plutarch, after recounting the rejection of Marcius'
suit to be consul, gives the reasons why he was "out of all
pacience": "For he was a man too full of passion and choler,
and too much given to over self-will and opinion, as one of
a high mind and great courage, that lacked the gravity and
affability that is gotten with judgement of learning and rea-

son, which only is to be looked for in a governor of state: and that remembered not how wilfulness is the thing of the world, which a governor of a commonwealth for pleasing should shun, being that which Plato called solitariness. As in the end, all men that are wilfully given to a self-opinion and obstinate mind, and who will never yield to others' reason but to their own, remain without company, and forsaken of all men." [18]

While in *Hamlet* and *Lear* the dramatic line of development can be likened to a journey — a journey which the heroes are forced to embark upon in order to discover themselves and the truth about the world they live in — there is no such journey towards painful discovery in *Coriolanus*. The Coriolanus of the first scene is the same Coriolanus at the end of the play. His opinions and attitude undergo no change. And it is Coriolanus' character and disposition which Shakespeare neutrally and dispassionately exposes to understanding.

Consider the function of the scene immediately preceding the battle before Corioli's gates. We are transported to a room in Marcius' house. The action of the play is not advanced in any way, but our understanding of Marcius is. It is the mother, Volumnia, who has shaped Marcius' character, as First Citizen has intimated in the first scene. Thus her talk of honor and fame explains his dependence upon her and the nature of his own values. Moreover, since the very next scene will show Marcius in battle, a deliberate contrast is established between her imaginings of the son's words and deeds in war and his actual performance.

As Volumnia tells Marcius' wife Virgilia, honor is to be prized more than love. Her values, like Marcius', are based entirely on deeds of war; and like her son, she looks forward to battles with an almost sensual delight; she too revels in thoughts of violence, power, blood. She pictures her son in battle:

> His bloody brow
> With his mail'd hand then wiping, forth he goes,
> Like to a harvest-man that's task'd to mow
> Or all or lose his hire.
>
> (I.iii.37)

And her fierce spartan outlook stands out when the gentle
Virgilia, in contrast, recoils in horror at the thought, "His
bloody brow! O Jupiter, no blood!" Whereupon Volumnia,
incensed, reveals her own character, and by indirection, her
son's:

> Away, you fool! it more becomes a man
> Than gilt his trophy. The breasts of Hecuba,
> When she did suckle Hector, look'd not lovelier
> Than Hector's forehead when it spit forth blood
> At Grecian sword, contemning.
>
> (I.iii.42)

One need only compare Plutarch's account of Volumnia
to see how Shakespeare departs from his source and changes
her characterization so that he might use her as a dramatic
reflector of Coriolanus' character. Both Plutarch and Shakespeare attribute Marcius' training to the mother, but Plutarch suggests that the education was faulty and that Marcius
gained success in spite of the deficiencies of his mother's
training. While Shakespeare presents Marcius as mirroring
his mother's sternness, Plutarch ascribes this to his faulty
upbringing.[19] Further, Shakespeare, to explain fully Coriolanus' own concept of honor as an objective value, the heroic
feats of war, has Volumnia make explicit to Virgilia that she
purposefully sent her son to the wars to seek honor. But
Plutarch gives a different interpretation:

the only thing that made him to love honour was the joy he saw
his mother did take of him. For he thought nothing made him so
happy and honourable, as that his mother might hear everybody
praise and commend him, that she might always see him return
with a crown upon his head, and that she might still embrace
him with tears running down her cheeks for joy.[20]

In the play, it is not with tears that Volumnia welcomes her son from the war. While Virgilia fearfully cries out, "O! no, no, no" (II.i.132) when Menenius inquires whether Marcius was wounded in battle, Volumnia proudly proclaims: "O, he is wounded; I thank the gods for't" (II.i.133). Volumnia not only explains and prefigures Caius Marcius' actions in war, she also prefigures his attitude towards the men he leads, even anticipating his very words:

> Methinks I hear hither your husband's drum;
> See him pluck Aufidius down by the hair;
> As children from a bear, the Volsces shunning him.
> Methinks I see him stamp thus, and call thus:
> "Come on, you cowards! You were got in fear,
> Though you were born in Rome."
>
> (I.iii.32)

In the very next scene we hear how closely Volumnia has approximated the tone of her son's speech when he cries out at his retreating troops:

> All the contagion of the south light on you,
> You shames of Rome! you herd of — Boils and plagues
> Plaster you o'er, that you may be abhorr'd
> Further than seen, and one infect another
> Against the wind a mile! You souls of geese,
> That bear the shapes of men, how have you run
> From slaves that apes would beat!
>
> (I.iv.30)

If this scene in Marcius' house were eliminated from the play, the plot would not be affected, for crucial information and action are not introduced. Its functional value is great, however, and its importance can be assessed if we consider what would be missing were it cut from a production. First, the scene has a single compositional center, Volumnia; it has two dominating points of reference, Marcius and war. Viewed through the eyes of Volumnia, nobility and worth, indeed life itself, have meaning only when rooted in the heroism of battle. If we recall Second Citizen's defense of Marcius in the first scene, "What he cannot help in his nature, you account a vice in him" (I.i.42), this scene enlarges our understanding of the remark, for Marcius' character and values are seen in perspective as but a reflection of his mother. The scene also serves to throw Marcius into sharp relief by prefiguring his character and action in war. Everything in this scene has its focus in war; even the recital of the grisly butterfly chase, Shakespeare's own invention, previews the father's disposition in battle. Volumnia's comment on hearing this is: "One on's father's moods" (I.iii.72). And Valeria, using the term "noble" in the very particular way in which Marcius and Volumnia conceive it, remarks, "Indeed, la, 'tis a noble child" (I.iii.73).

In one way this scene is a flashback explaining the force which from childhood shaped Marcius' character. At the same time, mainly through Volumnia's talk of war and her vision of her son's gory progress through battle, the scene projects Marcius' figure into the oncoming encounter at Corioli. Thus, Shakespeare objectively frames Marcius and we are invited to observe him from the outside, comparing the view of Marcius presented in this scene and his actual performance in the scenes immediately following. Forced to look upon the hero in this perspective, an audience is removed from the immediacy of his experience. It is forced to take the role of judge, to verify multiple views of the hero, or mediate between them. Judgment involves suspension of allegiance; it compels an audience to withhold active sympathy, to remain aloof. The audience's position as judge holds true for almost every moment of the play. We rarely enter into Coriolanus' own perspective to see the world through his eyes.

When the scene shifts swiftly from Marcius' home to the battlefield, the same perspective, the objective framing of Marcius, continues. To set forth the military attributes of Marcius which disqualify him as a leader in time of peace, Shakespeare, always aware of the value of contrast, plays off Marcius' words and actions against those of Cominius, his commander-in-chief. In the first attack on Corioli, when the Romans are beaten back, Marcius hurls ugly curses at them (I.iv.31). He threatens to "leave the foe/ And make my wars on you" (I.iv.39). We might remember, in contrast, King Harry in *Henry the Fifth* rallying his troops at Harfleur, "Once more unto the breach, dear friends, once more" (III.-i.1). But more important, we hear Cominius' words to his retreating troops:

> Breathe you, my friends; well fought. We are come off
> Like Romans, neither foolish in our stands
> Nor cowardly in retire.
>
> (I.vi.1)

And we hear, contrasted to the shrill abuse of Marcius, who stands alone, feeling superior to his men, the encouragement of Cominius, who evinces a bond with his men:

> March on, my fellows!
> Make good this ostentation, and you shall
> Divide in all with us.
>
> (I.vi.85)

In the test of battle Marcius finds his proper fulfilment, becomes a giant among "geese,/ That bear the shapes of men" (I.iv.34). Mantled in his own blood, appearing "as he were flay'd" (I.vi.22), he heedlessly ranges among his foes, experiencing all the while a kind of sensual delight, "As merry as when our nuptial day was done,/ And tapers burn'd to bedward" (I.vi.31). His actions are both awe-inspiring and the mark of "fool-hardiness" (I.iv.46) as his soldiers protest when they refuse to follow him into the city of Corioli.

Marcius is a heroic fighter; he is no great leader of troops.[21] He achieves his epic triumph within Corioli's walls single-handed. And the closing of the city gates upon him focuses upon his isolation, the alienation from his troops. Plutarch's Coriolanus, it should be noticed, enters Corioli "with very few men to help him";[22] he is not completely isolated and alone. Marcius' stature, magnified beyond all bounds in battle, points to the difficulties that will be encountered when, in time of peace, to gain an honor which depends upon the people, he will no longer be able to trust in himself alone. His personality presages the struggle he will wage with himself and with the people he despises.

6

Hardin Craig has suggested that the vitality of Elizabethan drama is partly due to the age's intense interest in issues of every kind; that at the time of Shakespeare there was a stir of ideas, a zest for controversy. Consequently, Mr. Craig argued, "It is no wonder that drama flourished, which is itself an art of contest, dialogue and debate, agreement and disagreement." [23] Mr. Craig then proceeded to develop an idea which has relevance to our understanding of *Coriolanus*: that the Renaissance conception of truth "suspends truth, not between hypothesis and verification, but between the affirmative and the negative in debate. In such circumstances truth becomes not a fixed proposition, but a shifting, elusive, debatable thing to be determined by dialectical acumen. . . . It follows also that every question has two sides, and that the acutest minds would habitually see both sides. Now, drama itself, as just said, its debate, and the issues it loves to treat are debatable issues. Shakespeare, the acutest of Renaissance thinkers, has a boasted breadth of mind, an ability to see both sides of a question, and a sympathy with all sorts and conditions of men." [24]

These observations on the collision of opposites are in substantial agreement with Lionel Trilling's concept that the form of a literary work is an idea, and we have an idea when two contradictory emotions are made to confront each other and are required to have a relationship with each other.[25]

When in *Coriolanus* the action shifts from the battlefield to a public place in Rome in the second act, there is a collision of opposites in the form of a debate on Marcius' worth.

Brutus and Sicinius accuse Marcius of many faults, particularly stressing his pride, while Menenius extols his value to the state: "Yet you must be saying Marcius is proud; who, in a cheap estimation, is worth all your predecessors since Deucalion" (II.i.99). A series of such debates recurs throughout the play; all are concerned with analyzing Marcius' worth; all give balancing estimations of Marcius. In the first scene of the play, First and Second Citizens were the first to give such balanced views: First Citizen attacked Marcius for being an enemy to the people, for being proud; Second Citizen countered by calling attention to Marcius' wartime services which benefited the country.

In these debates the balance of praise and blame is always divided in the same way: the virtue of Coriolanus inheres in his wartime service; his vice lies in his pride, his contempt for the common people. Serving as a chorus to an oncoming event, Coriolanus' election to consulship, two army officers discuss the hero with a similar balance of judgment:

> *1. Officer.* Come, come, they are almost here. How many stand for consulships?
>
> *2. Officer.* Three, they say; but 'tis thought of every one Coriolanus will carry it.
>
> *1. Officer.* That's a brave fellow; but he's vengeance proud, and loves not the common people.
>
> *2. Officer.* Faith, there hath been many great men that have flatter'd the people, who ne'er loved them; and there be many that they have loved, they know not wherefore; so that, if they love they know not why, they hate upon no better a ground. Therefore, for Coriolanus neither to care whether they love or hate him manifests the true knowledge he has in their disposition, and out of his noble carelessness lets them plainly see't.
>
> *1. Officer.* If he did not care whether he had their love or no, he waved indifferently 'twixt doing them neither good nor harm; but he seeks their hate with greater devotion than they can render it him, and leaves nothing undone that may fully discover him their opposite. Now, to seem to affect the malice and displeasure of the people

is as bad as that which he dislikes, to flatter them for their love.

2. *Officer.* He hath deserved worthily of his country; and his ascent is not by such easy degrees as those who, having been supple and courteous to the people, bonneted, without any further deed to have them at all into their estimation and report. But he hath so planted his honours in their eyes and his actions in their hearts that for their tongues to be silent and not confess so much were a kind of ingrateful injury; to report otherwise were a malice that, giving itself the lie, would pluck reproof and rebuke from every ear that heard it.

1. *Officer.* No more of him; he's a worthy man. Make way, they are coming.

(II.ii.1)

The officers, anticipating Marcius' appearance on stage, provide a perspective for viewing the hero. Though they discuss his vice, the final judgment, First Officer's, "No more of him, he's a worthy man," is an evaluation which stems from a military point of view. When, however, Marcius is seen from the citizens' viewpoint, though there is a balance of praise and condemnation, the final judgment is inevitably negative. Brutus, tribune of the people, has justification for saying, "we shall be blest" to honor Marcius for his military achievements,

> if he remember
> A kinder value of the people than
> He hath hitherto priz'd them at.

(II.ii.62)

Since Marcius has always despised the citizens, were he to gain the power of consul, his attitude unchanged, he would threaten them and their representatives. Though Marcius is their enemy, Brutus and Sicinius continually qualify their attacks on him by alluding to his martial worth. Speaking to the people after they have chosen Coriolanus consul, Brutus is not treacherous and irresponsible as most critics have suggested;[26] his analysis, from his own vantage point, is quite valid:

Could you not have told him
As you were lesson'd: when he had no power,
But was a petty servant to the state,
He was your enemy, ever spake against
Your liberties and the charters that you bear
I' th' body of the weal; and now, arriving
A place of potency and sway o' th' state,
If he should still malignantly remain
Fast foe to th' *plebeii*, your voices might
Be curses to yourselves? You should have said
That as his worthy deeds did claim no less
Than what he stood for, so his gracious nature
Would think upon you for your voices and
Translate his malice towards you into love,
Standing your friendly lord.

(II.iii.184)

And in other pronouncements on Coriolanus there is also
this balancing of judgment. Brutus affirms that "When he
did love his country,/ It honour'd him" (III.i.304); Sicinius
voices the wish that Coriolanus "had continued to his coun-
try/ As he began, and not unknit himself/ The noble knot
he made" (IV.ii.30). And Brutus' statement,

Caius Marcius was
A worthy officer i' th' war, but insolent,
O'ercome with pride, ambitious past all thinking,
Self-loving, —

(IV.vi.29)

can serve as the prototype for his position. The citizens themselves put forth similarly balanced judgments of Coriolanus:

> *3. Citizen.* . . . if he tells us his noble deeds, we must
> also tell him our noble acceptance of them. Ingratitude
> is monstrous, and for the multitude to be ingrateful were
> to make a monster of the multitude; of the which we be-
> ing members, should bring ourselves to be monstrous
> members.
>
> *1. Citizen.* And to make us no better thought of, a little
> help will serve; for once we stood up about the corn, he
> himself stuck not to call us the many-headed multitude.

(II.iii.8)

Third Citizen's statement, "I say, if he would incline to the people, there was never a worthier man" (II.iii.42), captures the essence of the conflicting judgments on Coriolanus.

Since these views are balanced, their conclusions depending on the speaker's vantage point, on his being patrician or plebeian, or officer of the army, the distinction between the good and evil in Coriolanus becomes shadowy indeed. The ability to distinguish between good and evil is of course predicated upon the concept that there is in the world a core of order. In the worlds of *Hamlet, Lear, Macbeth,* for example, there is a moral order, and its violation can have world-shaking consequences, so all-pervading that the macrocosm itself often reflects the upheaval in the microcosm. In these plays evil can be recognized. There is no final doubt about the villainy of Claudius, Edmund, of Goneril and Regan, or of Macbeth. In the clash between opposing worlds or conflicting emotions there might be temporary equivocation about the course of imminent action; there is no doubt where evil finally resides.

In *Coriolanus* evil is not localized; no single person — neither Brutus, Sicinius, Aufidius nor Coriolanus — is wholly villainous or an exponent of pure evil like the weird sisters, Iago, Edmund. Vice and virtue are so intermingled in Coriolanus that both are at different times judged to be noble. Henry the Fifth observed that

> There is some soul of goodness in things evil,
> Would men observingly distil it out.
> *(Henry the Fifth, IV.i.4)*

And Friar Laurence rounds out the idea:

> Virtue itself turns vice, being misapplied;
> And vice sometime's by action dignified.
> *(Romeo and Juliet, II.iii.21)*

In *Coriolanus* Volumnia and Aufidius take up this same idea: that excessive virtue can become vice; that virtue often must be tempered by the exigencies of the time.[27] Volumnia would have her son use gentle words to the citizens, though these words be "but bastards and syllables/ Of no allowance to your bosom's truth" (III.ii.56). She commends the nobility of his unswerving position, but with qualification:

> You are too absolute
> Though therein you can never be too noble,
> But when extremities speak.
>
> (III.ii.39)

And in a lengthy speech at the end of Act IV, Aufidius, serving as a kind of chorus, reviews all the opinions presented until that point, and holding them in equipoise, still proclaims the greatness of Coriolanus' merit:

> First he was
> A noble servant to them, but he could not
> Carry his honours even. Whether 'twas pride,
> Which out of daily fortune ever taints
> The happy man; whether defect of judgement,
> To fail in the disposing of those chances
> Which he was lord of; or whether nature,
> Not to be other than one thing, not moving
> From th' casque to th' cushion, but commanding peace
> Even with the same austerity and garb
> As he controll'd the war; but one of these, —
> As he hath spices of them all — not all, —
> For I dare so far free him, — made him fear'd;
> So, hated; and so, banish'd; but he has a merit
> To choke it in the utt'rance. So our virtues
> Lie in th' interpretation of the time.
>
> (IV.vii.35)

Upon the interpretation of the time depends the estimation of Coriolanus' nobility. The battles over, the military hero returns to civilian life amidst the cheers of the commoners he has despised and railed against. But in the world of peace and politics he is out of place, for he would still adhere single-mindedly to his own conception of honor based on his service in battle. When he stands before the citizens to ask for the consulship, and First Citizen inquires, "What hath brought you to't," Marcius' answer reveals his own conception of himself, "Mine own desert" (II.iii.71). Citizens and patricians agree that this "desert" or "merit," the nobility of valor, deserves Rome's honor; to do otherwise is to be ungrateful. But the citizens, recognizing his wartime worth, ask more: that he temper his hatred of them; for if he is to be consul he must incline to the people. For the patricians, however, Coriolanus' service is of sufficient value to merit Rome's honor in peacetime. Cominius, for example, after the people have reversed their approval of Coriolanus for consul, says that Coriolanus has not "Deserv'd this so dishonour'd rub, laid falsely / I' th' plain way of his merit" (III.i.60); Volumnia lashes out at the tribunes for their incapacity to judge "fitly of his worth" (IV.ii.34); and when Coriolanus joins the Volscians, Rome's enemies, his rival Aufidius greets him as a "noble thing," and calls Rome "ungrateful" (IV.v.136).

The play therefore deals not only with the clash between the worlds of the military and the civilian but also between opposing conceptions of honor and opinion. In the end, Coriolanus is destroyed by the very trait that made him so great a hero. He gained his stature and worth through individual deeds, honors obtained without the aid of other men. This trait of individual action is purposefully stressed throughout the play. Contemning his men, Coriolanus fought his battles unaided. When the soldiers return to Rome after battle, a Herald makes but a single announcement:

> Know, Rome, that all alone Marcius did fight
> Within Corioli gates; where he hath won,
> With fame, a name to Caius Marcius; these
> In honour follows Coriolanus.
> Welcome to Rome, renowned Coriolanus!
>
> (II.i.179)

Cominius, recounting to all Marcius' achievements in war, calls attention to this single encounter:

Alone he ent'red
The mortal gate of th' city, which he painted
With shunless destiny; aidless came off.

(II.ii.114)

And when, in the final moments of the play Aufidius enrages
Coriolanus with the epithet, "Boy of tears!" (V.vi.101), Coriolanus, bolstering himself, calls to memory his singular feat:

If you have writ your annals true, 'tis there
That, like an eagle in a dove-cote, I
Flutter'd your Volscians in Corioli;
Alone I did it. "Boy!"

(V.vi.114)

Coriolanus stands alone in his self-sufficiency. While the
various debates on his worth and the various analyses of his
character agree on his wartime merit, the multiple points of
view towards the hero's worth in time of peace shift as he is
seen through the eyes of the citizens or patricians or army
officers. In the background are shifting frames of reference;
in the foreground is Coriolanus himself. And it is only by
seeing how Shakespeare has Coriolanus present himself that
we gain a more precise indication of the dramatic point of
view established towards him.

Scrutinizing Marcius' language, we find no progressive
change in the course of the play. Strictly a military hero
whose life is rounded with battles and bloody thoughts, he
recognizes only the values of the battlefield and he views
everything from that vantage point. Never does his speech
betray a radical change in vision. In battle he invokes "Mars"
(I.iv.10) to aid him; he calls upon "the fires of heaven" (I.-
iv.39) as witness to his intent to war on his own men if they
retreat. When he asks a favor of Cominius he beseeches, "By
all the battles wherein we have fought, / By th' blood we
have shed together" (I.vi.56). The battles over, there is no
change from the references of war. The worlds of war and
peace are so fused that even in peacetime he continually sees

the world as if he were still in battle. When his wife tearfully greets his return from the wars, his comment is characteristic:

> Ah, my dear,
> Such eyes the widows in Corioli wear,
> And mothers that lack sons.
>
> (II.i.194)

Dealing with the tribunes, he is incapable of acting in a politic way, as Volumnia and Menenius counsel; he would "throw their power i' th' dust" (III.i.171). After a brief skirmish with the tribunes and citizens he speculates: "On fair ground / I could beat forty of them" (III.i.242). Called "traitor" by Sicinius, he turns again to thoughts of death and destruction:

> Within thine eyes sat twenty thousand deaths,
> In thy hands clutch'd as many millions, in
> Thy lying tongue both numbers, I would say
> "Thou liest" unto thee with a voice as free
> As I do pray the gods.
>
> (III.iii.70)

Again, when he is banished from Rome, he invokes the carnage of a battlefield as he tells the citizens that he prizes their love "As the dead carcasses of unburied men/ That do corrupt my air" (III.iii.122); while his last wish is that they become "Abated captives to some nation" (III.iii.132). Even in the farewell speech to his family after his banishment he has recourse to the imagery of war, asking Cominius to "tell these sad women/ 'Tis fond to wail inevitable strokes,/ As 'tis to laugh at 'em" (IV.i.25). And in a soliloquy before Antium his thoughts are not of the bitterness of exile nor of the anguished concern for justice, but of war:

> A goodly city is this Antium. City,
> 'Tis I that made thy widows; many an heir
> Of these fair edifices 'fore my wars
> Have I heard groan and drop. Then know me not,

Lest that thy wives with spits and boys with stones
In puny battle slay me.

(IV.iv.1)

If there is a truly tragic conflict in the play, it is not within
Coriolanus, but rather, in the conflict of ideas, the clash of
differing concepts of nobility which is the repeated concern
of the debates on Coriolanus' worth. These points of view
illuminate Coriolanus from the outside: now he is seen as
the noblest of Rome, now as the potential tyrant. But Coriolanus himself is as unchanging as his language. Brutus and
Sicinius know his personality so well they can foretell the
details of his downfall. And like a mechanical puppet, Coriolanus acts in strict accordance with their predictions. Sicinius
was quite right in his judgment:

He cannot temp'rately transport his honours
From where he should begin and end, but will
Lose those he hath won.

(II.i.240)

And the remarks of Brutus and Sicinius are absolutely correct
in the analysis and anticipation of future events:

Brutus. We must suggest the people in what hatred
He still hath held them; that to 's power he would
Have made them mules, silenc'd their pleaders, and
Dispropertied their freedoms, holding them,
In human action and capacity,
Of no more soul nor fitness for the world
Than camels in the war, who have their provand
Only for bearing burdens, and sore blows
For sinking under them.
Sicinius.   This, as you say, suggested
At some time when his soaring insolence
Shall touch the people — which time shall not want,
If he be put upon't; and that's as easy
As to set dogs on sheep — will be his fire
To kindle their dry stubble; and their blaze
Shall darken him for ever.

(II.i.261)

When, in every detail, Marcius acts as Brutus and Sicinius predict, he strengthens the idea that he is a mechanical being, that he is incapable of change. He cannot bend to the requirements of political considerations. And it is not accidental that Shakespeare sets up a pattern of "stooping" or "bending" images that are associated with Coriolanus, who is most strikingly likened to a noble tree which is so straight and firm that it cannot bend to external forces, for if it does, it will crack and be torn apart. Coriolanus himself refers to such an image when his mother kneels before him to beg that Rome be spared:

> Your knees to me? to your corrected son?
> Then let the pebbles on the hungry beach
> Fillip the stars; then let the mutinous winds
> Strike the proud cedars 'gainst the fiery sun,
> Murd'ring impossibility, to make
> What cannot be, slight work.
>
> (V.iii.57)

Anticipating what would be expected of him were he to ask for the consulship, Coriolanus tells his mother, "I had rather be their servant in my way/ Than sway with them in theirs" (II.i.219). Third Citizen, using the same metaphor, with its perspective changed, however, sees Coriolanus' bending to the people as the only quality lacking to fulfill his potential greatness: "if he would incline to the people, there was never a worthier man" (II.iii.42). Menenius sympathizes with Coriolanus' reluctance to "stoop to the herd" (III.ii.32) but argues, like Volumnia, that "The violent fit o' th' time craves it as physic/ For the whole state" (III.ii.33).

Rome's enemies, the Volscians, also characterize Coriolanus in the same way. Second Guard calls him "the rock, the oak not to be wind-shaken" (V.ii.117) when Coriolanus refuses Menenius' petition to spare Rome. And after Coriolanus finally yields to his mother's pleas that he not war against his country, Aufidius tells how

He bow'd his nature, never known before
But to be rough, unswayable, and free.

(V.vi.25)

And the Third Conspirator draws a parallel with Coriolanus' behavior in Rome:

Sir, his stoutness
When he did stand for consul, which he lost
By lack of stooping, —

(V.vi.27)

showing how Coriolanus' present situation is related to his past, thus fixing the hero's unbending nature in full perspective.

G. Wilson Knight would have us believe that Coriolanus' bending to Volumnia and the sparing of Rome mark love's triumph over pride and the "metallic world"; that at this moment Coriolanus enlists our total sympathy because he undergoes a change in his entire personality.[28] And yet, looking carefully at this event we must seriously question whether Coriolanus experiences that moment in tragedy when the individual comes to understand the meaning of his plight and his true relationship with society and the universe. When Virgilia, Volumnia, Valeria and young Marcius come to intercede for Rome, Coriolanus attempts to steel himself against natural instinct:

I'll never
Be such a gosling to obey instinct, but stand
As if a man were author of himself
And knew no other kin.

(V.iii.34)

Volumnia asks that he do nothing poisonous to his honor; tells him that he can honorably reconcile Volsces and Romans in peace. When he fails to reply to her entreaties, she too concentrates on his overweening pride which so many other characters in the play have continually focused upon:

> Speak to me, son.
> Thou hast affected the fine strains of honour,
> To imitate the graces of the gods;
> To tear with thunder the wide cheeks o' th' air,
> And yet to charge thy sulphur with a bolt
> That should but rive an oak.
>
> (V.iii.148)

When Marcius does relent, it is not because he undergoes any change of vision; Volumnia does not force him to see the consequences of pride, which has already cost him the consulship and caused his banishment from Rome. There is only his recognition that the act of submission to his mother will be his undoing:

> O my mother, mother! O!
> You have won a happy victory to Rome;
> But, for your son, — believe it, O believe it — ,
> Most dangerously you have with him prevail'd,
> If not most mortal to him. But, let it come.
>
> (V.iii.185)

Once again in this incident Shakespeare's dramatic technique throws light on the character of Coriolanus. Aufidius has already framed this moment for us. In a previous scene (IV.vii) devoted wholly to a discussion of Coriolanus' character, Aufidius had complained that Marcius

> bears himself more proudlier,
> Even to my person, than I thought he would
> When first I did embrace him; yet his nature
> In that's no changeling, and I must excuse
> What cannot be amended.
>
> (IV.vii.8)

In his last words of the scene, Aufidius looked forward to the moment

> When, Caius, Rome is thine,
> Thou art poor'st of all; then shortly art thou mine.
>
> (IV.vii.56)

And when Coriolanus yields to his mother, Aufidius' aside points to the catastrophe which must inevitably follow:

> I am glad thou hast set thy mercy and thy honour
> At difference in thee. Out of that I'll work
> Myself a former fortune.
>
> (V.iii.200)

Aufidius' remarks frame Coriolanus' action and character in the same way that Brutus and Sicinius previously framed him. All three understand Coriolanus completely, while Coriolanus has no insight into himself. They can easily manipulate him to bring about his own downfall. This framing technique has the effect of making Coriolanus into a kind of predetermined, unalterable being.

Twice in the drama Coriolanus rises only to fall. He gains glory at Corioli and falls before the citizens because, in Aufidius' words, "he could not / Carry his honours even" (IV.vii. 36). Joining the enemy Volscians, he again rises to universal acclaim only to fall. In both instances Coriolanus shows an unchanging nature: because of his pride and growing power he is a threat to the authority of Sicinius, Brutus, and Aufidius, and incurs their enmity. In both situations his antagonists praise his noble valor while they plot to overthrow him; and they are assured of his downfall beforehand because they know his unbending nature so well that they can foresee how he will react in a given situation. That Coriolanus' character undergoes no change during the play is evident in a comparison of the scene in which the tribunes goad him into exile, and the scene in which Aufidius incites him to his death. In both scenes the same word — "traitor" — forces Marcius to lose control over himself and brings upon him the hatred of the people. Aufidius goes further, calling him "boy of tears" (V.vi.101). In both scenes, it is important to note, as soon as Marcius' character is impugned, he immediately thinks in terms of violence. To the tribunes and Roman citizens he shouts that he would "throw their power i' th' dust"

(III.i.171); to the Volscians he recalls how single-handed he defeated them at Corioli. And after his banishment from Rome and his death among the Volscians, similar evaluations are made of him: Brutus and Sicinius praise his deeds in war, but point, at the same time, to the danger to all had he gained the consulship. Aufidius and a Volscian Lord call to mind Coriolanus' nobility which deserves mourning, but Aufidius balances his estimation:

> My lords, when you shall know — as in this rage,
> Provok'd by him, you cannot — the great danger
> Which this man's life did owe you, you'll rejoice
> That he is thus cut off.

> (V.vi.137)

7

We have witnessed the acting out of a debate on nobility, honor, worth. We have seen a dispassionate analysis of how the unbending warrior is incapable of fulfilling a role in time of peace. And when death shapes the end we are left with such a balancing of Coriolanus' worth that sympathy and compassion are held in check.

Coriolanus stands as the embodiment of an absolute position; his individuality and his vision of the world are less important than the function he plays in the working out of the drama's ideas. His fulfillment in character, as has been shown, is always in terms of what has been presented beforehand in the form of prefiguring or debates on his worth. Volumnia anticipates his values, his words and deeds in battle; Brutus and Sicinius correctly preview his actions in dealing with the citizens. Even Coriolanus' final yielding to his mother has been dramatically prepared in a careful way, for repeatedly emphasized in the play is his dependence on her. Existing within a framework already fashioned, Coriolanus neither transforms his view of the world, nor our view of him. That Sicinius and Brutus and Aufidius so analyze him that they can anticipate his crucial actions is an indication of the extent to which he has been molded to translate

idea into action — a method of characterization which typi-
fies a play of ideas.

Coriolanus' own perspective is so cramped and so confined
to the concept of martial valor, his emotions so egocentric,
and his knowledge of himself and his world so negligible
that he fails to make an intimate rapport with the audience,
just as he fails to establish a rapport with his own society.
Even in soliloquy — there are only three in the play (II.iii.
119–131; IV.iv.1–5; IV.iv.13–26) — his view narrows upon
himself and never reaches out to touch other human beings
or lead beyond, to a transforming vision.

Almost all critics consider the play and its hero to be un-
satisfying. An analysis of the play's construction, and particularly the point of view established towards the hero, enables
us to understand the technical reasons for this dissatisfaction.
In *Coriolanus* Shakespeare was concerned with what happens
to a particular man, not with what happens within that man.
We watch, as from a distance, the way the world goes. We
look at Coriolanus through the eyes of those who analyze his
actions, so that we are continually put in the position of
judging and evaluating him. Arthur Sewell has suggested a
most appropriate gloss on *Coriolanus,* Ulysses' words to
Achilles in *Troilus and Cressida:*

> . . . no man is the lord of anything,
> Though in and of him there be much consisting,
> Till he communicate his parts to others;
> Nor doth he of himself know them for aught,
> Till he behold them form'd in the applause
> Where they're extended; who, like an arch, reverberates
> The voice again; or, like a gate of steel,
> Fronting the sun, receives and renders back
> His figure and his heat.

CHAPTER V

CONCLUSION

SHAKESPEARE usually gives his audience a view of what the tragic hero's personality was like before his world began to fall apart. Ophelia, confronting a tortured and dishevelled Hamlet, grieves that the "expectancy and rose of the fair state, / The glass of fashion and the mould of form" should be transformed into a being whose "noble and most sovereign reason" is jangled and out of tune (III.i. 158). Recalling the vision of Hamlet's perfections, she poignantly reminds us of the ideal man who would have flourished had some terrible occasion not intervened. And when the players visit the court of Denmark we gain a further insight into what the hero was like before disintegration began. We see Hamlet as scholar and courtier and man of action. He displays a thorough and sensitive understanding of the theater; he renders the courtesies due to guests at court; above all, we see a Hamlet capable of decisive action: he has the intelligence and the disposition to direct others purposefully; he has the talent for composing a play to catch the conscience of the king.

In *Othello*, also, there is presented a vision of ideal man, the heroic soldier "whom passion could not shake." But Lodovico comes upon an Othello overcome with rage, sees him strike Desdemona, hears him call out his disgust at a world of lascivious animals, "Goats and monkeys!" Completely corrupted by Iago, Othello even assimilates his view that the world is bestial and diseased. And it is at this point in the play that the startled Lodovico highlights for an audience the disparity between the Othello he once knew, ideal man, and the fallen figure he now sees:

> Is this the noble Moor whom our full Senate
> Call all in all sufficient? Is this the nature
> Whom passion could not shake? Whose solid virtue
> The shot of accident nor dart of chance
> Could neither graze nor pierce?

(IV.i.275)

In the tragedies Shakespeare clearly defines a standard of excellence. Hamlet, Othello, and Macbeth fall away from the image of what ideal man should be; Lear grows into that ideal. Antony, once the greatest of men, can return to the world of absolute manhood only through remembrance. Coriolanus, who achieves perfect virtue in war, cannot live successfully in time of peace.

Why, we might ask, does Shakespeare so often show us the hero as ideal man, and in violent juxtaposition, the hero as fallen man? A simple answer is to point to the tradition of *De Casibus* tragedy and say that the dramatist, by means of contrast, makes us intensely aware of the great height from which the hero has fallen. Certainly in *Hamlet*, as Ophelia laments, we have the fall of a man from great height: "'T' have seen what I have seen, see what I see!" (III.i.169) is her cry of despair. What is stressed, however, is not merely the fall from prosperity and high estate; these are outward and secondary considerations. Something more profound is involved finally, and Herman Melville aptly describes this in his own way: "man, in the ideal, is so noble and so sparkling, such a grand and glowing creature, that over any ignominious blemish in him all his fellows should run to throw their costliest robes." [1] What is emphasized in *Hamlet*, as well as in *Othello*, is this idea: that perfection, that the rose, is being cankered. Hamlet, Ophelia says, was the "expectancy and rose of the fair state." Lodovico, Desdemona — even Emilia — remember Othello as the noble and dignified paragon of men and are appalled to see him reduced to the level of a beast. In Hamlet and Othello and Lear we have the image of ideal man; for society's well-being we would wish that great potentiality to be realized. For our own sake we would see Hamlet grow into perfection, Lear live with his new-found truth and love, because in them an audience apprehends that image of the ideal of which it yearns to be part.

King Lear acquires an identity; Macbeth loses his humanity and descends to the bestial. One journeys to find himself, the other, to lose himself. In both plays, however, an audience sees events primarily from within the protagonist's own consciousness. This is true neither of *Antony and Cleopatra* nor of *Coriolanus,* where our view of the protagonists is primarily from without, through the eyes of *raisonneurs* who subject them to relentless analysis. Because Antony, Cleopatra, and Coriolanus have little insight into themselves, commentators provide the understanding they lack. There is another reason why an external point of view prevails in these plays: absolute value does not inhere in the protagonists; the values are imposed by *raisonneurs.* This becomes strikingly apparent in *Macbeth* where there is a pronounced shift in point of view when the protagonist ceases to project his recognition of what his true conduct should be, when he becomes hardened in evil and there is no longer inner conflict between right and wrong. Then we have a distancing of his personality; *raisonneurs* hold up standards of action and provide moral judgment.

A study of the point of view in Shakespeare's plays leads to an objective understanding of character and structure; above all, it explains the kind of rapport that will exist between actor and spectator. When we view character from without, we are concerned not so much with a private inner life as with public life and the world's opinion. And when the protagonist does not develop insight into himself and his world, when others expose his situation for our understanding, an audience feels little identification or compassion, for judgment engenders superiority and moral detachment. Furthermore, what is missing in *Antony and Cleopatra,* in *Coriolanus,* and in the final scenes of *Macbeth* is the sense that despite all outward differences the inner world of one individual is akin to the inner world of all. A particular personality cannot effect rapport between audience and protagonist, only an experience which is universal; and all men share a spiritual realm which has no localized time or place.

King Lear is Shakespeare's greatest tragedy because it is most universal. Lear grows into a perfection that has little relation to the personal authority or costly trappings of kingship. When he identifies himself with the natural community, enlisting an audience in the defense of a dignity and humanity common to all, he commands his greatest respect. Undergoing what Keats calls the "provings and alterations and perfectionings" in "a World of Pains and troubles," he schools the "intelligence," acquires "identity," and becomes a "soul." [2] Spectators of the drama, sharing his torments and his point of view, become participants in a ceremony of innocence: an attempt to re-create a state of bliss, to transcend a personal life and realize its ideal. It is inherent in the human condition that man's vision exceeds his deeds. Since man is finite and imperfect and continually fashions for himself a heroic image which would deny his insignificance, does an audience not feel the loss of its own potential perfection with Lear's death? But there is, at the same time, an awareness that perfection can be realized, though its cost be enormous.

NOTES

CHAPTER I: KING LEAR

1. M. Steeven Guazzo, in *The Civile Conversation*, trans. George Pettie (London, 1581), II, 47, exhorts the courtier that Princes are "Gods on earth," and to "call into question their dooinges, is nothing else, but with the Gyants, to lay siege to heaven." Hence the courtier is called upon to give the Prince "the love, fidelitie, diligence, and reverence, whiche is due to Princes"; the Prince being "a God on earth, it behoveth him to doe him honoure as to a sacred thing" (III, 55–56). William Baldwin, in his dedication "To the nobilitye and all other in office" in *The Mirror for Magistrates*, ed. Lily B. Campbell (Cambridge, England, 1938), p. 65, asserted a view that had widespread acceptance; that a king governs "Gods owne office" and "therefore hath God established it with the chiefest name, honoring & calling Kinges, & all officers vnder them by his owne name, Gods." King James, indeed, vigorously espoused such doctrines, boldly asserting the divine right of kings: that no subject had the right to question the justice of any royal act "for Kings are not onely God's Lieutenants vpon earth, and sit vpon Gods throne, but euen by God himselfe they are called Gods. . . . That as to dispute what God may doe is Blasphemie . . . So is it sedition in Subiects, to dispute what a King may do in height of his power" (*Political Works of James I*, ed. Charles H. McIlwain, Cambridge, Mass., 1918, pp. 307, 310). Bacon, in his fragmentary "Essay of a King," also voiced the idea that "A King is a mortal God on Earth, unto whom the living God hath lent his own name as a great honour" (*Works of Francis Bacon*, ed. James Spedding, Robert L. Ellis, Douglas D. Heath, London, 1861, VI, 595). For a detailed presentation of the divine right of kings in England as well as France, see J. W. Allen, *A History of Political Thought in the Sixteenth Century* (London, 1941). See also, Ruth L. Anderson, "Kingship in Renaissance Drama," *Studies in Philology*, 41: 136–155 (1944).

2. For discussions of Elizabethan order, see Alfred Harbage, *Shakespeare and the Rival Traditions* (New York, 1952), pp. 133–185; Theodore Spencer, *Shakespeare and the Nature of Man* (New York, 1955), pp. 1–92; E. M. W. Tillyard, *The Elizabethan World Picture* (New York, 1944).

3. Pierre de La Primaudaye, *The French Academie*, trans. T. B[owes] (London, 1602), pp. 494, 501, 507.

4. *Shakespeare and the Popular Dramatic Tradition* (London, 1944), p. 71.

5. Charles Lamb, "On the Tragedies of Shakespeare," in *Shakespeare Criticism: A Selection*, ed. D. Nichol Smith (London, 1949), pp. 204–205.

6. *Shakespeare's Tragic Heroes: Slaves of Passion* (New York, 1952), p. 189.

7. *The Wheel of Fire* (London, 1954), pp. 172, 162.

8. *This Great Stage: Image and Structure in King Lear* (Baton Rouge, 1948), p. 86. Such pattern abstractions, while at times illuminating, often neglect dramatic interrelations of character and distort the structure of the work. One can see this tendency in Heilman, whose major tenet is that from the plot of the play we can discern only "partial outlines of tragic form" which must be "amplified or corrected by the evidences of the symbolic language" (p. 32). For a penetrating analysis of the excesses of Heilman's technique, see W. R. Keast, "Imagery and Meaning in the Interpretation of *King Lear,*" *Modern Philology,* 47: 45–64 (1949).

9. *The Fool: His Social and Literary History* (New York, 1935), p. 267.

10. Arthur Sewell has formulated this extremely useful concept of the character's "address to the world" in his book *Character and Society in Shakespeare* (Oxford, 1951).

11. Herman Melville, *Moby Dick* (Modern Library ed., New York, 1930), p. 166.

12. *The Heritage of Symbolism* (London, 1943), p. 197.

13. *Archetypal Patterns in Poetry* (London, 1934), pp. 15–17.

14. *The Chronicle History of King Leir,* ed. Sidney Lee (London, 1909).

15. A. C. Bradley has characterized the figures of Goneril, Regan, Edmund, Cornwall, and Oswald as "hard self-seeking," while suggesting that Cordelia, Kent, Edgar, and the Fool represent "unselfish and devoted love." The two forces, Bradley maintained, "are set in conflict, almost as if Shakespeare, like Empedocles, were regarding Love and Hate as the two ultimate forces of the universe" (*Shakespearean Tragedy,* London, 1905, p. 263).

Enid Welsford has portrayed the two groups in a similar manner. On the one hand are those who are "erring men, warm-hearted but self-willed," having in common the capacity for "fellow-feeling"; and in sharp contrast, those who are calculating, who could never be considered "candidates for the cap and bells" (*The Fool,* p. 257).

Harley Granville-Barker pictured Goneril and Regan as "realists. Their father wants smooth speech of them and they give it. . . ." (*Prefaces to Shakespeare,* Princeton, 1952, I, 301). This characterization was also arrived at by W. H. Clemen in his analysis of the imagery of their speech: "They speak rationally; they address their words to their partner, and converse in a deliberate and conscious manner. They have a goal which they seek to attain and everything they have to say is bent upon this. Their language does not betray to us what is taking place within them — in the form of 'imaginative visions'; it reveals to us solely their aims and attitudes, and how they intend to put these into practice" (*Development of Shakespeare's Imagery*, London, 1951, p. 135).

Edwin Muir (*The Politics of King Lear*, Glasgow, 1947, p. 24) has characterized the world of Edmund and Goneril and Regan as one where "the man of policy in the latest style . . . regards the sacred order of society as his prey, and recognizes only two realities, interest and force, the gods of the new age."

In an extensive investigation of Shakespeare's doctrine of nature in *King Lear*, John F. Danby found that "Edmund and the sisters see society as a competition" (*Shakespeare's Doctrine of Nature: A Study of King Lear*, London, 1949, p. 108), while R. B. Heilman, in a study of metaphorical patterns in the play, concluded that they are pragmatists who see in "nature no intensified claim of Nature but only an aspect of the physical world to be properly estimated and used"; that they represent "a new order which is coolly calculating, on the make, quick to take advantage of flaws which sharp minds detect in the old men whose roots are in the past" (*This Great Stage*, pp. 141, 279).

For D. A. Traversi, Goneril, Regan, Edmund and their cohorts exemplify the "ruthless exercise of the acquisitive instinct in its determination to break the bonds of 'nature' and custom in the free following of its own unlimited desire for power" ("*King Lear*, II," *Scrutiny*, 19: 137, 1953).

Hiram Haydn (*The Counter-Renaissance*, New York, 1950, p. 638) views the whole play as "unmistakably concerned with a dying order, in which the protagonists of Nature and Stoicism fight for supremacy."

16. Richard Hooker, *Ecclesiastical Polity*, in *Works*, ed. John Keble (Oxford, 1885), I, 223.

17. *Antonios Revenge*, in *Plays of John Marston*, ed. H. Harvey Wood (London, 1934), I, 109.

18. *The Prince*, ch. xv, trans. W. K. Marriott (Everyman ed., London, n.d.), pp. 121–122: "But, it being my intention to write a thing which shall be useful to him who apprehends it, it appears to me more appropriate to follow up the real truth of a matter than the imagination of it . . . because how one lives is so far distant from how one ought to live, that he who neglects what is done for what ought to be done, sooner effects his ruin than his preservation; for a man who wishes to act entirely up to his professions of virtue soon meets with what destroys him among so much that is evil.

"Hence it is necessary for a prince wishing to hold his own to know how to do wrong, and to make use of it or not according to necessity."

19. *Ibid.*, p. 123: "And again, he [the prince] need not make himself uneasy at incurring a reproach for those vices without which the state can only be saved with difficulty, for if everything is considered carefully, it will be found that something which looks like virtue, if followed, would be his ruin; whilst something else, which looks like vice, yet followed brings him security and prosperity."

20. See George T. Buckley, *Rationalism in Sixteenth Century Literature* (Chicago, 1933); Hiram Haydn, *The Counter-Renaissance.* For Montaigne's influence on Shakespeare, now accounted as negligible, see Alice Harmon, "How Great Was Shakespeare's Debt to Montaigne?" *PMLA,* 57:988–1008 (1942).

21. See Heilman, *This Great Stage,* p. 141.

22. *Laws,* I.vi, in *Cicero: De Republica, De Legibus,* trans. Clinton W. Keyes (Loeb Library ed., London, 1928), p. 317.

23. Regan calls Gloucester "ingrateful fox" (III.vii.28) and "dog" (III.vii.75) in a tense and dramatic situation. But this is an isolated case, and Gloucester is not otherwise depicted in such language.

24. *New English Dictionary,* X (Part II), 250.

25. See E. Catherine Dunn, *The Concept of Ingratitude in Renaissance English Moral Philosophy* (Washington, D. C., 1946).

26. *Moby Dick,* p. 655.

27. While almost every writer on *Lear* elaborates on some of these parallels, George R. Kernodle has devoted an entire article to them: "The Symphonic Form of *King Lear*" in *Elizabethan Studies and Other Essays in Honor of George F. Reynolds* (Boulder, Colorado, 1945), pp. 185–191. For an early (and most thorough) study of Natural Law in *Lear,* see Hardin Craig, "The Ethics of *King Lear,*" *Philological Quarterly,* 4:97–109 (1925).

28. *Troilus and Cressida,* II.ii.26.

29. *Aristotle on the Art of Poetry,* ed., trans. Ingram Bywater (Oxford, 1909), xiii, p. 35. For ideas on Shakespeare's appeal to the audience I am greatly indebted to Harry Levin, "An Explication of the Player's Speech," *Kenyon Review,* 12:273–296 (1950), and to Arthur Sewell, *Character and Society in Shakespeare.*

30. *Character and Society in Shakespeare,* p. 21.

31. *Die Tragödie vor Shakespeare* (Heidelberg, 1955).

32. In "The Salvation of Lear," *Journal of English Literary History,* 15:93–109 (1948), Oscar J. Campbell, after presenting an incisive account of Elizabethan Stoic thought, interprets Lear as a completely unstoical man. Hiram Haydn, in *The Counter-Renaissance,* pp. 642–651, sees the entire drama as a "Stoic play," and characterizes Kent, Cordelia, and Edgar as stoics, and Lear as unstoical.

33. *Meditations,* Bk. VIII, ch. 47, trans. George W. Chrystal (Edinburgh, n.d.), p. 150.

34. *Moby Dick,* p. 4.

35. Trans. Constance Garnett (Modern Library ed., New York, 1950), p. 344.

36. (London, 1950), p. 35.

37. *Religion in the Making* (New York, 1926), p. 16.

38. *Brothers Karamazov,* p. 408.

39. *Ibid.*

40. Letter 123: "To George and Georgiana Keats," in *The Letters of John Keats*, ed. Maurice B. Forman (Oxford, 1948), p. 336.
41. *Shakespeare* (New York, 1953), p. 204.
42. *Brothers Karamazov*, p. 387.
43. "The Family in Modern Drama," *Atlantic Monthly*, 197:40 (1956).
44. *Ibid.*, pp. 36–37.
45. Letter 32: "To George and Thomas Keats," in Forman, p. 71.
46. "The Family in Modern Drama," p. 41.

CHAPTER II: MACBETH

1. Waldegrave, 1603. Reprinted in *Publications of the Scottish Text Society* (Edinburgh, 1944), ed. James Craigie, XVI, 25.
2. "Hegel's Theory of Tragedy," *Oxford Lectures on Poetry* (London, 1923), p. 88, note 1.
3. For a survey and study of villain-heroes, see Clarence V. Boyer, *The Villain as Hero in Elizabethan Tragedy* (London, 1914).
4. Holinshed, *Chronicles* (London, 1808), V, 265.
5. *Ibid.*
6. *Ibid.*
7. *Ibid.*
8. *Ibid.*, p. 269. Kenneth Muir, in the introduction to the Arden Edition of *Macbeth* (Cambridge, Mass., 1953), p. xliii, presents these reasons for Shakespeare's departure from Holinshed: "Shakespeare suppresses these facts, partly because he wished for dramatic reasons to accentuate Macbeth's guilt and to minimize any excuses he might have had, and partly for accidental reasons. Macbeth was the murderer of James I's ancestor, and could not be depicted in a favourable light, and because of 'the triumph of primogeniture during the twelfth and thirteenth centuries' the method of succession which existed in Macbeth's day was not fully understood in Shakespeare's, even by Holinshed."
9. Holinshed, *Chronicles*, p. 269.
10. Cf. Willard Farnham, *Shakespeare's Tragic Frontier: The World of His Final Tragedies* (Berkeley, 1950), p. 79: "*Macbeth* is a morality play in terms of Jacobean tragedy."
11. For an exhaustive treatment of the influence James I might have had on the composition of *Macbeth,* see Henry N. Paul, *The Royal Play of Macbeth* (New York, 1950).
12. "How Many Children Had Lady Macbeth?" *Explorations* (London, 1946), p. 29.
13. "Hegel's Theory of Tragedy," *Oxford Lectures*, pp. 87–88.
14. *Explorations*, p. 36. Caroline Spurgeon offers a good example of the critical judgment which results from imagery study. She has pointed out the clothes imagery associated with Macbeth (I.iii.108; I.iii.144;

I.vii.32; I.vii.36; II.iv.37; V.ii.15; V.ii.20) and from these would construct a unified characterization (*Shakespeare's Imagery and what it tells us,* New York, 1936, pp. 326–327): "This imaginative picture of a small, ignoble man encumbered and degraded by garments unsuited to him, should be put against the view emphasized by some critics (notably Coleridge and Bradley) of the likeness between Macbeth and Milton's Satan in grandeur and sublimity. . . . He is great, magnificently great, in courage, in passionate, indomitable ambition, in imagination and capacity to feel. But he could never be put beside, say Hamlet or Othello, in nobility of nature; and there *is* an aspect in which he is but a poor, vain, cruel, treacherous creature, snatching ruthlessly over the dead bodies of kinsman and friend at place and power he is utterly unfitted to possess. It is worth remembering that it is thus that Shakespeare, with his unshrinking clarity of vision, repeatedly *sees* him."

However, should we not object — as did Cleanth Brooks, "Shakespeare as a Symbolist Poet," *Yale Review,* 34:642–665 (1945) — that this interpretation makes primary what is only one aspect of the garment imagery. Whether Macbeth be large or small is not the foremost concern of these images. These are not his garments; they are stolen; they do not fit him properly. Clothing imagery is also used to convey other meanings; it designates the hypocrite, the man who cloaks his true nature under a disguise. There is also a danger in saying that the garment imagery used by Macbeth's enemies, Caithness and Angus, points to Shakespeare's conception of Macbeth as a poor and somewhat comic figure.

15. For a differing view, see D. A. Traversi, *An Approach to Shakespeare* (New York, 1956), p. 151: "*Macbeth* is, in the first place and above all, a play about the murder of a king; and there is a very real sense in which the centre, the focal point, of the conception is to be found neither in the criminal usurper nor in the wife who urges him to his first crime, but in the figure, too easily neglected in its central, normative function, of Duncan."

16. *Shakespeare, His Mind and Art* (New York, 1900), p. 222. Elmer Edgar Stoll, "The Dramatic Texture in Shakespeare," *Criterion,* 14: 603 (1935), holds the same opinion as Dowden: "I mean that whereby the fatal influence, of which the Weird Sisters are the voices, asserts itself and permeates the action. As on his first appearance in the third scene the hero echoes their last words in the first . . . . the relation is established before (in keeping with their purpose) they have met him."

Willard Farnham, *Shakespeare's Tragic Frontier,* p. 106, presents a very similar interpretation: "The words of prophecy instantly place before Macbeth an image which they could not so soon have brought to an utterly innocent man, a horrid image which, as he says a few lines later, makes his seated heart knock at his ribs. Thus the witches offer their suggestion of murder to a man who has already prepared himself to receive it, who has, we may say, summoned them by his thoughts, and who has shown that there is a mysterious affinity between him and them by his unconscious echoing of their 'Fair is foul, and foul is fair' in the first words that we hear him speak: 'So foul and fair a day I have not seen.' "

In *Shakespeare and the Natural Condition* (Cambridge, Mass., 1956), p. 68, Geoffrey Bush would also have us believe that Macbeth's first appearance on stage establishes his inclination to evil: "When he is hailed by the Witches, his ambition is given a shape and voice that stops him on the road and greets him; he is made to hear the address of part of himself. The suggestion of the Witches is his own suggestion. . . ."

17. *Chronicles*, pp. 268–269.

18. M. M. Morozov, "Humanism in Shakespeare's Works," *Shakespeare Association Bulletin*, 18:57 (1943).

19. A straightforward gloss of Macbeth's words has been suggested: that they simply mean, *"Foul* with regard to the *weather,* and *fair* with reference to his *victory"* (Elwin, *Shakespeare Restored*, 1853, quoted in *The Arden Shakespeare,* ed. Muir, p. 15). There is no reason to dismiss this explanation because it lacks sufficient subtlety; it is quite plausible. However, there is this objection: Macbeth's statement is cryptic; that it needs a gloss, that it has occasioned considerable interpretive speculation, points to its puzzling nature. If Shakespeare had wanted to contrast the foulness of the weather with the glory of victory, would he not have given Macbeth a more detailed exposition? We must remember that in the absence of elaborate scenery the spoken word created atmosphere for Shakespeare's audience.

20. *Shakespeare's Imagery,* p. 329.

21. *Shakespearean Tragedy* (London, 1905), p. 340.

22. Lily B. Campbell, "Bradley Revisited: Forty Years After," *Shakespeare's Tragic Heroes: Slaves of Passion* (New York, 1952), pp. 265–266.

23. For a review and a questioning of this argument, see Alwin Thaler, "The 'Lost Scenes' of *Macbeth*," *PMLA,* 49:835–847 (1934).

24. L. L. Schücking, *Character Problems in Shakespeare's Plays* (New York, 1922), pp. 77–78, disregards Macbeth's moral qualms, his sense of guilt. He reduces Macbeth completely, calling him a "weak man" who is "a victim of his nerves": "No doubt of their diseased condition can arise when we find him suffering from unmistakable hallucinations of the visual and auditory organs. . . ."

25. *Character and Society in Shakespeare* (London, 1951), p. 76.

26. Richard Hooker, *Ecclesiastical Polity,* in *Works,* ed. John Keble (Oxford, 1888), I, 220, 222.

27. "Hawthorne and his Mosses," in *The Portable Melville,* ed. Jay Leyda (New York, 1952), p. 407.

28. Walter Clyde Curry, *Shakespeare's Philosophical Patterns* (Baton Rouge, Louisiana, 1937), pp. 85–86.

29. *Shakespeare's Tragic Frontier,* pp. 112–119.

30. *The City of God*, Bk. XII, ch. xiii, trans. John Healey (London, 1903).

31. *Lord Jim*, Modern Library ed., p. 157.

32. A. C. Bradley, for example, says of this and the following scene (*Shakespearean Tragedy*, p. 391): "I question if either this scene or the exhibition of Macduff's grief is required to heighten our abhorrence of Macbeth's cruelty. They have a technical value in helping to give the last stage of the action the form of a conflict between Macbeth and Macduff. But their chief function is of another kind. It is to touch the heart with a sense of beauty and pathos, to open the springs of love and tears."

33. *Ibid.*, p. 392.

34. *Shakespeare and the Nature of Man* (New York, 1955), p. 161.

CHAPTER III: ANTONY AND CLEOPATRA

1. *Prefaces to Shakespeare* (Princeton, New Jersey, 1952), I, 368.

2. *Ibid.*, p. 367.

3. *Art and Artifice in Shakespeare* (New York, 1951), p. 146.

4. *Shakespeare's Tragic Frontier: The World of His Final Tragedies* (Berkeley, 1950), p. 139.

5. *Shakespeare and the Popular Dramatic Tradition* (London, 1944), p. 117.

6. *Ibid.*, p. 129.

7. To list all the differing opinions about the play and its heroes would serve little purpose. But a sampling is helpful in showing the great range of disagreement. Concerning the main theme of the play we have a wide range of judgments. Mark Van Doren, at one extreme, has stated that the writing of the play "has to be wonderful because it is not supported by anything that Aristotle would have called a plot" (*Shakespeare*, New York, 1939, p. 273). A. C. Bradley is representative of those who find the morality of the protagonists so unpleasant that, "With all our admiration and sympathy for the lovers we do not wish them to gain the world. It is better for the world's sake, and not less for their own, that they should fail and die" (*Oxford Lectures on Poetry*, London, 1923, p. 304).

There are even proposals to label the play a satire. Brents Stirling characterizes it as such, though he qualifies his position: the play is a "satirical tragedy," he says, though not a "tragic satire"; it limits and satirizes tragic noblesse and yet remains a tragedy (*Unity in Shakespearian Tragedy: The Interplay of Theme and Character*, New York, 1956, pp. 157–192). In an article in the *Shakespeare Quarterly* (Daniel Stempel, "The Transmigration of the Crocodile," *SQ*, 7:59–72 [1956]), *Antony and Cleopatra* is discussed as a pointed satire meant to inculcate an important political lesson: "The morbid disease which has destroyed him [Antony] must be removed completely as a source of danger to the state" (p. 72). In this interpretation the death of Cleopatra is neither pathetic nor tragic, but the ironic culmination of serpent imagery: "What more fitting end for the serpent who has fed Antony with delicious poison than to die by her own weapon?" (p. 71). For another radically different outlook we can turn to critics who view the end of the play not as a damnation, but a redemption. The work of G. Wilson Knight has had great influence on Shakespeare criticism, and his chapter title "The Transcendental Humanism of Antony and Cleopatra" in *The Imperial Theme* (London, 1951 — first published in 1931) serves to describe the final judgment of those who find, like Mr. Knight, that the play "sees man as he is transfigured under the intense ray of love and keenest poetic vision" (p. 210). J. Dover Wilson spoke of "the marvellous *Antony and Cleopatra*, in which love lifts a libertine and a harlot into the sublime atmosphere of Romeo and Juliet" (*The Essential Shakespeare*, Cambridge, England, 1935, p. 127). In *The Voyage to Illyria: A New Study of Shakespeare* (London, 1937) by Kenneth Muir and Sean O'Loughlin, *Antony and Cleopatra* is described in this way: "Metaphysically, it is a poem of the conquest of death by love" (p. 209). The opinion that in the play death transforms ignominy into a kind of beatitude is to be found in W. K. Wimsatt Jr.'s statement that "What is celebrated in *Antony and Cleopatra* is the passionate surrender of an illicit love, the victory of this love over practical, political and moral concerns, and the final superiority of the suicide lovers [*sic*] over circumstance" ("Poetry and Morals: A Relation Reargued," *Thought*, 23:294, 1948). This position is also put forth in a French study, Henri Fluchère's *Shakespeare* (trans. Guy Hamilton, London, 1953): "Antony's death is a triumph and Cleopatra's a transfiguration" (p. 258).

8. London, 1901, p. xxvii.

9. *The Imperial Theme*, p. 217. Cf. John Danby (*Poets on Fortune's Hill*, London, 1952, p. 13) who refuses to entertain either the judgment of Philo or Antony's own words: "The deliquescent truth is neither in them nor between them, but contains both. *Antony and Cleopatra* is Shakespeare's own critique of judgment."

10. *Shakespeare's Imagery and what it tells us* (New York, 1936), p. 352.

11. *Shakespeare's Plutarch,* ed. C. F. Tucker Brooke (London, 1909), II, 25–26.

12. *Ibid.,* pp. 138–139.

13. *Oxford Lectures on Poetry,* p. 300.

14. *Poets and Playwrights* (Minneapolis, 1930), p. 13.

15. *Prefaces to Shakespeare,* I, 443.

16. *Coleridge's Shakespearian Criticism,* ed. Thomas M. Raysor (Cambridge, Mass., 1930), I, 86.

17. Preface to *Three Plays for Puritans,* p. xxvii.

18. *Antony and Cleopatra* (Glasgow, 1944), p. 27.

19. The relationship of valor to manhood in *Macbeth* and *Antony*

and Cleopatra is discussed by Eugene M. Waith, "Manhood and Valor in Two Shakespearean Tragedies," *Journal of English Literary History,* 17: 262–273 (1950). In this essay Mr. Waith calls attention to Plutarch's statement that in Rome valor was considered as an all-inclusive virtue. However, Mr. Waith's final conclusion is that Cleopatra is not a temptress but an ideal; and through her Antony fully achieves self-realization. His downfall, therefore, is his greatest triumph.

    20. *Prefaces to Shakespeare,* I, 371.

    21. *Poets on Fortune's Hill,* p. 149.

    22. *Ibid.,* pp. 144–148.

    23. "Symbolism and Fiction," in *Contexts of Criticism* (Cambridge, Mass., 1957), p. 200.

    24. *Shakespeare and the Popular Dramatic Tradition,* p. 124.

    25. *Ibid.,* p. 129. Harold S. Wilson, *On the Design of Shakespearian Tragedy* (Toronto, 1957), p. 161, offers a variant interpretation: "symbolically, it is the ageless contrast and conflict of East and West; the East, with its mystery, its sensuous delights and rapturous abandonment, against the matter-of-fact, efficient, materially powerful West. Antony tries to mediate between the two. He fails. But he gains his love. And that is what finally counts in the play."

    26. *Poetics,* trans. S. H. Butcher, in *Aristotle's Theory of Poetry and Fine Art,* 4th ed., 1951, pp. 25–27.

    27. *Ibid.,* pp. 27–29.

    28. Willard Farnham, *Shakespeare's Tragic Frontier,* p. 182, gives plausible consistency to Enobarbus' character: "He has a soldier's morality of a sort which distinguishes sharply between finding a riggish Cleopatra splendid and irresistible when there is no work to do and finding her so when there is a battle to fight, especially a battle for the rulership of the world."

    29. For exponents of this view, see note 7.

    30. *Oxford Lectures on Poetry,* p. 305.

    31. *Character and Society in Shakespeare* (Oxford, 1951), p. 82.

    32. *Ibid.,* p. 122.

    33. *Shakespeare's Plutarch,* II, 96.

    34. *Ibid.,* pp. 88–89.

    35. *Ibid.,* p. 97.

    36. *Ibid.,* pp. 100–101.

    37. *Character and Society in Shakespeare,* p. 124.

    38. In Plutarch's *Life of Marcus Antonius* Enobarbus is very briefly mentioned on three occasions. Elkin Calhoun Wilson, "Shakespeare's Enobarbus," *Joseph Quincy Adams Memorial Studies,* ed. James G. McManaway *et al.* (Washington, D. C., 1948), p. 391, points out that "There is no trace of Enobarbus in any of the French, Italian, German, and English plays about Antony and Cleopatra — Estienne Jodell's *Cléopâtre Captive* (1552), Robert Garnier's *Marc-Antoine* (1578), Nicolas de Montreux's *Tragédie de Cléopâtre* (1595), Alessandro Spinello's *Cleopatra* (1540), Cesare De' Cesari's *Cleopatra* (1552), Celso Pistorelli's

Marc' Antonio e Cleopatra (1576), Battista Giraldi Cinthio's *Cleopatra* (1583), Hans Sachs's *Tragedi* (1560), the Countess of Pembroke's *Antoine* (1592), Samuel Daniel's *Cleopatra* (1594), and Samuel Brandon's *The Vertuous Octavia* (1598)."

39. *Shakespeare and Spenser* (Princeton, 1950), p. 34.

40. *Shakespeare's Plutarch*, II, 123.

41. Levin L. Schücking (*Character Problems in Shakespeare's Plays*, New York, 1922, p. 134) finds a sharp contradiction between the wanton Cleopatra of the early scenes and the tragic queen of the last two acts and explains this in terms of his theory that Shakespeare "composed according to the 'single-scene' method." E. M. W. Tillyard (*Shakespeare's Last Plays*, London, 1951, p. 22) also finds a radical change in the last two acts: "The vacillations of Antony and his neglect of duty, the cunning and cruelty of Cleopatra, find no part in the creatures who are transfigured in death; they remain unassimilated, held in tension against the pair's expiring nobilities. The reason why *Antony and Cleopatra* is so baffling a play (and why the rhapsodies it provokes tend to be hysterical) is that the effort to see the two main characters simultaneously in two different guises taxes our strength beyond our capacities. And yet that effort has to be made. Those who see Antony as the erring hero merely, and his final exaltation as ironic infatuation, are as partial in their judgment as those who think that his final heroics wash out his previous frailties. Both sets are part right, but each needs the other's truth to support it."

42. "Shakespeare and the Stoicism of Seneca," in *Selected Essays* (London, 1951), p. 131.

43. *Troilus and Cressida*, III.iii.183.

44. Letter 123: "To George and Georgiana Keats," in Forman, p. 317.

CHAPTER IV: CORIOLANUS

1. Quoted in *The Variorum Shakespeare: Coriolanus*, ed. Horace H. Furness (Philadelphia, 1928), p. 663.

2. *Ibid.*

3. Oscar James Campbell, *Shakespeare's Satire* (New York, 1943), pp. 198–217.

4. *Ibid.*, p. 204.

5. Investigators of Shakespeare's imagery have analyzed the role of the body and disease imagery with widely varying conclusions. In concentrating on different clusters of images without a balancing study of the play's structure, imagery studies can arrive at such widely differing conclusions as to render them suspect. While Caroline Spurgeon has suggested that *Coriolanus* "has a central symbol," that of the body politic introduced by Menenius' fable, and has detailed the "images arising out of this central theme of the body and sickness," she concluded that this symbol "has not been born out of the creator's feeling

of the tragedy; it has just been taken over by him wholesale, with much else, from North's *Plutarch*" (*Shakespeare's Imagery and what it tells us*, New York, 1936, p. 347).

A perceptive analyst of Shakespeare's language, W. H. Clemen, saw the imagery emphasizing and repeating the play's main theme, "The contrast between the commanding figure of Coriolanus and the baseness of the 'rabble'" (*The Development of Shakespeare's Imagery*, London, 1951, p. 154).

G. Wilson Knight, emphasizing the hard and metallic nature of city and war imagery which fuses with the theme of Coriolanus' iron-hearted pride, theorized that "In *Antony and Cleopatra*, the two values, War and Love, oppose each other: the same contrast is at the core of *Coriolanus*" (*The Imperial Theme*, London, 1951, p. 154).

In analyzing Menenius' "belly" fable, D. A. Traversi concluded that "Greed and satiety are the main images by which we are prepared for the tragedy of *Coriolanus*" (*An Approach to Shakespeare*, New York, 1956, p. 221). Stressing the machine-like imagery used to characterize Coriolanus ("he walks like an engine" and so on), Mr. Traversi argued that, "The failure of Coriolanus is a failure in sensitivity, a failure in living; and it represents a failure on the part of a whole society" (p. 233).

6. *Shakespeare's Plutarch*, ed. C. F. Tucker Brooke (London, 1909), II, 138–139.

7. See James E. Phillips Jr., *The State in Shakespeare's Greek and Roman Plays* (New York, 1940), pp. 3–18, for a survey of critical opinions on this subject.

8. Cf. Barrett Wendell, *William Shakespeare* (New York, 1894), pp. 330, 334: "The fate of Coriolanus . . . comes from no decadence, no corruption, no vicious weakness, but rather from a passionate excess of inherently noble traits, whose very vitality unfits them for survival in this ignoble world about them . . . . in *Coriolanus* we finally find Shakespeare, with almost cynical coldness, artistically expounding the inherent weakness of moral nobility, the inherent strength and power of all that is intellectually and morally vile."

W. H. Clemen also came to a somewhat similar conclusion in his study of the play's imagery through which he found the main theme to be, "The contrast between the commanding figure of Coriolanus and the baseness of the 'rabble'" (*The Development of Shakespeare's Imagery*, p. 154).

9. Willard Farnham propounds such a view in a fine book, *Shakespeare's Tragic Frontier: The World of His Final Tragedies* (Berkeley, 1950), which treats *Timon of Athens, Macbeth, Antony and Cleopatra* and *Coriolanus* as constituting Shakespeare's last tragic world, a world whose heroes are all "deeply flawed," "paradoxically noble": "Under one aspect *Coriolanus* is the tragedy of a great spirit who cannot stoop to flattery in the way of the world. But the nobility of Coriolanus is never simple or outright; one may be led to qualify, or even reject, the praise of his nature offered by the loquacious Menenius in those well-

known lines: 'His nature is too noble for the world:/ He would not flatter Neptune for his trident,/ Or Jove for's power to thunder' " (p. 223). To validate his judgments, however, Professor Farnham very often depends upon Elizabethan "outside reading." At one point, for example, after analyzing Coriolanus' refusal to flatter the mob in Act III, scene iii, to support his thesis that the hero is "supremely guilty of pride the vice and at the same time supremely noble in pride the virtue," he goes on to cite a number of texts which an Elizabethan might have read, and concludes: "Members of Shakespeare's audience might at first be led to condemn Coriolanus, in the light of contemporary ideas about the viciousness of the man guilty of pride, and then be led to reconsider their condemnation, in the light of contemporary ideas about the virtuousness of the man incapable of flattery. The virtue of the nonflatterer could only too easily, in a corrupt world, be mistaken for envy or pride, as they might remember having been told in some such words as these: 'The world is growne to that corruption that he that cannot flatter is either accompted enuious or reputed proud and arrogant.' So one might have second thoughts, or even third and fourth thoughts, about the degree to which Coriolanus should be condemned for that pride which leads to his banishment" (pp. 254–255).

10. E. C. Pettet, "Coriolanus and the Midlands Insurrection of 1607," *Shakespeare Survey*, III, 34–42, suggests that Shakespeare altered Plutarch's account to give the play the topicality of recent events — the peasants' revolt of 1607 against enclosures in the Midlands.

11. Oscar James Campbell, *Shakespeare's Satire*, p. 204: "In the midst of the uproar Menenius appears. He is the chief of the many commentators and expositors in this play who serve as Shakespeare's mouthpiece."

Brents Stirling, *The Populace in Shakespeare* (New York, 1949), p. 38: Menenius is a "humor character designed for choral commentary: 'What I think, I utter, and spend my malice in my breath'; and that what he thinks and what he utters is intended by Shakespeare as the truth about the populace is corroborated by the equally quixotic contempt for commoners uttered by one of their own number, the Third Citizen of Scene 3."

E. C. Pettet, "Coriolanus and the Midlands Insurrection of 1607," *Shakespeare Survey*, III, puts forth the view that being a landowner, Shakespeare must have been concerned with the important agrarian problem of enclosures involved in the 1607 Midlands disturbances; that he therefore "expanded his Plutarch original because it afforded him the opportunity of saying something that he very much wanted to say; and this suggestion is strengthened by the fact that never before had he voiced the conventional political theory behind his parable with such earnestness and vigorous, homely eloquence" (p. 37).

12. Kenneth Muir, "Menenius' Fable," *Notes and Queries*, 198: 240–242 (1953), discusses various parallels to Menenius' fable and points out that the fable is also to be found in "Dionysius of Hali-

carnassus, in Livy and in Aesop's Fables, whence it found its way into Caxton's collection. A variant is to be found in John of Salisbury's *Polycraticon*, and Camden paraphrased this in his *Remaines*. Sidney told the story briefly in his *Defence of Poesy*, and William Averell in *A Meruailous Combat of Contrarieties* expanded it, at the time of the Spanish Armada, into a piece of patriotic propaganda. It is also mentioned in Erasmus's *Copia* and Shakespeare doubtless came across it at school in one form or another" (p. 240).

Also see M. W. MacCallum, *Shakespeare's Roman Plays* (London, 1910), pp. 454–457, for a discussion of the fable's sources. MacCallum also suggests (p. 457) that Shakespeare might have read Philemon Holland's translation of Livy.

13. *Shakespeare's Plutarch*, II, 145.

14. *Ibid.*, p. 138.

15. Harley Granville-Barker, *Prefaces to Shakespeare* (Princeton, 1951), II, 156, pointed out that, "the spiritual crisis in which he [Marcius] decides for his renegade revenge on Rome, is boldly and neatly sidestepped. It is strange, says Marcius in that one short soliloquy, how quickly enemies may become friends and friends turn enemies. 'So with me;/ My birth-place hate I, and my love's upon/ This enemy town.' We are (this is to tell us) past the play's turning point already. The crucial change in the man has already taken place; and of the process of it we learn nothing. . . . *Was* there any such explicable process? He is not a man of reason, but of convictions and passionate impulses, which can land him in a sudden decision — and he will not know how he came by it."

I would suggest that from the beginning Shakespeare presents Marcius as mainly concerned with his own private worth; that his deeds in battle are performed for their own sake, their service to the country being only incidental. His sudden joining of the Volscians is therefore understandable and in keeping with his character. But I do not think Shakespeare gave sufficient dramatic preparation at the moment when Marcius actually decides to join the Volscians.

16. Preface to *The Wings of the Dove* in *The Art of the Novel: Critical Prefaces by Henry James*, ed. Richard P. Blackmur (New York, 1950), p. 300.

17. *Prefaces to Shakespeare*, II, 153–154.

18. *Shakespeare's Plutarch*, II, 162.

19. *Ibid.*, pp. 137–138.

20. *Ibid.*, p. 142.

21. Cf. Paul A. Jorgensen, "Shakespeare's Coriolanus: Elizabethan Soldier," *PMLA*, 64: 221–235 (1949). Mr. Jorgensen's primary aim in this article is to relate the play to Elizabethan personalities and military treatises. Thus, in commenting on Coriolanus' solitary entrance into Corioli, Mr. Jorgensen is not so much concerned with its dramatic significance as with its "resemblance to Elizabethan military adventurers" (p. 222). And concerning Coriolanus' refusal to show his wounds, Mr.

Jorgensen again derives his explanation from the age rather than the play: "Displaying one's wounds and boasting of military services bore an unusual stigma in Shakespeare's time, largely because of the shameless beggars and rogues who disgraced the military profession" (p. 230).

22. *Shakespeare's Plutarch*, II, 149.

23. *The Enchanted Glass* (New York, 1952), p. 156.

24. *Ibid.*, p. 157.

25. Peter Alexander, *Hamlet: Father and Son* (London, 1955), applied Trilling's formulation to *Hamlet* (p. 30) and proposed that when Hamlet and his father meet in the closing scenes of the first act, "not merely two types, but two ages confront one another. Wittenberg — the University — is face to face with the heroic past. From this opposition are generated the two conflicting emotions that constitute the idea that informs the play" (p. 35).

26. For a sympathetic treatment of the tribunes, see John Palmer, *Political Characters of Shakespeare* (London, 1945), pp. 250–310.

27. Alfred Harbage, *As They Liked It: An Essay On Shakespeare and Morality* (New York, 1947), pp. 66 ff., traces in a range of Shakespeare plays "the idea that vice and virtue are not absolutes, and that excessive virtue becomes vice."

28. *The Imperial Theme*, pp. 195–198.

CHAPTER V: CONCLUSION

1. *Moby Dick* (Modern Library ed., New York, 1930), p. 166.

2. Letter 123: "To George and Georgiana Keats," in *The Letters of John Keats*, ed. Maurice B. Forman (Oxford, 1948), p. 336.

INDEX